POLITICAL JOURNALISM IN TRANSITION

POLITICAL JOURNALISM IN TRANSITION

WESTERN EUROPE IN A COMPARATIVE PERSPECTIVE

Edited by RAYMOND KUHN
and RASMUS KLEIS NIELSEN

REUTERS
INSTITUTE for the
STUDY of
JOURNALISM

Published by I.B.Tauris & Co. Ltd in association with
the Reuters Institute for the Study of Journalism, University of Oxford

The Reuters Institute would like to acknowledge the assistance of Paolo Mancini and John Lloyd as readers on behalf of the Institute.

Published in 2014 by I.B.Tauris & Co. Ltd
6 Salem Road, London W2 4BU
175 Fifth Avenue, New York NY 10010
www.ibtauris.com

Distributed in the United States and Canada Exclusively by Palgrave Macmillan
175 Fifth Avenue, New York NY 10010

ISBN: 978 1 78076 677 5 (HB); 978 1 78076 678 2 (PB)

A full CIP record for this book is available from the British Library
A full CIP record is available from the Library of Congress

Library of Congress Catalog Card Number: available

Printed and bound in Great Britain by T.J. International, Padstow, Cornwall

In memory of my father, Roman Kuhn (1922–2012) (RK)

To my family, past and present (RKN)

Contents

Acknowledgements

In addition to the contributors to the book and Sarah Oates, now at the University of Maryland, Cornelia Fuchs from the German newsweekly *Stern*; Ferdinando Giugliano, editorial writer at the *Financial Times*; Patrick Diamond, former adviser to prime ministers Tony Blair and Gordon Brown; and Ric Bailey from the BBC all kindly took part in a roundtable discussion on the practice of political journalism at a workshop in Oxford in March 2012, from which some of the chapters in this book originate. John Lloyd and Paolo Mancini agreed to serve as reviewers of the manuscript and offered many constructive comments.

We are grateful to the Reuters Institute for the Study of Journalism and its director, David Levy, for hosting the workshop and supporting this publication, and to the School of Politics and International Relations, Queen Mary University of London, and the Department of Politics and International Relations at the University of Oxford for providing financial support. Rasmus Kleis Nielsen's work on the publication was in part supported by the Open Society Foundations as part of a larger project on the changing business of journalism and its implications for democracy.

Tables and Figures

Tables

Figures

Contributors

Olivier Baisnée is Associate Professor at Sciences Po, Toulouse.

Philip Baugut is Research Associate at Ludwig-Maximilians-University Munich.

Mark Blach-Ørsten is Associate Professor at Roskilde University.

Alessio Cornia is Postdoctoral Researcher at the University of Perugia.

Stephen Cushion is Senior Lecturer at Cardiff University.

Aeron Davis is Professor at Goldsmiths, University of London.

Frank Esser is Professor at the University of Zurich.

Raymond Kuhn is Professor at Queen Mary University of London.

Rasmus Kleis Nielsen is Associate Professor at Roskilde University and Research Fellow at the Reuters Institute for the Study of Journalism at the University of Oxford.

Carsten Reinemann is Professor at Ludwig-Maximilians-University Munich.

Andrea Umbricht is Research Associate at the University of Zurich.

Kevin Williams is Professor at Swansea University.

1

Political Journalism in Western Europe: Change and Continuity

Rasmus Kleis Nielsen and Raymond Kuhn

> The gallery in which the reporters sit has become a fourth estate of the realm. The publication of the debates, a practice which seemed to the most liberal statesmen of the old school full of danger to the great safeguards of public liberty, is now regarded by many persons as a safeguard tantamount, and more than tantamount, to all the rest together. (Macaulay, 1828)

> Burke said there were Three Estates in Parliament; but, in the Reporters' Gallery yonder, there sat a Fourth Estate more important far than they all. It is not a figure of speech, or a witty saying; it is a literal fact. ... [Publishing] is equivalent to Democracy. ... Whoever can speak, speaking now to the whole nation, becomes a power, a branch of government, with inalienable weight in law-making, in all acts of authority. (Carlyle, 1841)

Introduction

In its self-conception, the popular imaginary, and the social sciences, political journalism is regarded as a key part of democratic politics and at the very heart of the journalistic vocation. The venerable notion of the 'fourth estate', attributed to the eighteenth-century conservative politician and philosopher Edmund Burke (though probably first developed by

1

Thomas Macaulay and then later ascribed to Burke by Thomas Carlyle) still captures the ideal and to some extent the actual position of political journalism. It is a formally independent institution that is part and parcel of representative politics, engaged in criticising those in positions of power, promoting particular political actors, issues, and views, keeping people at least to some extent informed about public affairs and mobilising citizens for political action – all often done in concert with other estates, but never simply as their instrument. Political journalism is about professional achievement, personal fulfilment, and often money – especially after the commercialisation of the press and later broadcasting – but it is also about politics, power, and what Macaulay called 'the safeguards of public liberty'. It is, in short, as much about democracy as it is about the media.

In its paradigmatic late twentieth-century form of mass politics pursued by mass parties covered by mass media, political life in Western European democracies was intimately intertwined with different, distinct national varieties of political journalism, developed within newspapers and broadcasters that reached far wider audiences than the nineteenth-century reporters Macaulay and Carlyle wrote about. Today, in the early twenty-first century, journalism is still, for good and ill, at the heart of politics. Yet many parts of the equation are changing across Europe. Popular political participation is on the decline (or at least changing) in many countries. Parties have lost both their mass membership and the firm loyalty of previously committed voters in a process of partisan de-alignment evident across different political systems. Consolidated mass media environments defined by print and broadcast media have begun to give way to much more diverse, fragmented, and digital media landscapes that give audiences many more options for active engagement and selective use. Just as politics today is different from the politics of the immediate postwar period and the media of today are different from the media of the 1970s, political journalism today is different in many respects from that of previous generations. It remains deeply shaped by historical legacies and is still practised in the shadow of inherited norms and ideals associated with an earlier age, supported by news organisations developed in another time and oriented towards predominantly national political systems that reflect centuries-old political and constitutional theories and distinct paths to democracy. But political journalism is also changing and reinventing itself as a craft and as a profession. Journalists find themselves faced with audiences that are often more sceptical, less interested, and more scattered; they work on their own or for media companies facing ever harsher competition and a rapidly changing business environment; and they confront a political world undergoing its own profound changes. In short, political journalism in Western Europe is in transition.

What we know about political journalism in Western Europe

This book presents an overview of the combination of change and continuity that characterises political journalism in Western Europe in the early twenty-first century, a time of considerable turmoil especially in the media industries that have traditionally underpinned reporting, but also in how political actors and ordinary citizens relate to journalism. It is concerned with political journalism broadly understood as including at its core the coverage produced by dedicated political reporters who in many countries do their daily work in constant and close contact with elected officials and their aides. It also embraces running political commentary provided by various pundits, news coverage by general assignment reporters and others that deal with issues of political importance, and even some coverage labelled as 'foreign affairs' or 'international news' that actually overlaps with domestic democratic politics (for example, news about the European Union). While political communication is a much broader phenomenon, including activities such as grassroots canvassing, professionally produced campaign communications aiming to circumvent journalistic scrutiny, and the mediation of politics through entertainment shows and other forms of political culture, conventional news coverage remains the single most important source of information about public affairs for most European citizens (Bennett and Entman, 2001; Richardson et al., 2013). Political journalism is thus worth examining in its own right.

In this book we ask a set of simple but important questions about political journalism. How does it work in our selected countries? What are the similarities and differences in how it operates? How is it changing? Finally, which issues cut across national borders? We address these questions by covering both national developments in five different Western European countries (France, Italy, Germany, Denmark, and the United Kingdom) and a range of cross-cutting issues including coverage of the European Union, the role of public service broadcasting, and long-term trends in reporting styles and international news. Throughout the book we examine political journalism as it is practised at the intersection between

3

political and media systems, as part of politics as much as part of the media (Blumler and Gurevitch, 1995; Cook, 1998; Kuhn and Neveu, 2002). The focus is on how political journalism, understood primarily as the product of interactions between professional journalists and political actors and oriented towards a popular audience still generally seen as consisting of mostly passive receivers, operates in Western Europe today, and how it has changed in recent decades as part of wider economic, social, and technological transformations sweeping across the continent.

Self-reflexive journalistic scrutiny of political coverage, personal accounts by prominent political journalists and politicians, and a growing body of academic work focused on political journalism mean we know much more about this topic than we did. Comparative studies of political journalism allow us to outline from the outset a number of shared characteristics of Western European political journalism at the turn of the century. It is a form of journalism that has become increasingly independent of narrow party-political or proprietorial agendas and is increasingly driven by its own professional, organisational, and – in the case of private-sector media – commercial logics. It generally covers politics in ways that are focused on personalities and political manoeuverings more than parties and policies, on successions of individual events more than drawn-out processes, and on conflict more than compromise and cooperation. It focuses overwhelmingly on a narrow and partial range of political issues, actors, and institutions, subjecting to the light of publicity only a small subset of the political processes playing out at any given point in time, paying attention only to a small minority of those involved, and covering leading figures from national parliaments and governments far more than other important arenas like local government, interest groups, and the governance networks they are part of or, for that matter, European Union-level institutions. Yet, for all its shortcomings, it also keeps those who actually follow the news consistently better informed about public affairs than those of their peers who do not (Curran et al., 2009).

Political journalism is a journalism that generally shares with the majority of politicians, social scientists, and European citizens a 'legitimist vision' of electoral politics, accepting the latter's basic legitimacy as indisputable and its importance as a given, and often by implication regarding any outside challenge to this system with considerable scepticism (whether confronted by the populist comedian-turned-anti-politician Beppe Grillo in Italy, the Pirate Party in Germany, or the

Occupy movement in the United Kingdom). It is a form of journalism that is, all talk of 'citizen journalism' aside, overwhelmingly practised by salaried white-collar professionals working for legacy news media organisations such as newspapers and broadcasters (including their online operations). It is a journalism that in Western Europe is deeply shaped by the particular combination of private-sector elite newspaper journalism with often pronounced partisan overtones (in Northern Europe combined with a pronounced populist streak in the form of widely read tabloids) and a generally strong tradition of widely used public service broadcasting that differentiates it from, for example, American political journalism. All these characteristics have been highlighted in academic studies of political journalism especially from the 1990s onwards (Blumler and Gurevitch, 1995; Brants and Voltmer, 2011; Kuhn and Neveu, 2002; Norris, 2000). All of these features remain relevant today, underlining how contemporary political journalism is in many key respects a continuation of well-known decades-old trends.

Different models of Western European political journalism

Just as broadly similar developments rooted in the 1990s or even before continue to define the practice and output of contemporary political journalism, older, deeper-rooted institutional differences also continue to shape the news produced. Throughout the book, chapter after chapter confirms that historically inherited national differences remain pronounced even within the relatively similar family of Western European democracies. Europe is not internally homogenous. Even after more than half a century of European political and economic integration, different countries have significantly different domestic political systems, economic structures, and nationally oriented news media. While on-the-ground variation is considerable and does not always neatly follow national borders or theoretical expectations, comparative media researchers interested in political journalism often use a conceptual typology developed by Daniel C. Hallin and Paolo Mancini (2004) to categorise European media systems on the basis of: (a) how developed their media markets are, (b) the extent to which media organisations are directly or indirectly intertwined with the political system, (c) the development of journalistic professionalism, and (d) the degree and character of state intervention in the media sector.

On the basis of these four variables, Hallin and Mancini offer three ideal types that several contributors return to in later chapters, but are worth introducing briefly here. The first is a 'liberal' model, characterised by the relative dominance of market mechanisms and commercial logics across the media sector. The United States is seen as the clearest example of this model; it is not common in Europe, where virtually every country has some sort of public service broadcasting provision and many newspapers have stronger roots in politics than in the market. The second is a 'democratic corporatist' model, characterised by the co-existence of commercial media, media with roots in civil society and political groups, and public service media. Germany is seen as a particularly important example of this model, the Low Countries and the Nordic countries also. The third is a 'polarised pluralist model', characterised by weakly developed commercial news media, a high level of interpenetration between media and politics, and substantial state intervention in most media sectors. Many Mediterranean countries, including Italy, Spain, and Portugal, are seen as close to this model.

Although some countries, including France and the United Kingdom, are hard to place, Hallin and Mancini's typology offers a useful way of thinking about high-level differences and similarities even within – from a global perspective – a relatively homogenous region like Western Europe. (All the countries covered here are by global standards affluent and politically stable, as well as enjoying high levels of media freedom.) The three stylised models capture important variations in the structure of media industries and their relations to politics – and thus the structural frameworks within which political journalists operate – though research suggests that one should not assume that such systemic differences always translate directly into parallel differences in terms of news media use, news media content, or indeed into professional journalistic self-conceptions (Dalen, 2012; Esser et al., 2012; Hanitzsch, 2011; Pfetsch, 2004; Shehata and Strömbäck, 2011). Media environments and their relations to the political system are important in shaping political journalism, but professional milieus also have their own internal dynamics and ultimately the impact of political journalism also depends on how citizens relate to it – whether they pay attention to it, whether they feel it is relevant for them, and whether they trust it.

Structural changes affecting Western European political journalism

While the shared trends of personalisation, an emphasis on politics over policy, some tendencies towards popularisation, and the enduring importance of inherited institutional differences represent important continuities, change is also afoot. Western European political journalism is changing in response to both external and internal factors. In this opening chapter we focus principally on those *external* variables that are largely shared across different national Western European systems. The individual national case study chapters deal in greater detail with the *internal* factors that vary from one country to another. Political journalists across Western Europe have to contend with a structural transformation in the industries that have sustained and constrained the profession for decades (especially in the case of newspapers); with changing audiences who are less credulous, deferential, and patient, as well as increasingly empowered by various digital media and a growing number of media options to choose from; and with political actors who often dedicate more and more resources to handling their media relations (often in part by hiring experienced journalists as advisers).

All five Western European countries dealt with in detail in this book have increasingly diverse media markets, high levels of social media use, and far more internet users per capita than the global average. All have newspaper industries undergoing a rapid and often exceedingly painful transition as print circulation declines and advertising revenues erode, in many cases with direct consequences for the number of journalists covering politics. All of them have seen political parties, interest groups, government agencies, and major corporations invest in expanding their public relations efforts. A few quantitative indicators provide a sense of the scale and scope of change in the media sector. Figure 1.1 charts the decline in paid printed newspaper circulation in Denmark, France, Germany, Italy, and the United Kingdom from 2000 to 2009. (The figure in parentheses is the accumulated drop in circulation over this ten-year period.) While inherited differences in newspaper circulation continue to shape these national media systems, clearly separating countries with historically strong commercial newspaper industries from those without, overall print circulation is declining. This is undermining the business models of many newspaper companies even as they reach more readers online than ever before (newspapers dominate online news provision in France, Germany,

7

and Italy, and loom large in Denmark and the United Kingdom, though public service broadcasters dominate the sector in the UK in particular).

While paid print newspaper readership has declined over the last decade, overall television viewing has remained stable. What has changed is what people watch. Most Western European countries have moved from limited channel choice and a few big audiences as recently as the late 1990s to a multi-channel environment first with cable and satellite pay-TV and later with digital terrestrial free-to-air transmission. In the early 2000s a limited number of channels still attracted substantial audiences, but many more channels drew limited niche audiences. In terms of the number of people reached and the time spent engaged, television remains the single most important and most extensively used source of news across Western Europe, while print, though still important, is in decline. On the rise, in contrast, are digital media, as people get news online – often from legacy media companies like broadcasters or newspapers – via desktops, laptops, and increasingly via mobile devices like smartphones and tablets. The spread and domestication of digital and networked communication technologies have been so fast and so thorough, especially amongst affluent Northern Europeans, that it is easy to forget what a dramatic shift we have seen in media use in recent years – comparable perhaps only to the rapid rise of television in the 1960s. A survey conducted by the Reuters Institute for the Study of Journalism captures how widely used various ways of accessing news were across Western Europe as of 2012 (see Table 1.1).

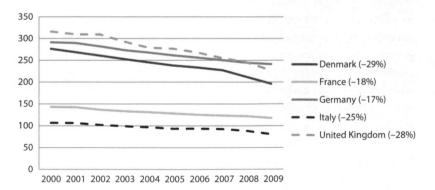

Source: adapted from Nielsen (2012a) with additional data from the World Press Trends database.

Figure 1.1 Paid newspaper circulation per 1,000 population

Table 1.1   Weekly access of news by source

	Denmark	France	Germany	United Kingdom
Television	81%	80%	87%	76%
Online	82%	77%	61%	82%
Print	57%	57%	68%	54%

Source: from the 2012 Reuters Institute Digital News Report (Newman, 2012). 'Which of the following news sources have you used in the last week?' Conducted with a representative sample of the online population in each country, Denmark (N=1002), France (N=1011), Germany (N=970), United Kingdom (N=2173). Given the methodology, the results do not reflect the media habits of adults with no regular internet access, estimated to about 10 (Denmark) and 20 (France, Germany, and the UK) per cent of the population in 2012.

The media sector is not the only one that has experienced significant change over the last decade. Western European politics has also changed, in part as a continuation of older trends towards de-alignment, changes in party organisations, and the loosening of corporatist networks between governments and interest groups, in part also as a result of institutional change, especially at the European Union level, and in part because of sharply dropping public confidence in many countries after a decade of political problems, scandals, and the recent financial and economic crisis (Dalton, 2007). Eurobarometer survey data ten years apart, from 2002 and 2011/2012, illustrate some of these changes in our five selected national case studies (see Figure 1.2). In Germany and particularly Denmark, relatively stable and sizeable proportions of the population responded in both 2002 and 2012 that they 'tend to trust' national political institutions. In France, trust increased substantially in the same period. In both Italy and the United Kingdom, however, there was a marked decline in confidence (the Eurobarometer surveys suggest this was also the case in many other EU member states). In the United Kingdom, the proportion who expressed some trust in national political institutions declined from about three in ten in 2002 to only one in five in 2012. In Italy, where in 2002 fewer than one in three had said that they 'tended to trust' national political institutions, by 2012 the figure was fewer than one in ten (only 4 per cent of respondents expressed any trust in political parties).

It is important to keep in mind that stable and relatively high levels of public confidence in national political institutions, especially in Northern Europe, undermine the idea that all Western democracies face a crisis of

9

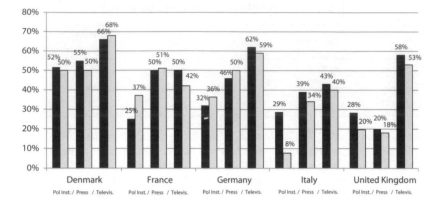

The first two bars for each country represent trust in political institutions. The second two bars represent trust in the press. The third two bars represent trust in television. The black bars represent data from 2002 and the grey bars, data from 2012. 'Political institutions' is the average of the number of people who say they 'tend to trust' national governments, parliaments, and political parties.

Source: data from Eurobarometer 57 (2002), Eurobarometer 76 (2011) and Eurobarometer 77 (2012).

Figure 1.2 Percentage of people who 'tend to trust' political institutions, press, and TV (2002/2012)

legitimacy today. Yet clearly many established democracies suffer from a 'democratic deficit', with representative political institutions seen as delivering less than citizens expect (Norris, 2011). Interestingly, however, the same Eurobarometer surveys that document the growth of this deficit (especially in Italy and the United Kingdom) also suggest that in all five of our national case studies television is generally trusted by more people than are national political institutions. Moreover, although trust in the media has dropped in several of them, the decline is not as sharp as the decline in confidence in political institutions.

Faced with changes in the media and in the citizenry they seek to appeal to, political parties have in many countries tried to expand their own independent campaign communications as well as their public relations efforts (Davis, 2002; Esser et al., 2001). Across Western Europe overall campaign expenditures have grown and political actors have invested more in media management. Yet although the resources involved have increased, things need to be kept in perspective. In France, the official cap for presidential campaign spending is €22.5 million per candidate. In 2012, around 35 million votes were cast in the decisive second round, which suggests that about €1.30 was spent by the two major candidates combined for each vote cast (although the actual expenditure of the Sarkozy campaign was put under investigation). In Germany, the combined campaign budgets of the major parties was about €70 million in the 2009 federal elections; 43 million votes were cast, suggesting about €1.60 spent for each vote. In the United Kingdom, the three major parties spent a combined £30 million (€35 million) in the 2010 general election; 27 million votes were cast, suggesting about €1.30 per vote cast. By contrast, recent elections in Brazil saw major party expenditures in the region of €4.00 per vote cast, and in Mexico's presidential elections about €3.00 per vote cast (Plasser and Lengauer, 2008). The extraordinarily expensive 2012 US presidential elections saw the two major candidates alone spend almost €7.00 for each vote cast.

These changes in part reflect parallel displacements in terms of the rise of digital media, the relative decline of print and the fragmentation of many media audiences, as well as increasing investments in political communication. But they also reveal persistent particularities and new peculiarities from country to country (Nielsen, 2012a). The relation between these structural changes and conditions on the ground are rarely simple or transparent. Consider legacy media, new media, and the political uses of PR. While newspapers are struggling to readjust across Western Europe, they have suffered far more in the United States; moreover, revenues have so far declined more in the United Kingdom (with its historically strong press) than in France (with its historically weak press) (Nielsen and Levy, 2010). Freesheets have established themselves as significant sources of news, especially in bigger cities in Denmark, France, Italy, and the UK, but are absent in Germany. Internet use has grown rapidly and is high by global standards across Western Europe, but it is far higher in Denmark and Germany than in Italy. Nevertheless, Italy has seen more spectacular examples of internet-assisted political activism and more innovative online-only journalistic start-ups in recent years than its Northern European neighbours (Bruno and Nielsen, 2012; Vaccari, 2011). Political actors are ramping up their public relations efforts in all these countries, but the resources at their disposal vary widely: from the vast personal fortunes of Silvio Berlusconi to the largely publicly funded Danish parties, with the fundraising-driven British parties somewhere in between (Davis, 2002; Elmelund-Præstekær et al., 2011). These pronounced cross-national differences matter as much as the similarities when it comes to understanding political journalism in Western Europe. That is why this book includes both country-specific chapters that examine political journalism as it is practised at the intersection between media, politics, and the public, and cross-cutting comparative chapters that have a more thematic focus.

Similarities and differences in the changes affecting political journalism

We have produced this book to provide an overview of political journalism in Western Europe in a transitional period characterised by both change and continuity. It is narrowly focused on Western Europe, understood here as the group of high-income, mixed-economy democracies that remained free of authoritarian influence throughout the postwar period and aligned themselves with the so-called 'Western world' during the Cold War. Precisely because we believe historical inheritances and social, political, and economic differences are key to understanding political journalism, we do not believe that these countries are representative of all of Europe, let alone the rest of the world. Nonetheless, we consider that these countries, lumped together in one corner of a wider and much more diverse world, with their approximately 300 million inhabitants, their dominant role in the European Union – the largest economy in the world and the most ambitious and painful experiment in supranational economic and political integration – and the distinct democratic, journalistic, and political challenges they face at the turn of the century, merit close analysis on their own terms. From a global perspective Western Europe is a very odd place – more affluent, more secular, well past its imperial 'peak', with political systems and media companies sometimes tracing their roots back all the way to the eighteenth century and the democratic revolutions of the nineteenth century, profoundly shaped by its unusual twentieth-century commitment to public service broadcasting. It is worth examining as the oddity it is, not because of any universal pretensions.

The starting point for the analyses presented in the rest of the book has been the overarching question of how much similarity and difference contemporary developments in political journalism exhibit across Western Europe. Here we suggest that three trends in particular cut across all the countries covered in this volume:

- an accelerated news cycle, driven especially by 24/7 rolling news channels and continuously updated newspaper websites, and increasingly also social media sites like Twitter. This results to some extent in 'churnalistic' tendencies, where pre-produced material substitutes for reporting;
- a general shift in the balance of power between increasingly time- and resource-pressed journalists on the one hand and increasingly professionalised political sources, especially around top politicians, major political parties, and well-organised interest groups, on the other; and
- a clear move from analogue to digital media on the supply side (allowing for clear generational differences in demand). This is a shift in which legacy news media organisations remain far more important than start-ups in terms of news provision, dominating online news almost as much as they do offline news.

It is noteworthy that the chapters in this volume identify these three trends in very different countries, with significant variation in the structure of media systems, political systems, and national economies. Germany, Italy, and the United Kingdom, for example, are very different countries with distinct journalistic traditions and political cultures. Yet the three trends of accelerated 'churnalism', empowered sources, and digitisation dominated by legacy media are to be found in all three countries. While these trends are certainly shaped in important ways by national variations in politics and culture, they seem driven for the most part by the combination of cross-cutting economic and technological forces and certain shared professional journalistic and political practices.

It is also worth highlighting, however, that some trends visible in other high-income democracies seem less present in Western Europe. This challenges the idea that contemporary economic and technological developments point in the same direction across the world, or even across the 'Western world'. For example, three trends that have been particularly evident in the United States in recent years seem much less pronounced in the countries covered in this volume. These are:

- a high degree of fragmentation of the largest news audiences (Prior, 2007; Stroud, 2011), driven by the decline of free-to-air television news viewership and print newspaper readership, combined with the rise of niche-oriented cable television and online news;

- an increased tendency towards more explicitly partisan political journalism (Baum and Groehling, 2008; Bennett and Iyengar, 2008), especially on new niche news media fighting to draw and retain a loyal audience, but also in the form of vibrant community blogs and smaller groups engaged in politically charged forms of 'guerilla journalism'; and
- a significant and growing proportion of the adult population who obtain a large part of their news about politics and public affairs through social networking sites and in the form of material that perhaps originates with legacy media organisations but is not accessed through channels they control (Williams and Delle Carpini, 2011; Wojcieszak and Mutz, 2009).

In terms of audience fragmentation, the largest television channels *are* losing share in Western Europe and newspapers' print audiences *are* declining. Yet across their analogue and digital offerings, large news organisations like the BBC in the UK (a public service broadcaster), TF1 in France and RTL in Germany (private broadcasters), *Ekstrabladet* in Denmark (a tabloid newspaper), and *La Repubblica* in Italy (a broadsheet newspaper) all reach very large audiences, in some cases larger than they ever have before. In terms of partisanship, partly this is nothing new in Western Europe, where elite (broadsheet) newspapers in particular have often had distinct and fairly political editorial lines, and partly the development of such forms of journalism is restricted by impartiality rules for licensed broadcasters, whether public or private. In terms of social media, most Western European countries have levels of internet use, broadband access, and social media use that equal or exceed levels in the United States; but recent surveys suggest that most Europeans, even though they use digital media frequently, have not made these a central part of the ways in which they routinely obtain news about public affairs or connect with political processes (Newman, 2012).

In short, although the same economic and technological forces that have helped propel the United States towards a media environment characterised by audience fragmentation, partisan polarisation, and an increasing reliance on social media over news media are at work across Western Europe, it is far from clear that the end result is the same, given the very different political and cultural contexts, as well as different histories, of individual countries. Stronger, more developed national media have retained a larger audience share in smaller, more homogenous

European countries and remain as popular online as they are offline. Partisanship, already being present, has not increased significantly even as new media have become available and competition intensifies. (Italy, with its highly politicised and polarised media, is a partial exception to this.) Though social networking sites are wildly popular across Western Europe, they have so far not become a particularly important platform for accessing news for the general population, who in 2012 still relied more on the analogue and digital offerings of legacy news media.

Power and public liberty: the politics of political journalism

The daily operations of political journalism in different Western European countries – as well as the direction of change in this transitional period – are shaped in part by social, economic, and technological factors largely external to the profession itself (including those we have dealt with in this chapter) and in part by dynamics internal to journalism and its institutionalised relationship with the political world (later chapters deal with these in greater detail). The independent and enduring importance of different journalistic traditions and different kinds of relationships between reporters and their political sources is demonstrated time and again throughout the book, underlining that even at a time of great structural change in the media sector, we cannot understand political journalism without also understanding politics (Blumler and Gurevitch, 1995; Cook, 1998; Pfetsch, 2004). This fundamental point was the one Thomas Carlyle made Edmund Burke emphasise when he attributed the idea of the 'fourth estate' to him and called journalism not only 'a power' but also 'a branch of government'. By highlighting the physical location of nineteenth-century reporters inside parliament itself, in the gallery, he also underlined how close political journalism is to politics. The physical, social, and symbolic proximity between journalists and politicians and the potential for the use and abuse of power that such proximity represents constitute significant themes more than 150 years later across Western Europe. It is striking that both British and Danish journalists use the same metaphor and describe politicians, political reporters, and pundits as parts of the 'Westminster bubble' and 'Christiansborg bubble' respectively. Moreover, in both countries research shows that many people often feel political journalists cover politics on its own terms, using its internal language, and thus making it hard for citizens to make sense of the news, let alone the substantive issues covered (Couldry et al., 2010; Harrits, 2006). In Germany, there is talk of a 'politics–media village' or a Berlin 'spaceship', largely separated from the rest of the Federal Republic and the concerns of ordinary people. In France, relations between the journalistic and political elites are extraordinarily close (and sometimes intimate). In Italy, where individual top politicians and their entourages are sometimes defined as a distinct beat, the close everyday relations between reporters and officials seem almost formalised. In all these countries, it is clear that we need to pay close attention not only to the routine interactions between journalists and politicians, but also to the informal and formal ties that bind them together in relationships that are adversarial one moment and symbiotic the next, as well as to the paths via which some journalists move into politics (as advisers or candidates) and sometimes back to the news media.

In many cases, the ties between media and politics go well beyond the individual networks cultivated in these half-secluded social worlds of political gossip, technocratic jargon, and informal social exchanges. It is clear that in countries as diverse as France, Germany, and the United Kingdom, top politicians have cultivated high-level contacts with media owners and executives and through these have tried to influence news coverage. In France, President Sarkozy was seen as close to the Lagardère group with its many print and web publications as well as to the Bouygues group, which owns the commercial television station TF1. In Germany, press watchdog groups have expressed rising concern about political attempts to influence public service television, while several prominent politicians have been regarded as being too close to top editors at the tabloid *Bild*. In the United Kingdom, successive governments from both the centre-left and centre-right have assiduously courted Rupert Murdoch's News International titles (including the broadsheet *The Times* as well as the tabloid *Sun*) and the influential *Daily Mail*, as well as exerting extensive pressure on the BBC in an attempt to influence its coverage. In Italy, high-level ties between media and politics are far more than informal, taking on formal character in the *lottizzazione* practices that divide up editorial control of the main public service Rai channels between the political parties (Mancini, 2007a) and most obviously in the direct control former prime minister Silvio Berlusconi exercised over most of the commercial broadcast sector through his company Mediaset (as well as the control his brother Paolo exercises over the nationally distributed broadsheet that he owns, *Il Giornale*). Not only political journalism, but also the organisations that sustain and constrain it, can be highly politicised and never entirely free of political influence, as commercial media companies are in a regulation-sensitive business and public service media ultimately depend on political support.

It is important to be aware of these many and close ties between political actors, journalists, and media organisations and to critically examine their implications for political journalism and its role in democracy, but also to recognise that they may be a necessary part of journalistic work. Political journalists are in many cases uncomfortably close to the powerful people they cover, highly dependent on access to maintain their own professional standing, and tightly intertwined in their daily work with political institutions that many European citizens no longer trust. This can be a problem, but it is also part and parcel of what political journalism is – a profession that claims to serve the public and has to at least be seen as in part doing so in order to retain its special standing in contemporary democracies, while at the same time one that remains deeply dependent on political actors as it tries to do this. Political journalism is thus 'part of government' in Carlyle's terms, at least as much as it is a 'safeguard of public liberty' as Macaulay would have it. These two facets are not in direct contradiction with each other, a bad side and a good side of political journalism so to speak, but more in constant and necessary tension. The profession can only serve as a safeguard for public liberty insofar as it is seen as a power and is involved in processes of government. But being so risks compromising its ability to serve the public whenever it gets too close to those it covers and moves too far away from its popular audience. Almost 200 years after Macaulay first used the term, after the rise of first industrialised mass media and later digital, networked media, after many transformations in both journalism and political life, the notion of the 'fourth estate' remains a useful way of thinking about the position of political journalism. It is tightly intertwined with politics and always potentially compromised by this relationship, but it is also a potentially powerful safeguard of public liberty precisely because this relationship exists. In short, political journalism cannot be practised in splendid isolation.

As is made clear throughout these chapters, Western European political journalism in the early twenty-first century is in a transitional period, characterised by both change and continuity. It is that period we examine in this book, trying to capture both the structural changes

17

journalists have to contend with as well as the role their own profession and their relations to politics play in shaping the direction of travel. Political journalism always and continuously reinvents itself, changing in dramatic ways from the reporters of the time of Macaulay and Carlyle (who wrote for numerous competing limited-circulation periodicals) through to twentieth-century newspaper and television journalists (who could count on audiences in the hundreds of thousands and sometimes millions), and on to today's multi-tasking newsmen and newswomen (who produce around the clock for numerous platforms that range from mass audience evening news bulletins to social media updates read by a few hundred aficionados). Throughout each of these reinventions, political journalism has provoked complaints from critics about personalisation, an obsession with politics at the expense of policy, and tendencies towards popularisation. It has also occasioned warnings of a 'crisis of journalism', of a decline in standards, and of a trivialisation of public discourse – warnings that are as old as journalism, standards, and public discourse itself. These criticisms – both when they hit the mark and when they do not – are testimony to the importance contemporary societies assign to political journalism and the widespread belief that it occupies a special position, exercises real power, and, at best, helps make democracy possible – and thus calls for critical scrutiny as well as careful practice. It is a special position that each generation of political journalists has inherited since the nineteenth-century reporters Macaulay and Carlyle wrote about, but also one they have had to win anew as their vocation goes through various transitions – such as the early twenty-first-century one we analyse in this book. It is a position that journalists lose at their own and democracy's peril.

Structure of the book

In this opening chapter we have provided a brief overview of political journalism in Western Europe, highlighted some of the inherited differences that exist within this group of otherwise relatively similar countries, outlined what we see as the most important structural changes currently affecting Western European political journalism, and alluded to some of the ways in which developments in this part of the world differ from those in, for example, the United States. We have emphasised that this book is about change and continuity in Western European political journalism and these themes run through the different chapters that make up the rest of this volume.

Among the main *changes* are the effects of technological shift, including the impact of the decline of the business model for paid newspapers; the expansion of news provision in broadcast and online media; the huge amount of news and journalism available to audiences; and the professionalisation of sources. Evidence of all of these changes can be found in our five national case studies. Yet, as has been emphasised in this opening chapter and will be clear from a reading of these case studies, the precise impact of these changes varies, in part because of national variations in the institutional configuration of political systems and media systems, in part because of cultural differences that even in a globalised and regionally integrated Europe remain relevant. The *continuities*, including the continuing importance of national differences, can be seen clearly both in terms of the overall development of media industries from country to country, but also when one examines more qualitative phenomena like the close relationships that exist between political elites and journalists. The existence of such close relations is emphasised in all of the national case studies, and would appear to be a strong element of similarity across Western European political journalism, and not a surprising one. (It would be a strange environment indeed in which politicians and journalists did not regularly meet up, did not have off-the-record conversations, and did not sometimes trade favours, including information and sometimes exposure.) But when one examines more closely the character of these linkages, national differences, even amongst neighbouring countries, appear. For instance, while in France several prominent top politicians and political reporters have been openly romantically involved in recent years, across the Rhine in Germany, the use of the casual *du* rather than the formal *Sie* as a form of address is considered inappropriately intimate for reporters in their dealing with sources. As later chapters show, the more one drills down into the details of political journalism across Western Europe, the more it becomes clear that while there are evident similarities across the region, differences – sometimes structural and formally institutionalised, sometimes at the level of informal norms and everyday practices – are also pronounced.

The book is divided into two parts which provide more detailed analysis of the issues raised in this opening chapter. The first part consists of five national case studies, with chapters on France, Italy, Germany,

Denmark, and the United Kingdom respectively. Each of these chapters focuses on what the relevant author considers to be key features of contemporary political journalism in that particular country; hence, the organisational format of these national case study chapters is deliberately heterogeneous. We start with two examples of the so-called 'polarised pluralist' model (France and Italy) because they are quite different from the media systems and political cultures most familiar to the Anglophone world, then move on to the 'democratic corporatist' cases (Germany and Denmark) that together with the Mediterranean model dominate Western Europe, and finally examine the United Kingdom which, while having much in common with continental Northern Europe, also has some affinities with the more 'liberal' model of the United States.

In Chapter 2 *Raymond Kuhn* argues that several features of contemporary political journalism in France are national variants of broader cross-national trends that are commonly to be found in other Western European political communication systems. Notwithstanding this, however, he makes clear that there are certain features of the French case which, although they do not make its political journalism exceptional, differentiate it in certain important respects from that of many other Western European systems. These features include the very close relationship (both historic and ongoing) between the state and media, the particularly close nature of the interdependences between elite politicians and political journalists, certain norms and values prevalent in the journalistic culture, the lack of a tabloid press, and specific legal provisions such as the law on the protection of privacy.

In Chapter 3 *Alessio Cornia* shows how the close relationship between media and politics in Italy means that political journalism there has changed much less over the last decade than the wider Italian media system in which television retains its primacy as a means of political information and where newspapers still have limited print circulations. Cornia particularly emphasises the importance of the competitive framework of the national political system and the polarised nature of the country's political culture as explanatory variables for the current state of political journalism in Italy. Interestingly he also points to examples of what he calls a radicalisation of media partisanship which is affecting Italian political journalism in a context of significant political instability in terms of party competition.

In Chapter 4 *Carsten Reinemann and Philip Baugut* focus on Germany, arguing that the German media system has so far been less disrupted by the rise of digital media than many other countries' (the newspaper industry is doing relatively well, television audiences are eroding only slowly, and, while internet use is widespread, online news is still less important here than elsewhere). Nonetheless, German political journalism has actually changed in significant ways as a result of an accelerated news cycle, greater emphasis on chasing audiences, and growing reliance on increasingly professionalised political sources. They also note trends towards a further political media de-alignment, especially in the elite press, contrary to developments in France and Italy.

In Chapter 5 *Mark Blach-Ørsten* focuses on political journalism in Denmark and identifies parallel developments towards an ever more competitive news regime where political journalists – who still predominantly work for a few relatively strong newspaper companies and broadcasters – increasingly compete for stories (as the volume of production has increased to feed an accelerated news cycle and multiple new platforms), for attention (as citizens have more and more platforms to choose from), and for access (as top politicians and their PR people increasingly impose strategic control over the flow of information to select journalists). This results in 'churnalistic' tendencies even as the media system as such seems stable.

In Chapter 6 *Aeron Davis* paints a darker picture of the situation in the UK, arguing that UK political journalism is reeling under the double impact of the economic crisis and the internet on the media organisations that have historically sustained it (in particular newspapers). Increasingly overworked journalists are becoming ever more intertwined with the politicians they cover, dependent on press releases and strategic leaks in their coverage, lacking the resources to critically scrutinise the material they are offered, and increasingly oriented towards insular insider audiences. Many (although not all) of these trends are observable in public service media, such as the BBC, as well as in the commercial print and broadcast media. The political journalism emerging is, Davis suggests, more superficial and sensationalist, less informed and less investigative, more desk-bound, more cannibalistic, and generally prone to taking newsgathering short-cuts.

The second part comprises five chapters on cross-national themes. This section recognises that while political journalism in Western Europe remains deeply shaped by country-specific national traditions and contextual variations, there are also a range of important issues that cut across countries. In Chapter 7 *Olivier Baisnée* examines a very specific type of political journalism – coverage of the European Union. He analyses how the gulf between EU journalism and conventional political journalism grows ever wider. Though the supranational union is clearly political and of great substantial importance, its political processes provide a poor fit for forms of political journalism which are increasingly oriented towards well-known personalities (of which there are few in Brussels), focused on partisan conflict (which in the EU is replaced by fluid, temporary, and issue-specific coalitions), and concerned with fast-moving events (one thing EU decision-making is not). Baisnée's chapter invites us to carefully consider the boundaries of the concept and practice of political journalism in a decision-making context where politics is conducted in a quite distinct form from that of national political systems.

In Chapter 8 *Stephen Cushion* examines the role of public service media, especially licence-fee-funded, independent public service broadcasters like DR in Denmark, ARD and ZDF in Germany, and the BBC in the UK. Public service media are one of the most important sources of political news in most Western European countries, and set the region apart from much of the rest of the world.[1] While they have certainly not been immune to the tendencies towards personalisation, process-orientation, and popularisation that characterise Western European political journalism more generally, Cushion shows how public service media demonstrably contribute to keeping people more informed, and more evenly informed, than commercial news media alone – even in countries like France and Italy where they are less generously funded and less editorially independent than their counterparts in Northern Europe.

In Chapter 9 *Rasmus Kleis Nielsen* pursues the possibility of Western European exceptionalism even further, comparing recent developments in political journalism in the United States with trends in selected Western European countries, demonstrating the important, persistent, and systemic differences that exist on both sides of the Atlantic Ocean, but also identifying some similarities along the lines foreshadowed in this opening chapter. He highlights increased audience fragmentation, an accelerated news cycle, some tendencies towards partisan polarisation in the media, the increased importance of non-journalistic actors in shaping and sharing news, and declining trust in traditional sources of political news as five of the most important facets of current changes in American political journalism, comparing US developments in each of these areas with the situation in France and Germany.

In Chapter 10 *Andrea Umbricht and Frank Esser* adopt a longitudinal approach to the question of convergence or divergence in political journalism, presenting an extensive content analysis of print media reporting in a sample of five Western European countries and the US during the period from the 1960s to the 2000s. They identify both a remarkable consistency in how German and Swiss newspapers have covered politics over the last half-century as well as significant changes in coverage in France, Italy, the UK, and the US, but find little evidence to support the notion that national differences in the content produced by political journalists are fading away.

Finally, in Chapter 11 *Kevin Williams* adopts a historical perspective, focusing on contemporary concerns over the perceived decline of international news reporting. By going back to late nineteenth- and early twentieth-century discussions, he shows how the trope of decline has dominated discussions of foreign correspondence for more than half a century as European and American news organisations, tightly intertwined with imperial systems, retreated from the world after World War II. Williams' chapter is an important reminder that contemporary debates about the quantity and quality of journalistic coverage frequently echo the concerns of previous generations of commentators. His chapter also shows the methodological difficulties inherent in longitudinal comparison in the provision of a particular type of journalistic content, especially as in the internet age one might argue that the amount of information available about what is happening outside of one's national borders has never been more widely or easily available.

Note

1   Some non-European countries also have licence-fee-funded public service broadcasters, including Japan and South Korea, as well as the former British colonies of Australia, Canada, and New Zealand. However, in the rest of the world, many nominally 'public service' broadcasters are more properly understood as state broadcasters, under the control of sitting governments and directly dependent upon them for day-to-day funding.

Part I

National Case Studies

Part I

2

What's So French About French Political Journalism?

Raymond Kuhn

Introduction

A comprehensive account of the state of political journalism in contemporary France would need to address a broad range of factors, including the working conditions and career trajectories of political journalists, their status within the journalistic profession as a whole, the economic situation of the media organisations that employ them, the form and content of their product, and the nature of the upstream linkages with their sources as well as of the downstream relations with their audiences. Similarities and differences of practice between national and local or regional media on the one hand and within and across different media sectors (newspapers, magazines, radio, television, and the internet) on the other would also need to be included in the mix. While this chapter makes reference to some of these disparate variables, its central focus is necessarily limited. It aims to analyse and evaluate political journalism in France largely in terms of the interrelationship between journalists and elite politicians. The emphasis is therefore more on upstream newsgathering and production variables, than on detailed content analysis, patterns of audience usage, or media effects, although some reference is made to these aspects where appropriate.

With this focus in mind, the chapter argues that several features of contemporary political journalism in France are national variants of broader cross-national trends that are commonly found in other Western European political communication systems. Notwithstanding this, however, there are certain features of the French case which, although they do not make its political journalism exceptional, differentiate it in certain important respects from that of other Western European systems. From a comparative perspective, then, France is worthy of study because it *both* typifies some of the important changes in contemporary journalism in Western Europe *and* exemplifies particular elements of national distinctiveness.

The media system

Certain aspects of the French media system are nationally specific (Kuhn, 2011). In terms of the configuration of ownership, for instance, France has no equivalent of a powerful commercial media company such as Murdoch's News Corporation in the UK, Bertelsmann in Germany, or Berlusconi's Mediaset in Italy, all of which have extensive cross-media interests within their respective national markets. In other respects, however, the functioning of the French media is frequently a variant of broader cross-national patterns. For instance, as is the case across Western European media systems in general, the French newspaper sector, notably in its paid-for newsprint version, is in decline. In terms of supply there has been a decrease in the number of individual titles both long-term (since the high point of 1946) and more recently (the print versions of two national daily titles, *France Soir* and *La Tribune*, disappeared from the market in 2011–12). In terms of demand, daily newspaper sales per capita are low by the standards of many (though not all) Western European democracies, with a total print run of paid-for newsprint titles (national and regional dailies combined) of 7.5 million in 2010 for a population of around 65 million. In respect of newspaper circulation, therefore, France can be easily accommodated in Hallin and Mancini's 'Mediterranean or polarised pluralism model' (2004: 89–142).

This means that there is a distinct lack of high-selling national daily newspapers to act as agenda setters for a significant nationwide audience, with the most obvious gap on the supply side and the main reason for low total circulation being the absence of a mass title with tabloid journalistic values: France notably lacks the equivalent of the *Sun* in Britain or *Bild* in Germany. Instead, regional titles, well implanted in their geographic fiefdoms, dominate the daily newspaper market across the country. The national titles produced in Paris are important information providers and sources of comment for their predominantly upmarket readerships, including key decision-makers in the fields of politics and the economy. They devote significant attention to national and international politics and also exert an important indirect impact outside their primary readership through their influence on the news content of the broadcast media. Finally, free newspapers such as *Direct Matin* and *20 minutes* have boosted circulation figures in Paris and major provincial cities in recent years; their focus, however, is predominantly on 'soft news' and apolitical journalistic content (Rieffel, 2010).

The paid-for newspaper sector is in financial meltdown, even if some individual titles are performing better than others. The press's share of media advertising revenue has fallen in recent years, while for print versions of newspapers the costs of raw materials and distribution have substantially increased (Regards sur l'actualité, 2009). Meanwhile – and this is certainly not unique to France – no fully effective business model for the transition to online newspaper publishing has yet been discovered. Large amounts of state aid, recently increased under President Nicolas Sarkozy, are currently being pumped into the system just to keep some newspaper titles afloat (Antheaume, 2010). In contrast, weekly political news magazines, such as *L'Express* and *Le Point*, enjoy comparatively healthy circulations among their well-educated, elite target readerships.

The broadcasting sector has expanded as a result of public policy decisions originating in the 1980s and more recent technological change, notably the switchover from analogue to digital. In particular, the digital terrestrial television platform, rolled out between 2005 and 2011, has brought an array of free channels to those households not subscribing to cable or satellite pay-TV packages. The supply of political information by television was for many years dominated at the national level by the news programmes of TF1 (commercial) and France 2 (public service), with right-wing and uncommitted voters tending to opt for TF1 and left-wing voters showing a preference for France 2 (Vedel, 2013: 66). In recent years this dominance of the two main channels has been challenged by the less mainstream news formats of M6 and Canal+ as well as by rolling news channels such as i-Télé and BFM TV which are freely available on all digital platforms (in contrast to LCI for which viewer payment is required). While audiences for rolling news channels have been small, their content may feed the generalist news channels (for example, LCI is part of the TF1 group) and their presence also influenced the style of the 2012 presidential campaign with the staging of open-air meetings by several candidates in order to obtain 'live' television coverage. By far the biggest challenge for television news providers comes from a lack of interest towards the traditional format and content on the part of certain audiences, notably the young. In the radio sector, stations such as France Inter, RTL, and Europe 1 are important outlets for political news and comment, enjoy healthy audiences, and attract top national politicians in their early morning peak-time interview slots.

The internet has allowed a range of political actors – from the president to the tiniest pressure group – to distribute their messages directly to users without any mediating journalistic filter. During the 2012 presidential campaign, for instance, François Hollande's supporters were particularly active on Twitter; in contrast, by the end of the first-round campaign Sarkozy (with 600,000 'friends') was much stronger than Hollande (91,000) on Facebook (Amedeo, 2012). An online presence is *de rigueur* for established media outlets, both print and broadcasting, with the notable exception of the weekly newspaper *Le Canard enchaîné*, which excels in revelatory journalism and whose articles are often used as feeds by mainstream media because this allows them to cover stories at one step removed by quoting *Le Canard* as the source. Newspapers have launched sophisticated apps for usage via smartphones, tablets, and social media such as Facebook in an attempt to capture the youth market as well as retain existing readers who prefer to access content online. Newspaper websites are popular with the public: in January 2012, Lefigaro.fr was the most used news website in France, followed by the sites of *Le Nouvel Observateur, Parisien/Aujourd'hui en France*, and *Le Monde* (which benefited from the recent launch of a French version of the *Huffington Post* in which *Le Monde* is a stakeholder). Television management has been much slower to commit resources to a significant online news presence and there is nothing of the scale provided in the UK by the BBC and Sky.

Independent news websites such as Mediapart and Atlantico are also a notable feature of the contemporary online world of political journalism, although the business model for these 'pure play' ventures is not as yet established. A case in point is Rue89, which was founded by former journalists from the centre-left newspaper *Libération* in 2007 as an independent news outlet, but was taken over by weekly news magazine *Le Nouvel Observateur* at the end of 2011. While the direct influence on audiences of these independent news websites is small, they can play an important part in the agenda construction of mainstream media, as was shown by the revelations made by Mediapart regarding the Bettencourt affair in 2010 and the Cahuzac scandal in 2012–13, both of which were then taken up by various legacy media (Bruno and Nielsen, 2012: 60).

Across all media sectors, television has long been by far the main mass medium of political information for French citizens and this remained the case during the 2012 presidential election. This dominance of television is not surprising in the light of the medium's social implantation. Virtually every household has at least one television set; multi-channel output is available 'on tap' at no additional cost to users on top of the annual licence fee; television viewing is a well-established leisure activity; the visual qualities of the medium make its content easily accessible; and viewing some output is a ritual event in the daily routine of many citizens. In this regard it should be noted that while their hold over audiences is under threat in the more competitive conditions of the digital communications environment, the main evening news programmes of the national free-to-air channels TF1, France 2, France 3, and M6 still attracted a combined total of around 18–19 million viewers on a daily basis in 2011.

Surveys continue to put television well ahead of radio, the press, or the internet as the public's primary source of national and international news. For instance, at the start of 2013 television was the primary source of national and international news for 57 per cent of citizens, followed by 19 per cent for radio, 10 per cent for the press (down from 14 per cent in 2010), and 13 per cent for the internet (including 8 per cent via the websites of the legacy media and 5 per cent via other websites) (La Croix, 2013). Thus for the French citizenry as a whole television is a more frequent primary source for national and international news than radio, press, and the internet combined. However, news consumption patterns also show important generational differences. At the start of 2013 for all those aged under 35 the internet (24 per cent) came well ahead of both the press (6 per cent) and radio (14 per cent) though still behind television (55 per cent) as the most important source of national and international news. In contrast, among those aged over 65 the press (16 per cent, down from 23 per cent in 2012) came second after television (68 per cent, up from 57 per cent a year previously), ahead of both radio (14 per cent) and the internet (2 per cent) (La Croix, 2012, 2013). In the 35–64 age group radio remained the second most used medium for national and international news after television.

The politics–media nexus

Political journalism in France can be usefully analysed with reference to two features of the politics–media nexus. The first is the extent of press parallelism with political parties. The era of newspaper titles owned by or closely affiliated to political parties has long been over. No major daily newspaper – including the elite opinion formers *Le Monde*, *Le Figaro*, *Libération*, and *Les Échos* – is either owned by or has close organisational links with a party or any other formal political entity. Moreover, in terms of content and editorial line, newspaper titles are frequently reluctant to identify systematically with a particular party or leading political figure. This is most obvious in the case of the regional dailies. Their powerful sales position within particular geographical markets encourages regional titles to downplay any strong party-political views in reporting and editorial commentary for fear of alienating sections of their readership and thus compromising sales figures; commercial self-interest usually trumps any inclination towards overt political partisanship. National titles are more likely than the regional papers to adopt an overtly partisan stance, notably during election campaigns – witness the strong support from *Le Figaro* for Sarkozy and from *Libération* for Hollande in the 2012 presidential contest. The overall result is a complex picture of political parallelism in the contemporary French press, ranging from some editorially partisan titles (some national dailies, some news magazines) at one end of the spectrum to a marked reluctance to display overt and committed political leanings (regional dailies) at the other. This means that in terms of circulation the bulk of the French newspaper industry is uncommitted politically in a crude partisan sense.

The second feature of the politics–media nexus is the degree and nature of state intervention. The state has traditionally taken a close interest in the country's media through the exercise of its ownership, policy-making, regulatory, and financial patronage functions. For instance, state authorities have always enjoyed a close relationship with public service television, which has had difficulty establishing a strong sense of institutional autonomy vis-à-vis the political executive in part because of the path dependence created by the historical legacy of government control and in part because of the state's continuing intervention in terms of top appointments, funding, and remit. Nor is the close relationship between the state and television confined to the public service broadcaster, France Télévisions. Because of the existence of close structural and personal interlinkages between the state and commercial channels, especially under right-wing presidents and governments, even privately owned and advertising-funded television is not synonymous with political independence in France. For instance, the most popular free-to-air commercial network, TF1, has long been regarded as close to politicians from the right of the political spectrum in terms of the structure of the news agenda, the framing of issues, and the tone of coverage (Péan and Nick, 1997). There is also a well-established tradition of state intervention in the configuration of the newspaper market. In the complex negotiations in 2010 to find a new buyer for *Le Monde*, for example, President Sarkozy exerted significant pressure to try to ensure that the influential daily would be taken over by persons sympathetic to the right, although on this occasion the Élysée's efforts ended in failure (Benyahia-Kouider, 2011; Fottorino, 2012).

With reference to their relationship with the state it should also be noted that many of the commercial companies that own a stake in the French media are conglomerates that often bid for state contracts in France, and/or their interests are subject to state regulation, and/or they have business ventures in overseas countries where the French state traditionally exercises political influence (Chupin et al., 2009: 110). It is then a simple step to envisage a relationship based on mutual exchange: positive news coverage for the president and government in return for state decisions sympathetic to the companies' wider corporate as well as media interests.

One should, however, be mindful that deterministic explanations of news production that focus primarily on the dimension of ownership and control oversimplify the way in which news agendas are formed and issues framed on a day-to-day basis. Evidence from across Western democracies shows that the routine operationalisation of news values may result in critical news reporting of politicians even in those outlets where owners and top management are favourably pre-disposed towards them. The close links between the state and various commercial media barons during the Sarkozy presidency, for example, did not necessarily deliver favourable coverage for the President. As the 2012 presidential election approached, not even the best efforts of the Élysée spin machine could prevent journalists from highlighting the President's electoral unpopularity as registered in regular opinion polls, the various movements of industrial unrest that continued to plague France, and the increasing sense of unease about his re-election prospects within the ranks of his own party (Pilichowski, 2012).

Newsgathering and production

With particular regard to the newsgathering and production functions, political journalism in France is characterised by the following three features. First, there has been a professionalisation of elite political sources in terms of news-management strategies and techniques. Clear evidence of this development can be seen in the increased attention and resources allocated to mediated public communication by the political executive. The presidency, for instance, is a pivotal official source for political journalists, with various structural resources as primary definer embedded in the office – institutional centrality, issue expertise, political authority, and electoral legitimacy among others. Under President Sarkozy, the Élysée fully mobilised these resources in a holistic, strategic approach to news management that emphasised an exchange-style relationship with owners, senior management, and news editors in the commercial media and more traditional methods of top-down intervention and political instrumentalisation in the public sector (Kuhn, 2010). Other political actors – including parties, pressure groups, and regional and local government bodies – have also invested significant resources in mediated public relations activities, frequently implemented on the ground by former journalists who have converted into public relations and communication specialists (Gorius and Moreau, 2011). A notable recent example of this transition from journalism to political communication is President Hollande's communication adviser, Claude Sérillon, who was formerly a journalist and television news anchor.

Second, French political journalism operates in highly competitive media markets, the result of the huge expansion of broadcast and online media in recent years. There are not just significantly more media outlets than even ten or twenty years ago, but the processes of newsgathering and production (as well as distribution) have been revolutionised with the advent of digital media and the internet. The growth of online journalism in its different guises has not just posed a huge problem for the monetisation of journalistic content, but has also led to a re-evaluation of working practices within newsrooms, including most notably an emphasis on the multi-functionality of journalists who now need to be able to work across different media platforms. Several French newspapers, including *Le Monde*, were slow to begin the process of integrating their digital and newsprint journalistic staff into a single newsroom. Towards the end of 2012, France Télévisions still maintained separate newsroom staff for their television and online output; in contrast, the free newspaper *Metro* had embraced 'reverse publishing', with priority given to the production of the web version of the paper. The clickstream of audience hits on news stories provides managers and editors with real-time feedback on those stories that are attracting audiences and generating online debate, while user-generated content is now integrated with that of professional journalists (although its impact should not be overestimated – most news content remains the product of professional journalists).

Third, there has been a notable acceleration of the news or 'political information' cycle with the embedding of the 24/7 rolling news culture and the reporting of many events in real time. In the large part this has been driven by the aforementioned technological shift – or, more accurately, the incorporation of technological change into the practices of sources, journalists, and users. Events that may well have not been reported on by mainstream media in the relatively recent past can now go viral in a matter of seconds. Thus, when President Sarkozy directly insulted a member of the public who had refused to shake hands with him at a public event in 2008, the President's words – '*Casse-toi, pauv' con*' ['Get lost, asshole'] – were picked up and transmitted via social media in the instant. In the French case this acceleration of the news cycle was amplified by the political communication style of President Sarkozy, who deliberately strove to keep the news agenda moving on a fast-rolling basis. His hypermediated visibility, especially noticeable in the early period of his presidency, left journalists little time to follow up presidential initiatives in a sustained analytic or evaluative fashion. However, it is much more difficult, if not impossible, for those involved in news production, whether sources or journalists, to influence the process in the reverse direction – that is, to slow down the cycle. Journalists and political actors are trapped in a dynamic of permanent news flow and communication respectively.

It is not just the speed of information transmission that has made life difficult for political journalists. There is also the question of information overload, the bombardment of primary material (text, audio, video) by sources keen to impose their version of events on the news agenda and frame the political debate in a way that serves their partisan interests. Since journalists are now involved in producing content across platforms and informational genres (newspaper articles, blogs, tweets, interactive forums) the time to process incoming material and produce journalistic content has effectively been cut (Rieffel, 2012). In a parallel development the number of newsroom staff has frequently been reduced in response to the parlous financial situation of many media outlets. Political journalism in common with other journalistic genres has become a precarious professional activity for many of its practitioners. In the eyes of critics, these developments have led to a growing reliance on agency copy and news releases in political reportage and a resultant similarity in coverage (Cohen and Lévy, 2008). Meanwhile at the very summit of the profession, a small coterie of the same faces and voices is to be found commenting on political issues and events in newspapers and news magazines, on radio and television, and in books. Alain Duhamel, Franz-Olivier Giesbert, Laurent Joffrin, and Christophe Barbier among others form part of an elite guard of political commentators – a French version of the 'commentariat' (Hobsbawm and Lloyd, 2008) – from whose opinions on every aspect of national political life it is virtually impossible to escape.

In respect of these three features of newsgathering and production in the practice of political journalism, the French case represents a national variant of a common Western European pattern. All of these elements can be found with varying degrees of intensity in other Western European systems. What gives political journalism in France its particular national specificity, its Gallic flavour, lies elsewhere, notably in the journalistic culture and the particular nature of the interdependences between political journalists and elite politicians.

Journalistic culture

In her cross-national comparative study of government news management Barbara Pfetsch emphasises two features of journalistic cultures: first, the role definition of journalists as news-makers in the political arena and, second, the orientations of journalists towards political institutions. With regard to journalists' role definition, she states that this is influenced 'not only by the media they work for but also by the socially and culturally defined expectations that dominate in a national news system. Professional roles can range from neutral transmitter of politics to interpretative or even openly adversarial styles of news reporting' (Pfetsch, 2008: 88).

In the case of French journalistic culture there remains a strong tradition of 'opinionated' and advocacy journalism especially in the national press, the roots of which can be traced back to the literary and political origins of the journalistic profession (Ferenczi, 1993). This culture of political engagement and interpretative journalism, with individual journalists showing support for or opposition to particular parties, policies, or individual politicians, has meant that commentary and opinion have often been more highly prized than accuracy and objectivity (Chalaby, 1996; Ferenczi, 2005). In contrast, neither investigative nor watchdog journalism has ever been a particularly strong feature of the French news media culture, despite some progress from the 1980s onwards (Charon, 2009). Indeed, official sources frequently benefit from the prevalent news culture, whereby the French media, especially television, tend to be followers rather than leaders in the process of agenda construction – they are secondary rather than primary definers.

Critics, including journalists themselves, often point to the functional proximity between political journalists and elite politicians (Masure, 2009; Ridet, 2008), with both sets of actors enjoying close relations and functioning to a large extent in the same milieux. Although their professional career paths are clearly quite different, they operate in a relatively closed world in which they get to know each other well. None of this is particularly new; almost 40 years ago a leading political correspondent of *Le Monde*, Pierre Viansson-Ponté, eloquently alluded to this aspect of the political journalistic microcosm (Viansson-Ponté, 1976: 20–3). Nor is such functional proximity especially unique to France: indeed, the at times rather cosy relationship between politicians and journalists is one of the themes that emerges in the other national case-study chapters in this book. It is rather the particular closeness of the interdependence that is striking in the French case, as evidenced, for instance, in the number of publicly declared romantic liaisons, including marriages, between politicians (male) and journalists (female) in recent years. The most obvious current example of this phenomenon is the relationship between President Hollande and Valérie Trierweiler, who is a former political journalist for the weekly photo news magazine, *Paris Match*.

In much of the mainstream media, deference on the part of journalists to elite politicians remains more of a feature of occupational norms and behaviour in France than in Anglo-American democracies where a journalistic tradition of critical watchdog and 'Fourth Estate' thinking is more firmly implanted. The majority of French journalists remain less distant and less autonomous in their relationship with elite politicians than their counterparts in the UK and USA. This has resulted in a relationship that in the eyes of some commentators is based on overly close cooperation, collusion, and even connivance (Carton, 2003). One radical-left commentator has called the result of this interdependence an uncritical, reverential style of journalism (*un journalisme de révérence*) (Halimi, 2005: 17–48).

A lack of journalistic challenge towards politicians is especially notable in the broadcasting sector. In regional television, for instance, where the public service channel France 3 has a monopoly hold on news programming, institutional sources are privileged by the newsrooms as primary definers because of their 'seriousness' and 'geographic proximity', while the political contribution of regional news programmes is 'strongly marked by the predominance of political information of an official tenor' (Lafon, 2012: 187). Combined with the desire by journalists to reinforce their professional legitimacy by remaining 'neutral' in the partisan political debate and not challenging the original framing by sources, the resulting news product is characterised by what Lafon calls 'the consolidation of consensualism' (2012: 187).

Meanwhile, at the national level, French television interviews between leading politicians and broadcast journalists often seem tame compared to the cut-and-thrust of their equivalents in some other Western democracies. In France elite politicians are frequently given a platform from which to deliver their views, with the journalists posing questions but rarely putting the politicians on the spot or challenging their version of events. The French president in particular is frequently treated with kid gloves in set-piece television interviews on the major networks, being fed 'soft' questions rather than subjected to rigorous interrogation. Frequently more than one journalist is involved in the interview and in practice the president's advisers decide which journalists will be selected, often choosing the news anchors of the main free-to-air networks. These journalists are generalists rather than specialist political correspondents and lack the specific expertise (for example, in economic matters or foreign affairs) to ask probing questions even if they were minded to do so. Going head-to-head with the main evening news anchors from TF1 and France 2 can hardly be considered a trial by fire for an experienced political leader. Journalists may even be given advice regarding the subjects 'on which the president would welcome the opportunity of speaking' (Hayward and Wright, 2002: 93). Only occasionally are the rules of polite engagement infringed, as when Patrick Poivre d'Arvor, the TF1 news anchor at the time, asked Sarkozy prior to his first G8 summit meeting in 2007 if he did not feel like a 'little boy going into the big boys' playground' (*'petit garçon en train d'entrer dans la cour des grands'*). It was reported that Sarkozy had not appreciated the way in which the question had been framed by the interviewer and the news anchor lost his job a few months later.

What explains this journalistic subordination in broadcast interviews? One possible reason might lie in the institutional status of the president as head of state rather than simply head of government. In the Gaullian tradition the president of the Fifth Republic is supposed to be above party-political conflict. Yet the US president is also head of state and embodiment of the nation, but this does not stop the American broadcast media from on occasions adopting a critical stance towards the incumbent in interviews. Moreover, the public–private division in the ownership of the broadcasting media is not an important factor either: there is little appreciable difference between the journalists of TF1 and those employed by France Télévisions in their interviews with the president.

One factor might simply be fear on the part of television journalists that they may end up being pushed to one side within their news organisation if they step out of line. Another explanation might be sympathy on the part of the journalist towards the politician, either out of political conviction or opportunistic careerism. A quite different explanation, however, may lie with audience expectations. The elected politician is a representative of the Republic and a certain formal courtesy, even hierarchical deference, on the part of the journalist is simply part of the cultural protocol. It is not that French television journalists are incapable of being assertive, as has been clear in interviews with Marine Le Pen, where the leader of the National Front has been subjected to a tougher style of questioning than that accorded politicians of both mainstream left and right. Nor is it that French audiences are averse to critical journalistic commentary: there is a market for a range of mocking media treatment of politicians, including cartoon books, newspapers such as *Le Canard enchaîné*, the satirical puppet-based sketch show *Les Guignols de l'Info* on Canal+, and user-generated content on the web.

Yet in the context of a formal television interview with mainstream political leaders, most notably the president, French journalists often prefer to pull their punches. While in terms of content the audience is not best served by this practice, it may be that a full-on adversarial relationship between journalist and political leader in a formal television interview would quite simply not be considered acceptable in a mass audience news programme, especially to an older generation of French viewers. In contrast, in the press, journalistic critiques of the president can be forthright. One front cover of the news magazine *Marianne* accused

Sarkozy of being 'the hooligan of the Republic' ('*le voyou de la République*'), while in the early months of his presidential tenure Hollande was the target of widespread critical commentary. The 'media bashing' of Hollande did not escape the attention of audiences; in response to a question about the way in which Hollande was treated by the media in the early months of his presidency, 31 per cent responded 'unfavourably', while only 13 per cent responded 'favourably' (La Croix, 2013).

With regard to Pfetsch's second feature of the journalistic culture – the orientations of journalists toward political institutions – she argues that these 'can vary from respect and appreciation for the political system to cynicism and distrust' (Pfetsch, 2008: 88). In this context it is important to distinguish between journalists' attitudes towards the values and institutions of the political system on the one hand and to the politicians who seek and occupy office on the other (Blumler and Gurevitch, 1995: 55). Among political journalists in France there is strong support for the traditional values of French republicanism (universalism, secularism, the rights of man) as transmitted via the educational system and considerable respect for the supreme office of the presidency qua office. Yet alongside these views in support of republican values and institutions, French journalists show high levels of distrust, and occasionally cynicism, towards politicians as a class. This is perhaps not surprising, given the significant levels of voter scepticism and suspicion of politicians. At the same time, journalists themselves are regularly regarded by the public as too close to political interests: in 2012, while 28 per cent of citizens saw them as resisting pressures from political parties and the executive, 59 per cent thought the opposite (La Croix, 2012). A survey of voter attitudes published in early 2013 showed that 73 per cent of respondents thought that journalists were 'not independent' and 'had a tendency to give in to pressure from political authorities' (Sondage Ipsos Public Affairs, 2013). In addition, 72 per cent of respondents considered that journalists were 'cut off from reality and did not speak about the real problems of the French'.

Personalisation and scandal

Two aspects of the content of contemporary French political journalism are particularly noteworthy. The first is a strong focus on the personalisation of political issues and electoral competition. International summits, for instance, tend to be covered by the French media through a predominantly national prism that focuses on the key leadership role of the president. In this respect President Sarkozy dominated media coverage not just of domestic politics, but also of those European and international political issues, such as the global financial crisis, in which France was closely involved as a policy actor.

In large part this personalisation of political reportage is a direct consequence of the institutional make-up of the regime; the political system of the Fifth Republic, established by General de Gaulle in 1958, is highly personalised in terms of the concentration of power in the supreme office, with the president frequently called a 'republican monarch' (Duverger, 1974). Moreover, the presidential election has become by far the major political contest in France, with higher electoral turnout and much greater media coverage than the parliamentary election which now follows on a few weeks later.

Yet it is also the case that the news media have amplified this trend towards the personalisation of political reportage. Much coverage of the presidential campaign, for example, is candidate- rather than issue-centred, with an emphasis on the conduct of the campaign, 'horse race' coverage, and the electoral strategies of the leading candidates (Gerstlé, 2008: 115–51). Moreover, while an emphasis on personal leadership may be institutionally driven, the mediatised focus on the personal qualities of leadership is not. There has been a distinct move towards an emphasis on the emotional and psychological aspects of political leadership – the integrity, friendliness, honesty, and empathy of the politician – in journalistic coverage of politics, both during and outside election campaigns. This is a journalism of politics as spectacle, as emotional drama, as soap opera, as a sporting contest between individuals rather than a clash of ideas and ideological values.

What is driving this personalisation of journalistic coverage? There are political factors at work here. There is less ideological conflict between right and left than in the recent past; in 1981 the successful Socialist candidate for the presidency, François Mitterrand, spoke about the need to abolish capitalism and radically change society – a rhetoric that is articulated only towards the fringes of the party system nowadays. Politicians' own political marketing has also helped. Many, though not all, elite politicians are now willing to put aspects of their private lives into the public sphere as part of their electoral campaigning. As a result, there is now greater journalistic coverage about the everyday 'human' side of politicians, including the lives of their spouses or partners. This was particularly evident with Sarkozy. Hollande pledged in 2012 to reintroduce a dividing line between public and private, but this has proved difficult to enforce, in part because of contemporary media expectations regarding the role of the French 'first lady' and in part because his partner, initially at least, refused to stay out of the public limelight.

In addition, the scenography of the political landscape has changed. Globalisation and greater European integration have made an understanding of contemporary issues of resource allocation and conflict management more complex for citizens (and, indeed, for many journalists) than in the past; it is easier for journalists to construct and for audiences to understand a narrative centred on conflict between leadership figures. Ironically, this has come at a time when the French president (whatever the political complexion of the incumbent) has arguably less autonomous power to influence events, for example in domestic economic management, than his early predecessors in the Fifth Republic, such as General de Gaulle (1958–69) and Georges Pompidou (1969–74). Regular publication of opinion polls in the media also fuel the journalistic concern with personalised politics. Voters are asked about the personal qualities of politicians and the results are given high-profile media coverage. The popularity ratings of the president and other members of the executive act like a thermometer of public opinion and fuel speculation as to how executive figures will react when their popularity dips or goes into freefall.

The second feature of contemporary political journalism in France is the growing place accorded to coverage of scandal. Financial scandals have long been an integral part of the journalistic coverage of French politics. In recent years, for instance, the media have covered various scandals related to leading politicians of both right and left, notably in the field of financial malpractice where the media have called into question the probity of politicians and demanded greater transparency on behalf of the electorate. One of the most recent high-profile stories was the accusation in December 2012 by the news website Mediapart, tipped off by an opposition politician, that the budget minister in the Socialist government of President Hollande, Jérôme Cahuzac, had illegally held a secret bank account in Switzerland. The accusation proved to be accurate and not only resulted in the humiliating resignation of the minister (who ironically was responsible for the control of tax evasion), but also caused a full-blown political crisis for the Hollande presidency and led to the introduction of new legislation in April 2013 that was designed to clean up political life and introduce greater transparency into the financial affairs of ministers and parliamentarians.

While coverage of financial scandals has a long tradition, any whiff of sexual scandal has normally been covered quite differently. The French media have been much more cautious when it comes to reporting the sexual (mis)behaviour of their political leaders. Journalists have been quite happy to allude in more or less veiled terms to the sexual affairs of leading politicians in books, but not in newspapers and magazines or in the broadcast media. There has been a long-standing agreement between politicians, journalists, and the public that sexual relationships, including marital infidelity, belong to the private sphere and are off-limits to media coverage. The existence of strong privacy legislation is just one factor that helped act as a barrier to the media intrusiveness into the private lives of political leaders that is often found in other Western democracies (Stanyer, 2013), but the dominant norms of the journalistic culture also played a significant role in shoring up the division between public and private.

The most notorious example of media reticence in the face of an executive leader's sexual behaviour was President Mitterrand's extra-marital relationship with Anne Pingeot and in particular the product of their union, their daughter Mazarine. It was not until November 1994, when Mazarine was already nearly 20 years old, that Mitterrand's private secret was, with the tacit acquiescence of the President, made fully public in *Paris Match* (Chemin and Catalano, 2005: 225–43). Prior to this revelation journalists had cooperated, even colluded, with the Élysée to keep Mitterrand's secret out of the public realm, even though the news story contained elements of clear public interest, since state funds were being used for the purposes of Mazarine's accommodation and personal security (Schneidermann, 2010: 76–7).

More recently, the French media appear to have become much less reticent in their coverage of the sexual liaisons of their political leaders, as exemplified by the attention devoted to relations between President Sarkozy and his successive wives Cécilia Attias and Carla Bruni. For instance, the tempestuous on–off relationship between Sarkozy and Attias was a staple element of journalistic coverage until their divorce in October 2007, notably when she left the marital household in 2005 and her new relationship was covered in depth by the news media, including a front-cover picture in *Paris Match* that featured her with her new lover. This would certainly seem to indicate a new intrusiveness on the part of

French journalists into the private lives of political leaders, including the president.

Yet appearances can be deceptive. The media covered the downside of Sarkozy's relationship with Attias only because the politician had himself previously instrumentalised this relationship for political purposes: until their marital problems came to dominate the news headlines, the supposedly close relationship between Sarkozy and Attias had been mediatised at length by the then government minister. It was Sarkozy – not the media – who first stepped over the dividing line between public and private. Indeed, the extent to which Sarkozy used his personal life for political self-promotion was ground-breaking in the French context, especially in its focus on the intimate aspects of the private sphere (Dakhlia, 2008). Sarkozy complained bitterly about media coverage of Attias's new relationship and later helped secure the removal of the magazine editor responsible for the infamous cover photo (Genestar, 2008). However, by using his family for the purposes of electoral marketing, Sarkozy had in the eyes of many journalists given up his right to protection from media intrusion (Domenach and Szafran, 2011). The mediatisation of intimacy by Sarkozy helped to break down the public–private barrier for journalists, who considered that aspects of the private life of the president had been made fair game for journalistic coverage.

However, the incident that really called into question the manner in which French journalists had previously ignored the sexual behaviour of leading politicians was the Strauss-Kahn scandal. In May 2011, Dominique Strauss-Kahn, head of the IMF and widely tipped to be the Socialist Party candidate in the 2012 presidential election (and therefore favourite to win the presidency), was imprisoned in New York on charges of sexual assault and attempted rape of a hotel chambermaid. Many political journalists had been well aware of Strauss-Kahn's sexually predatory behaviour: a female member of the IMF staff who had been pressurised by Strauss-Kahn to have sex with him had already written publicly about his unacceptable behaviour, while a French journalist, Jean Quatremer, had in 2007 published on the website of the daily newspaper *Libération* (but this was not included in the print edition) a guarded indictment of Strauss-Kahn's relations with women (Quatremer, 2012). In general, however, journalists had not put the full story into the public realm as it was not considered relevant to his political career – it was deemed to be a purely private matter. Once the news of his arrest emerged, however, several journalists, especially but not exclusively female, started to question their previous silence. What the journalists (and the French public) found shocking was not that Strauss-Kahn had been unfaithful to his wife – hardly a newsworthy event in France – but that he had engaged in sexual harassment and, it seemed, violent behaviour to satisfy his sexual urges. That a man who regarded women in such a light could well have become president came as a wake-up call. The Strauss-Kahn scandal has arguably changed the boundaries in terms of journalistic coverage of the private lives of politicians. While respect for a politician's private life will still be more easily accorded than in some other Western European countries, it is possible that the fallout from the Strauss-Kahn affair may represent a turning point in opening up coverage by French journalists of the traditionally no-go area of politicians' sexual behaviour.

Conclusion

This chapter has argued that several features of contemporary political journalism in France are national variants of broader cross-national trends that are to be found across Western European political communication systems as a whole. What then is distinctive about the French case – what's so French about French political journalism? In response, one might point inter alia to the very close relationship between the state and media, particularities of the interdependences between elite politicians and political journalists, certain norms and values prevalent in the journalistic culture, the lack of a tabloid press, and legal provisions such as the law on the protection of privacy. While even in combination these variables may not make French political journalism exceptional, they do differentiate it in certain important respects from that of other Western European systems and make a national case study a valuable exercise.

Indeed, one of the interesting aspects of such a case study is that the more one drills down into examining a country's political communication system and culture of political journalism, the more nuanced and circumspect one becomes in making broad generalisations even *within* a single national context. For instance, in the French system in recent years the nature of the interdependence between journalists and the presidency was shaped to a considerable extent by the persona of Sarkozy, his governing style, and particular approach to news management. A new president, such as Hollande, with a different presidential style, will seek to influence journalistic coverage of his term in office in distinct ways from his predecessor. A change of presidential incumbent with a different constellation of communication advisers and favoured reporters allows at least the possibility for some change in the relationship between journalists and politicians in France, even with no modification of the institutional framework of the political system.

At the same time it is reasonable to ask whether elements of national specificity in French political journalism will endure – and, if so, for how long. After all, journalistic norms and practices have already considerably altered since the foundation of the Fifth Republic, in some respects quite markedly, as a result of broader cultural changes in society, the introduction of new technology, and the professionalisation and feminisation of journalistic employment (Neveu, 2009). More recently, French journalistic practice has incorporated aspects of so-called 'Anglo-American' journalism – such as the introduction of the fact-checking of politicians' claims as in the 'Désintox' page of *Libération* – as a result of the transfer of practices across national borders and greater formal training in journalism schools. While full-on UK-style tabloid coverage remains an unlikely prospect, it may be that French political journalism will in the future incorporate even more aspects of so-called Anglo-American journalism (Williams, 2006) – Mediapart, for instance, explicitly positions itself as oriented towards investigative journalism. It may also be the case that competitive conditions will encourage more journalists to move away from the 'pack' and that a younger and more highly educated generation of political journalists will prove to be less deferential towards elite political actors than has been the case heretofore. If so (and it must be stressed that such a prospect is by no means inevitable), the answer to the question 'What's so French about French political journalism?' could turn out to be 'considerably less than in the past'. At the same time, one should not overlook elements of national specificity that will in all likelihood endure: the national origin of the majority of French political journalism's sources, producers, and users; a huge swathe of nationally focused content (electoral contests, political personalities, historical reference points, and domestic policy issues); and the official language of the Republic in which most French political journalism will continue to be expressed.

3

Will Italian Political Journalism Ever Change?

Alessio Cornia

Introduction

The aim of this chapter is to analyse and explain the dynamics of change and continuity that exist in contemporary Italian political journalism. After a short section outlining certain key features of the media system, the main characteristics of the national tradition of journalism are analysed with reference to certain specificities of the media and political contexts in which it has developed. In particular, this section focuses on those enduring journalistic features that are heavily influenced by the close relationship between media and politics, the competitive framework of the political system, and the polarised nature of Italian political culture. Our argument is that because of these variables political journalism has tended to resist the process of change that is affecting the Italian media system in general. In contrast, in the final section some case studies are presented that illustrate innovative elements in the Italian political news environment. These examples are related to a wider tendency towards the radicalisation of media partisanship that is currently affecting Italian political journalism, with new technologies being used as innovative means to participate in the political debate.

The media system

The Italian media system is characterised by the predominance of television in attracting both resources and audiences. Television accounts for more than half the total revenues of the whole media system (its dominance is particularly evident in the advertising market) and is the main source of information for most Italians (see Table 3.1). In contrast, the media sector where most journalists are employed and where national political news is covered in most depth is the press.

Table 3.1 Revenues, source of news, and number of journalists by media sector (Italy, 2011)

	Overall revenues (%)	Number of journalists (%)	Media used to get information (%)
Television	51	22	89
Daily newspapers	17	45	62
Magazines	19	26	9
Radio	4	4	19
Internet	10	3	21
Total	100 N=17,540 million euros	100	% of interviewees using the media to get information

Source: author's processing of data from AgCom (2011; source of news) and AgCom (2012; revenues and number of journalists).

Both television and the press are characterised by close ties between media and politics and by a marked political parallelism (Hallin and Mancini, 2004). The party press played a central role in Italian political journalism up until a few decades ago. Today its readership has strongly declined: many outlets representing the specific views of a particular party are no longer available, while the economic survival of those still in existence is strictly dependent on state subsidies, which often represent most of the total revenue of this kind of newspaper (Cocconi, 2010; Gambaro, 2010). Public funding is considered one of the main factors that contribute to keeping the Italian political press separate from a purely market-driven approach. Yet, as pointed out by the Italian Communication Authority, in the light of the low readership of party newspapers, press subsidies are more effective in fragmenting and distorting the newspaper market than in assuring pluralism in the supply of news and political information (AgCom, 2012). Nonetheless, despite the party press playing a weaker role nowadays and the fact that its very survival is seriously at risk (because of the reduction of state support and the growth of a widespread belief that there is no convincing rationale for press subsidies any more), its presence has contributed to shaping the Italian journalistic culture, notably its tradition of advocacy and partisan journalism.

Another long-established feature of the Italian press is the absence of what Italian scholars call 'pure publishers' (Barile and Rao, 1992; Hallin and Mancini, 2004; Mancini, 2002; Mazzoleni et al., 2011; Seghetti, 2010). Most newspapers are owned by business people involved in other economic activities: their core business is not publishing but, for example, the construction industry, the financial sector, or private healthcare. These newspaper owners operate their media outlets not only because of the profit they expect to obtain by selling news, but also at least in part because they wish to play a role in Italian political life and influence the policy-making process in favour of their non-journalistic business interests. One Italian scholar has defined this phenomenon as 'Italian-style lobbying' (Ortoleva, 1997). Even today, for example, the car manufacturer FIAT owns *La Stampa* (one of the newspapers with the highest circulation in northern Italy), the national employers' federation Confindustria controls *Il Sole 24 Ore* (the main business newspaper), and Carlo De Benedetti (the former president of Olivetti, now involved in several businesses, such as the energy sector, healthcare, and finance) controls *La Repubblica*, one of the most popular national newspapers. The newspaper with the largest readership, *Il Corriere della Sera*, is controlled by a group of financial and construction companies.

Further evidence of the fact that the Italian press is conceived as an instrument to garner political support and to influence the government rather than a 'pure' business venture is the absence of tabloid-style newspapers: all Italian dailies are quality newspapers with a strong focus on political news and current affairs. The main target of the Italian newspapers' political pages, therefore, is not the mass audience, but rather the well-educated and powerful elites that the 'impure publishers' try to influence. Many years ago, Enzo Forcella, an Italian journalist, captured this aspect of Italian journalism by using the metaphor of the 'fifteen hundred readers':

> *A political journalist in our country can count on fifteen hundred readers: the ministers and under-secretaries (all of them), members of parliament (some), party and trade union leaders, the top clergy and*

those industrialists who want to show themselves well-informed. The rest doesn't count, even if a newspaper sells three hundred thousand copies. First of all, it is not clear whether the common readers read the first page of the paper, and in any case their influence is minimal. The whole system is organized around the relation of the journalist to that group of privileged readers. (Forcella, 1959, quoted and translated in Hallin and Mancini, 2004: 96)

Despite the fact that the Italian daily press has always reached a narrow audience and that it is currently facing a general decline in circulation, it still remains an important arena within the national political communication system. Politicians, ministers, business people, and other Italian elites strongly rely on these newspapers to obtain political information and, especially, to communicate among themselves. Through the daily press they follow and comment on the ongoing process of negotiation that characterises the complex multi-party system of contemporary Italy, they compete to build the public agenda, they signal positions and commitments, and they put pressure on one another (Hallin and Mancini, 2004). This kind of journalism is strongly elitist, self-referential, and mainly addressed to political insiders; but the daily press is *the* place where large amounts of news, opinions, scoops, and background information about Italian political life can be found, and its articles are often quoted by other media.

If newspapers' political information is mainly addressed to an elite, the main target of Italian television is the mass audience (Statham, 1996): all the main international statistics (for example, Eurobarometer and WAN-IFRA data) show that Italy, compared to other Western European countries, is particularly weak in newspaper circulation and strong in television consumption. However, an instrumental notion of the media has historically also prevailed in the broadcasting sector: the political parties have always conceived of television as a means to establish and maintain their cultural and political hegemony over Italian society (Padovani, 2009). Since the 1970s, the expression *lottizzazione* has been commonly used to describe the power sharing within Rai, the Italian public service broadcaster. As testified by many scholars, 'through the practice of *lottizzazione*, the control of the political parties over the state broadcasting media was institutionalised' (Statham, 1996: 515) and public television became 'a privatized sphere of political patronage' (Hibberd, 2001: 236).

This logic is still applied to the appointment procedures of the public broadcaster, but with new division-of-spoils mechanisms that are related to changes in Italian parliamentary representation:[1] the editor-in-chief of Tg1 – the main public news programme – is chosen by the main party in power; Tg2 is under the patronage of the right-wing parties; and Tg3 is controlled by the parties of the left. Moreover, *lottizzazione* affects not only the appointment of the members of Rai's Administrative Council, heads of the three channels, and editors-in-chief of the three news programmes, but also the choice of a large part of the personnel down through the organisation, journalists included (Hallin and Mancini, 2004). Indeed, the parties' influence over state television is reflected in its political coverage: each of the three public news programmes tends to support one of the three main parties (Statham, 1996).

Another historical peculiarity of the Italian media system concerns the level of ownership concentration. While the press market is quite fragmented, the television sector is structured as a duopoly: from the 1980s up until the early years of the twenty-first century, the three channels of Rai and the three of the commercial broadcaster Mediaset, owned by Silvio Berlusconi, attracted a combined audience share of approximately 90 per cent and an even larger proportion of the industry's advertising revenues. Italian commercial television does not benefit from a greater distance from political power than the public broadcaster and, since 1994 (when Berlusconi entered the political arena), the impact of the duopoly on pluralism has become a major democratic concern. Through the *lottizzazione* mechanisms, Berlusconi – as Italian prime minister and owner of the national private broadcaster – was able to control, directly and indirectly, all the commercial channels and two out of three of the public news programmes (D'Arma, 2010; Padovani, 2009). Moreover, Berlusconi also owns a newspaper and is involved in other businesses, such as advertising, finance, and a football club. As will be shown in this chapter, Berlusconi's unresolved conflict of interests and his influence on the mass media still contribute to the radicalisation of some of the most prominent features of Italian political journalism.

The main features of Italian political journalism

The main features of Italian political journalism have been quite stable over time and strongly linked to particular aspects of the media system,

51

the political system, and Italian political culture. The first point to note is that political journalism plays a central role within the overall journalistic culture in Italy: news coverage focuses strongly on politics and, very often, political content is covered on newspaper front pages and is accorded the most prominent position in broadcast news. In 2009, for example, domestic politics was the main topic in television news programmes: according to data released by Isimm Ricerche, all national news bulletins combined devoted 31.6 per cent of their time to domestic politics, compared with 16 per cent to foreign news and 7 per cent to economic coverage (Isimm Ricerche, 2010).[2] The centrality of politics in journalistic coverage seems to be particularly marked in the Italian context: cross-national comparative research carried out by the Osservatorio di Pavia showed that in 2008 the Italian public service news programmes devoted almost 35 per cent of their coverage to politics, compared with only 16.5 per cent in the equivalent output of a sample of other Western European public service broadcasters (see the first part of Table 3.2). Since politics is central in Italian news coverage, political journalists are perceived as having the highest status inside the journalistic field.

In addition, Italian coverage of politics is particularly focused on the activities of political parties: political journalists concentrate their attention on intra- and inter-party debates, strategic alliances, and the evolution of relations among political figures, rather than on the decision-making process and its policy outputs. The Isimm Ricerche data testify to the centrality of parties in Italian political journalism: in 2008 – a year characterised by national elections and consequently by an increased interest in political issues – the parties obtained 53.2 per cent of total news programme time devoted to institutional and political actors, whereas the government secured 32.4 per cent and the head of state and all other actors obtained only 14.4 per cent (Isimm Ricerche, 2009).

Furthermore, Italian political journalism assigns a central role to politicians' statements. The typical structure of an Italian news report (both print and broadcast) is a brief presentation of an event, followed by a larger focus on comments given by political actors (Hallin and Mancini, 2004). While politicians' declarations are also important in other journalistic cultures, very often for Italian journalists the politician's statement *is* the news. The second part of Table 3.2 shows that 55 per cent of Italian political news is based on sources' declarations, expressing an evaluation or a purpose, while less than half of the coverage is focused on actions or decisions taken by institutions. In contrast, coverage by

Table 3.2 Differences in television news programme content: comparison between Rai and other Western European public service broadcasters (PSBs)

	Rai*	Other Western European PSBs*
Political content in newscast coverage (%)		
Political news	34.8	16.5
Other kinds of news	65.2	83.5
Total	100	100
Kind of event on which the news is based (%)		
Actions/decisions**	45	74.6
Statements**	55	25.4
Total	100	100
Level of conflict in political news (%)		
News with a conflictual frame***	41.6	20.7
News without a conflictual frame	58.4	79.3
Total	100	100

* 'Rai' includes Tg1, Tg2, and Tg3. 'Other Western European PSBs' includes BBC One (UK), France 2 (France), TVE (Spain), and ARD (Germany). Content analysed: 14 editions of each news outlet in 2008.

** 'Actions/decisions' includes news focusing on the approval of bills and other activities of parliament or government; meetings between political and/or social organisations; conferences, conventions, etc. 'Statements' includes declarations expressing a purpose or an evaluation, polemics, etc.

*** 'Conflictual frame': news focusing on polemics, adopting narrative forms centred on the opposition between differing opinions.

Source: Osservatorio di Pavia (2008).

German, French, British, and Spanish public broadcasters is mainly focused on events and actions as well as on the outputs of the decision-making process. In similar comparative research, Canel et al. (2007) reached the same conclusion: Italian television journalists typically do not give an autonomous description of events; instead they limit themselves to reporting what politicians say about the events they take part in. From this perspective, Italian journalism is opinionated not only because journalists mix the facts they cover with their own opinions (a practice much more common in newspaper journalism), but also because their stories are built around the opinions of political sources.

A previous study of Italian journalism showed that the centrality of politicians' statements is one of the main differences between the typical working routines of Italian journalists covering the national political scene and those of Italian correspondents covering EU activities in Brussels (Cornia, 2010). As two Italian journalists explained:

> *The journalism in Brussels [...] is less opinioned, it is more factual. [...] In Italy we believe that journalism is 'to record' the opinions of Diliberto [an Italian political leader] who criticizes other politicians or the government. In Italy there is a journalism of opinions, of other people's opinions.*

> *In Italy [...] if you follow Berlusconi, 90 percent of the news is: 'the Berlusconi statements'. Then you embellish [the story] with the goings-on behind the scenes. (Interview with two Italian press journalists, quoted in Cornia, 2010: 375)*

This centrality of party politics and of politicians' statements in news coverage is linked to some of the particularities of the Italian political and media systems, notably the importance of parties in Italian political life and, consequently, their deep influence on the journalistic field. Considering that the political authorities control (directly or indirectly) several news outlets, notably in the television sector, it is easy to understand why journalists' reporting strongly focuses on politics and is structured around politicians' statements. Because of the *lottizzazione* logic, for example, Rai journalists have to account to several superiors (many deputy-editors-in-chiefs, desk editors, etc.), each one of whom is an 'informal representative' of a different political party inside the newsroom. A news feature structured around many (often too many) declarations by politicians is a direct consequence of the multiple political pressures television journalists have to deal with.

Statements released by politicians in public contexts are also important in press journalism, but the *retroscena* (background news) is considered the most prestigious journalistic product. Since the newspapers' political pages are mainly aimed at a narrow audience largely composed of insiders, journalists make a strong effort to uncover the 'behind-the-scenes' aspects of Italian politics, to reconstruct the 'real' reason why a politician said or did something, and to investigate the meaning of an 'obscure' political event. From this perspective, Italian press journalists do not limit themselves to describing an event; they activate confidential sources – and sometimes mix the reported facts with their personal evaluations – in order to offer to their audience a distinctive interpretation of what is going on in the political arena.

Hence, press journalists' newsgathering practices are often based on a personal relationship with a politician or with a political faction: they strongly rely on off-the-record information, on confidences given by politicians they are close to, and on rumours and gossip circulating inside the Transatlantico (the large hall of the Italian Parliament where deputies and journalists are accustomed to having informal interactions and where most political scoops emerge) (Cornia, 2010; Mancini, 1994). Newspapers' political information is widely based on the newsgathering work carried out by '*ad personam* journalists' – that is, reporters specialising in the coverage of one single leading political figure. Their function is to develop and consolidate relationships with the political leader and their staff in order to obtain more on-the-record statements and off-the-record information. The internet has not changed this aspect of Italian journalism: undoubtedly social networking sites are increasingly used as sources of information – for instance, it might be the case that the statements reported in the coverage of political debates are based on a tweet released by a leading political figure – but the typical newsgathering practices of Italian political journalism are always based on the informal interaction and personal relationships between politicians and reporters.

As journalists use politicians to obtain confidential information, so in turn politicians use journalists to secure positive media coverage. Therefore, boundaries between journalism and politics are blurred. An interpersonal relationship with a leading politician is often the reason why a journalist obtains advancement in their career. Moreover, journalists sometimes start a prominent political career in the party they are closest to. This was the case, for example, of Lilli Gruber and David Sassoli, two former Rai journalists who were proposed as candidates by the centre-left and elected to the European Parliament in 2004 and 2009 respectively.

Another feature of Italian political journalism is the centrality of conflict. Political coverage strongly focuses on political controversies and struggles between opposing interests or views of society. This is not surprising in a country marked by a polarised and conflictual political culture (Almond and Powell, 1966; Sartori, 1976), whose origins can be found in its history. Italian history has been studded with many conflicts that created long-lasting cleavages that still affect the contemporary political system. The confrontation between Church and State during the national unification process – to give just one historical example – has underpinned the still existing antagonism between clerical and secular forces. This history of conflict has crystallised a feeling of reciprocal hostility between political factions, which hampers cooperation between parties and prevents any unemotional, non-ideological, and rational political discourse. On the contrary, as observed by Sani (1980), the 'pattern of antagonism' characterising Italian political culture encourages political conflict, supports the predisposition of politicians to refuse compromise solutions, and reinforces the dissemination of ideologically oriented political viewpoints.

The high level of conflict represented in the news, therefore, certainly reflects a similar level of conflict among political actors. As other studies have demonstrated (Cornia, 2010), however, conflict is often particularly emphasised by Italian journalists: they tend to represent political topics by adopting a conflictual frame and by employing narrative forms and news structures that are centred on the contradiction between opinions. Conflict is undoubtedly an important news value in other journalistic cultures as well: as observed by Lengauer et al. (2011: 182), 'conflict-centred negativity is more "marketable" than positive news as it is more eye-catching, adds drama, stimulates interest, and is easy to understand even by uninformed audiences'. Nevertheless, other comparative studies have demonstrated that this general tendency is particularly predominant in the Italian journalistic tradition. The previously mentioned research carried out by the Osservatorio di Pavia, for example, shows that the conflictual frame is applied in more than 40 per cent of Italian political news, more than double the level of conflict registered in British, French, German, and Spanish news programmes (see Table 3.2 above).

Another well-known feature of Italian political journalism is its partisanship. Traditionally, journalists played an active role in the political struggles that characterised the nation's history; even today they often continue to mix facts with their own opinions and they openly show politically oriented bias (Hallin and Mancini, 2004). This is particularly evident in press and television talk-show journalism, where political commitment and commentary tend to be accepted – or even positively received – by audiences. Indeed, the political culture of the Italian electorate is also strongly polarised and characterised by widespread partisan commitment: a large number of Italian citizens are strongly politicised and are used to interpreting the world on the basis of their partisan affiliations (Sani, 1980). Therefore, while this may not be true of all citizens, relevant segments of the electorate look at the news to find interpretative elements that might confirm their personal views of society. For this reason, Italian information consumption, even today, is marked by a high level of selective exposure to the news: newspapers and news programmes supporting the centre-left parties are read and watched by persons with left-wing sympathies, while news outlets closer to the centre-right parties are used by persons with right-wing sympathies (Mancini, 2011). In 2006, for example, 87 per cent of Tg3 viewers (the traditionally leftist Rai news programme) voted for a centre-left party, while only 12 per cent voted for the centre-right coalition. In contrast, 75.1 per cent and 71 per cent of the audience of the two main news programmes on the channels owned by Berlusconi (Tg4 and Tg5) voted for his political coalition (Itanes, 2006). This selective exposure of Italians to news – as stressed by Paolo Mancini – does not 'encourage the sharing of a field of common interests and values; instead it pushes society towards a polarisation of political options and affiliations' (2011: 41).

The main features of Italian political journalism have not changed over the past few years. This is because the centrality of party politics, of politicians' statements, and of conflict, as well as the partisanship and informal newsgathering practices that characterise Italian journalism, are strictly tied to the context in which they have developed: in order to have change in Italian political journalism, major changes would have to occur in the political and media systems. Regarding the political system, the most important 'shake-up' in the last couple of decades has been the emergence of Berlusconi as a political figure. As emphasised by Giovanni Belardelli (2012), the centrality of Berlusconi in the Italian public sphere created a new cleavage, an opposition between 'berlusconism' and 'anti-berlusconism' that forced 'everything and everyone to define themselves primarily – and often only – with respect to Berlusconi'. The Italian political spectrum – traditionally fragmented into many ideologically differentiated parties – was forced to aggregate into two main coalitions on the basis of support for, or opposition to, Berlusconi. Yet as will be shown in the following sections, the opposition between these two political cultures and the digitisation of the media system have not altered traditional features of Italian political journalism; they have rather contributed to strengthening them and, in particular, to radicalising both its partisanship and its tendency to participate in political debate and conflict.

Change and continuity in the Italian media system

Is it possible that nothing has changed in Italian journalism? Is it possible that the arrival of digital terrestrial television (DTT) and the growth of news consumption through the internet have not changed the peculiarities of the political journalism field?

Despite the fact that in Italy – compared to other Western European countries – the level of broadband connection is particularly low, the number of Italians that regularly look for information on the internet has been constantly growing in recent years. This trend affects the traditional news industry, especially the press, which is facing a deep crisis mainly due to the significant decline in both circulation and advertising revenue.[3] Indeed, publishers are convinced that the downturn in newspaper sales is caused by the fact that the internet is producing a shift in the news consumption behaviour of Italian citizens: because of the growing availability of free information on the web, readers buy newspapers less frequently.

Newspaper publishers are trying to balance the revenues they are losing in their traditional sector by investing in the new market for online news. However, this market is quite fragmented and, despite the growth of online news consumption, the profitability of web advertising is still too low to allow publishers to break even. In contrast, the television sector is less affected by the crisis: the overall television audience has not declined and advertising revenues have begun to decrease later and less significantly than in the newspaper sector. As a result, the broadcasting business is less influenced by the shift in content consumption caused by the web and, consequently, it has tended to invest fewer resources in the online news market.[4]

Table 3.3 shows the online audience for the websites of the main traditional media (whose business originated in the press and television sectors) and of the new players that have started to distribute news only on the internet. The statistics demonstrate that the only players able to reach a large audience (and consequently to make profits) are the online versions of the traditional media. The scenario of online news partially corresponds to the structure of the traditional Italian media system. The two most successful online news outlets are *La Repubblica* and *Il Corriere della Sera*, the two players that sell the highest number of copies in the traditional newspaper sector. However, unlike in the traditional media system, in the online news environment television does not reach a wider audience than the press. This is because Italian broadcasters do not consider the internet a profitable market. The public service broadcaster, for example, has never considered online activities as a priority, as is shown by its low success in web hits. Indeed, as reported by the Italian scholar Benedetta Brevini, 'lack of resources and of political support has led to insufficient investments on the internet offer'. In addition, 'the web offer of Rai is still mainly entertainment-oriented rather than focused on news and public affairs and, for this reason, internet users look for news content from other web sources' (Brevini, 2010: 355, 359). The only broadcaster able to reach a large audience on the internet is Mediaset: it has recently strengthened its online information provision by investing resources in TgCom, a news outlet based mainly on the web, but also broadcast on the channels made available by the switchover to DTT.

The internet facilitates the entry of new players into the news market. In recent years many outlets without a previous background in the traditional journalistic field have tried to establish themselves as news sources on the web. Undeniably, these purely online players have increased the level of pluralism and enriched the Italian public sphere with new interpretations, opinions, and information about current affairs. However, they are still unable to reach an audience size that can guarantee their future survival in the online news market (see Table 3.3). In their study of online journalistic start-ups in Western Europe, Bruno and Nielsen (2012) focused on three of the above-mentioned outlets launched between 2010 and 2011: Il Post, a blog run by a small newsroom that mainly aggregates and comments on mainstream media news; Lettera43, a website run by a larger newsroom that tries to compete with the traditional players with a mixed offer of current affairs coverage, quality commentaries, soft news, and gossip; and Linkiesta, an outlet providing independent investigative reporting and commentary. As emphasised by Bruno and Nielsen, these journalistic start-ups are continuously struggling to survive in a market dominated by strong and already well-established legacy outlets. So far they have been operating at a loss: their limited niche audiences are largely insufficient to generate the online advertising revenues necessary to

Table 3.3 News websites: internet unique visitors (daily average in 000s, 2008–12)

	Circulation and category	2008	2009	2010	2011	2012
Main newspapers' websites						
La Repubblica	National, news	1,034	1,148	1,368	1,445	1,492
Corriere della Sera	National, news	960	1,109	1,060	1,192	1,279
Gazzetta dello Sport	National, sport	507	544	634	676	687
Il Sole 24 Ore	National, business news	308	270	252	407	436
La Stampa	National,* news	184	213	277	352	394
Il Fatto Quotidiano	National, news	n.a.	n.a.	n.a.	257	265
Il Giornale	National, news	n.a.	164	150	173	193
Il Messaggero	National,* news	n.a.	117	110	102	159
Main broadcasters' websites						
TgCom (Mediaset)	News	n.a.	n.a.	476	621	719
Mediaset (total**)	News and entertainment	726	680	975	982	1.228
Rai	News and entertainment	304	314	333	311	371
Sky	News and entertainment	n.a.	214	250	258	248
La7	News and entertainment	n.a.	22	30	31	66

Main purely online news outlets

Dagospia.com	Gossip, politics and business news	n.a.	43	n.a.	56	61
Lettera43.it	News	n.a.	n.a.	n.a.	34	45
Il Post.it	Blog, news	n.a.	n.a.	27	22	34
Blitzquotidiano.it	News	n.a.	13	26	n.a.	33
Linkiesta	News	n.a.	n.a.	n.a.	n.a.	17
AgoràVox.it	News	n.a.	3	5	n.a.	n.a.

* *La Stampa* and *Il Messaggero* have a national circulation, but are mainly distributed in the areas of Turin and Rome respectively.

** Mediaset includes TgCom, Mediaset Premium, Mediaset.it, SportMediaset, VideoMediaset.

n.a. = data not available

Source: author's processing of Audiweb data (May 2012, September 2011, September 2010, September 2009, October 2008) for the project *The Changing Business of Journalism and Its Implications for Democracy* (Levy and Nielsen, 2010).

finance a newsroom. As a result, their survival still depends on the initial funding they collected from private investors (Bruno and Nielsen, 2012: 69–91). So far these new players have not represented a major change in the Italian journalistic system. This is not only because they reach small niche audiences, but also because their journalistic activity does not have a significant impact on the Italian public sphere: they have not yet produced any scoops or journalistic investigations of high public relevance (Mazzoleni et al., 2011). In addition, even if their organisational models and their layout formats are innovative, their substantive coverage does not seem to break with the tradition of Italian political journalism. As observed by Bruno and Nielsen (2012: 90):

> So far, [...] [these] online start-ups have been innovative in their use of web-native formats more than in the content of their reporting, their journalistic styles, or their business situation. [...] Most of them still work within the opinionated world of Italian journalism – full of partisanship, commentary, and long-form analysis, less heavy on hard news reporting and investigative journalism, commercially opaque and often tied in with numerous outside interests, rarely breaking even on the basis of their own work.

With the exception of Lavoce.info – a website launched in 2002 by a group of economists, whose authoritative current affairs analysis is followed by journalists and political and economic elites – the only purely online outlet capable of having an impact on mainstream media coverage and political debate is Dagospia, a website launched in 2000 that has specialised in gossip and behind-the-scenes coverage of Italian political and economic life. Even in this case, however, the journalism model adopted by Dagospia can be situated within the Italian political journalism tradition: most of the scoops produced by this site are based on rumours and insider information that its founder, Roberto D'Agostino, is able to obtain thanks to his close relations with the powerful elites he is gossiping about.

Therefore, the internet – and the growth of the online news market – is not changing the consolidated features of journalism in Italy: there are no signs that Italian political journalism is less close to political and economic elites, less opinionated, more market-oriented, or more targeted towards a mass audience. Instead, the internet seems to have exerted a significant impact on politics itself: in recent years, for instance, many civil society movements have successfully exploited the opportunities of the web to expand their reach, to mobilise their supporters, and to organise protests and demonstrations (Mazzoleni et al., 2011; Mosca and Vaccari, 2011). The best known is the case of Beppe Grillo, a former television comedian who, starting with his blog, organised a political movement (Movimento Cinque Stelle – Five Stars Movement) that had several representatives elected in the 2008 and 2012 local elections and obtained an unprecedented success in the 2013 general election. The success of this movement – characterised by a radical critique of the traditional parties and of the legitimacy of the current political system – shows how new media, by allowing political actors to communicate with the public without journalistic mediation, can promote a polarisation of political discourse.

With regard to the television system, the Rai/Mediaset duopoly has been partially weakening in recent years: their total combined audience share decreased from 90.2 per cent in 2003 to 75.8 per cent in the first five months of 2012.[5] This reduction is mainly due to the introduction of digital terrestrial television, a process that started in the early 2000s and concluded in 2012. Undoubtedly Italian television is going through a (relatively slow) process of audience fragmentation, but Rai and Mediaset are still overwhelmingly dominant in both audience and advertising revenue shares. Indeed, as pointed out by many observers, the legislators have missed the opportunity offered by DTT to remove anomalies in the Italian system. Rather than facilitating the emergence of new content providers and distributors, the spectrum allocation policies have favoured the incumbents, who obtained many of the available new channels (D'Arma, 2010; Mazzoleni et al., 2011).

Moreover, since broadcasters have mainly aimed at expanding their entertainment provision, the increase in DTT frequencies is not producing a significant transformation in the political information landscape. The few novelties on the digital terrestrial platform are produced by traditional media organisations: Mediaset recently launched a brand new all-news channel, TgCom24; *La Repubblica* created its own channel RepubblicaTV (which mainly broadcasts the audiovisual content produced for its website); and RaiNews, the public service all-news channel, was made available on the terrestrial platform in addition to its original satellite version. However, the audiences of all three of these initiatives are so far minuscule.[6]

An important change in the Italian television system comes from the satellite platform Sky Italia. The network owned by Rupert Murdoch entered the Italian pay-TV market in 2003 and it has now become a strong player: in 2012, with around 5 million household subscriptions, it obtained 29.9 per cent of the total revenue share of the television market (AgCom, 2012). From an economic perspective, Sky Italia is the only real competitor to Rai and Mediaset. However, its news provision does not produce significant results in terms of audience share and advertising income. For example, although the network invested resources in SkyTg24 – an all-news channel that is generally considered free from political ties and loyalties (Mazzoleni et al., 2011) – its potential audience is limited to Sky Italia subscribers. As a result, its audience share is marginal (see Figure 3.1).

The major change in the Italian television political information landscape is represented by La7. This is a broadcaster that in the early years of the twenty-first century started to compete with Rai and Mediaset in the free-to-air analogue television market. Since until recently La7 was controlled by Telecom Italia, the major Italian telecom company, it could

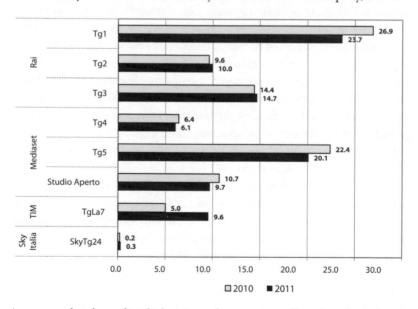

Average market share of total television audience at time of broadcast (inclusive of analogue, DTT, and satellite platforms).

Source: AgCom (2012).

Figure 3.1   Audience share of evening editions of the main Italian national television news programmes (2010–11)

be regarded as another case of an 'impure publisher'; however, contrary to the Rai and Mediaset situations, this broadcaster is generally considered free from political influence. La7 does not play a strong role in the television market overall – in 2011 its network collected only 1.8 per cent of the total resources of the television system (AgCom, 2012) – but it plays an important role in the political news field: particularly in recent years, La7 has invested heavily in the strengthening of its news provision.[7]

Since political journalism has become the channel's distinctive characteristic, its audience share has been growing: from 1.8 per cent in 2002 to 3.8 per cent in 2011.[8] The most important achievement of La7 has been the enrolment of Enrico Mentana as editor-in-chief of its news programme, TgLa7. In 1992, Mentana founded and for 12 years ran the main television bulletin of Mediaset, Tg5, without openly supporting the political line of Berlusconi, the network owner. In 2009, this well-known journalist became a symbol of professional integrity and autonomy when he resigned from Mediaset because of deontological disagreements. In an autobiography published the same year Mentana explained that his growing unease about working inside Mediaset was due to the fact that the network was becoming Berlusconi's election committee (*comitato elettorale*), a propaganda instrument to support the election campaigns of its proprietor (Mentana, 2009; Stella, 2009). In July 2010, Mentana became editor-in-chief of the La7 news programme. He conceived a high-quality product, strongly focused on national politics, rich in opinions, analyses and commentaries, but without any evident partisan bias and affiliation. In a few months, the audience share of TgLa7 increased from 2.26 per cent to 8.05 per cent.[9] As Figure 3.1 shows, while the main news programmes of Rai and Mediaset are losing viewers and all the other television news programmes are quite stable, TgLa7 is the only one that continues to increase its audience share.

The radicalisation of Italian media partisanship

Except for the TgLa7 case, all the other innovative elements in the Italian mainstream political information landscape seem to indicate a trend towards a radicalisation of journalistic partisanship, an increase in the news media's political engagement, and a polarisation of Italian political discourse.

A first example is the case of *Il Fatto Quotidiano*, a daily newspaper founded in 2009 by (among others) Marco Travaglio, a journalist well known for his coverage of trials and judicial inquiries. *Il Fatto Quotidiano* specialises in investigative journalism – it has produced several journalistic inquiries and scoops that have received wide coverage in the mainstream media. It is also characterised by a political line openly opposed to Berlusconi but – in contrast to other newspapers such as *La Repubblica* – without supporting the parties of the centre-left. In addition, the editorial policy of this newspaper could be considered one of the best examples of the more general 'anti-political class' (*anti-casta*) tendency of Italian journalism, which manifests itself in a widespread anti-political attitude that runs through a huge number of newspaper articles, television programmes, and best-seller books that focus on cases of corruption, political patronage, privileges, and waste in public expenditure. Although *Il Fatto Quotidiano* does not have any official affiliation with a traditional political party, some consider it to be close to the (anti-)political positions of Beppe Grillo's movement.[10]

The *Fatto Quotidiano* case is important because it exemplifies how – despite the phase of deep crisis faced by the newspaper industry – a newcomer has managed to successfully enter the market by addressing a specific target market defined from a political and ideological perspective, a niche audience looking for aggressive, investigative journalism and characterised by a marked *anti-berlusconism* and *anti-casta* approach.[11] Moreover, this newspaper stands out because it is considered by its readership to be a rare case of journalistic independence and 'pure publishing'. First, it is one of the few Italian newspapers that does not receive any public funding – and this is prominently emphasised in the line that features below the newspaper's title. Second, its company statute sets specific rules that prevent a single shareholder from owning more than 16 per cent of the total capital share, while 30 per cent of the shares are reserved for the newspaper's own journalists (Mazzoleni et al., 2011).

Another important example of the radicalisation of Italian journalistic partisanship is the Minzolini case. Augusto Minzolini is a former newspaper '*ad personam* journalist' who followed Berlusconi's activities and specialised in behind-the-scenes news. In June 2009, at the time of the Berlusconi government, he was appointed as editor-in-chief of Tg1, the main public service news programme. Although according to the well-consolidated practice of *lottizzazione* it is considered normal that the editorial policy of Tg1 favours the government and parties in office, Minzolini's management was the object of much polemical controversy. This is because under his stewardship the programme's political coverage was particularly biased, much more so than under all of his predecessors. Minzolini was accused by his critics of omitting to publish news that could have put Berlusconi in a negative light and, above all, of introducing a new practice that was not usual in public service news output – showing video-editorials and commentaries openly supportive of Berlusconi during the prime-time news programmes. He clearly expressed his personal point of view and took a stand on Berlusconi's trials and on disputes inside his political coalition, often denigrating the prime minister's opponents. During Minzolini's period of management, Tg1 registered a significant decrease in audience figures as well as in the index of viewers' perception of the news programme's reliability.[12] Unlike the other cases discussed in this section, the radicalisation of Tg1 partisanship seems to be the reason for its decline.

The final two cases to be discussed typify the extent to which in recent years the political engagement of the Italian media has been increasing, also thanks to new technology. The first concerns the e-petition campaigns organised by *La Repubblica*. This newspaper has always been an example of a partisan media outlet, with a tendency to participate actively in the political sphere – closer to the centre-left, but without any direct financial or organisational connection with a specific party. Since 2009, *La Repubblica* has launched several online petitions (collecting readers' 'digital signatures') and other forms of campaigning to mobilise its public and pursue political goals. In 2009, for example, it launched a cross-media campaign against the so-called 'gagging law': the Berlusconi government's draft law imposing restrictions on criminal investigations and curbing, in particular, police wiretaps and their publication in newspapers. On this occasion *La Repubblica* website collected and published a huge number of photos taken by readers who held up placards and wore masks in a protest against censorship. As reported by the Italian scholar Cristian Vaccari (2011), as a result of *La Repubblica*'s successful campaigns, the right-wing partisan newspapers – *Il Giornale* and *Libero* – launched their own online petitions against opponents of the Berlusconi government. According to Vaccari, these initiatives show how the possibility of promoting participation through online tools has enabled Italian partisan media to adopt mobilisation techniques and organisational arrangements typical of political parties and social movements. Indeed, with the aim of influencing the policy-making process these initiatives were instrumental in showing tangible signs of popular support for the newspapers' policy preferences.

The final example concerns Michele Santoro, a popular talk-show host and former Rai journalist, who left the broadcasting corporation in June 2011 after a long series of public disputes with Rai management. These controversies – generated by Santoro's explicit stance against Berlusconi and, more generally, against the excessive political pressures put on the public broadcaster – were made evident and highly dramatised even during the 'live' broadcasting of his Rai talk show *Annozero*. In order to avoid any limits being placed on his editorial autonomy and to assert his freedom to set the agenda and the slant of his television programme, in November 2011 he launched his own journalistic show, *Servizio Pubblico* (Public Service). This weekly talk show was totally innovative in the Italian media landscape. The first reason was its cross-media nature: the programme was distributed by a heterogeneous multi-platform network (which he assembled on an *ad hoc* basis) composed of local television channels, Sky Italia satellite and DTT channels, radio stations, and several websites (the show was available in 'live' streaming on the websites of *La Repubblica*, *Il Corriere della Sera*, and *Il Fatto Quotidiano*). The second reason is that he produced a successful show without relying on the funding, organisational support, and distribution infrastructure of any single traditional publisher. Instead, the business model was based on a mix of advertising revenue and voluntary subscriptions: his public directly contributed to the production of the show by donating more than €1 million. The results of this experiment were very impressive: although the cross-media network was composed of channels not used to attracting a large public, the average-per-minute audience of the first episode of *Servizio Pubblico* consisted of 2.8 million television viewers (11.87 per cent of overall television audience share), while those who watched the online 'live' streaming of the show totalled 500,000 (Mele, 2011).

The success of this experiment – in terms of audience figures and popular subscription – demonstrates that in Italy there is a significant segment of the public that is seeking a partisan and polarised kind of journalism. Santoro represents the archetype of a media figure who is becoming increasingly popular in the Italian media field: the anti-berlusconism star. On several occasions, journalists and satirical comedians (such as Michele Santoro, Marco Travaglio, Enrico Luttazzi, and Sabina Guzzanti) have taken advantage – in terms of both popularity and political support – of the criticisms and political pressures directed at their television programmes by politicians, institutional actors, and television managers close to Berlusconi. The Santoro case also demonstrates that in a phase of weakness in Italian politics, journalism gets stronger, radicalises its partisanship, and manifests its tendency to play an active role in the political sphere. Today, the strongest politically engaged media are not directly tied to a political party (as used to be the case in the 'golden age' of the party press), but are *against* something or someone: their editorial policy is recognisable because it is markedly *against* a political faction, *against* a specific policy, or even *against* the entire political class (the so-called *anti-casta* tendency). As observed by Beppe Servergnini, a well-known Italian journalist, 'nowadays partisan media don't support political factions, they replace them'. If in the past they limited themselves to recording the statements of Italian politicians and to emphasising political conflict, 'now they themselves become actors who shout', willing to mobilise support to achieve political goals (Servergnini, 2010).

In terms of audience appreciation, this trend towards radicalisation might appear to produce contradictory results. Indeed, the Minzolini and Mentana cases seem to demonstrate that an excess of partisanship does not please the news programme audience: Tg1 has lost a significant share of its viewers because of the partisan bias of its editor-in-chief, whereas the new management of TgLa7 has been successful in part because it represents an alternative to the other politically affiliated news programmes. In contrast, *Il Fatto Quotidiano*, *La Repubblica*, and the Santoro cases seem to demonstrate that Italian audiences appreciate politically committed journalism. These differences reflect the dual profile of the Italian political news public. On the one hand, newspapers, television political talk-shows, and (in part) news websites mainly address an elite audience, already well defined in terms of political affiliation, that looks to partisan journalism to find confirmation of its own personal viewpoints and values. On the other hand, television news programmes address the mass audience, which constitutes a larger percentage share of the public, which has a lower interest and involvement in politics, and which looks for a kind of information that is more distant from the political domain and, possibly, free from clear partisan commitment.

Conclusion

According to our analysis, the main features of Italian political journalism are not changing. The centrality of party politics, of conflicts, and of informal newsgathering practices, as well as the proximity of journalists to politicians, are enduring traits that still resist the transformation process of the media sector engendered by new technology. Neither digital terrestrial television nor the growth of online news consumption is undermining the traditional basis of the culture of Italian political journalism. In particular, they have not favoured the entrance of new important and 'pure' players into the information market. The cases analysed in this chapter demonstrate that the few journalistic start-ups have so far been marginal in terms of audience results and, moreover, are still in line with the tradition of Italian journalism in terms of content, style, and business models. In contrast, the evidence from Beppe Grillo's blog, *La Repubblica* e-campaigns, and Michele Santoro's cross-media network indicates that new technologies – by creating new opportunities for social movements and for politically engaged news providers to interact directly with their public in order to mobilise support for their political initiatives – are fostering a polarisation of politics and contributing to the tendency of Italian media to participate actively in the political sphere.

The culture of Italian political journalism seems to be quite stable because it is deeply rooted in the context in which it has developed: the national political system and political culture have always been strongly polarised, while the Italian media have always been important instruments – or even active participants – in the historical conflicts among diverse ideological factions. Undoubtedly, the entry of Berlusconi into the political sphere and the consequent contraposition between 'berlusconist' and 'anti-berlusconist' journalisms radicalised the already existent partisanship and political engagement of the Italian media. Yet the proximity between Italian media and politics is not limited to the Berlusconi experience. It is rather a structural element of Italian public life that will persist even after Berlusconi's exit from the political arena. As the first steps of Beppe Grillo's movement seem to suggest, even if the new media should prevail over the traditional and even if the Berlusconi-inspired conflict of interests were to be overcome, Italian journalism will find new figures around which to organise their political conflicts.

Notes

1   Traditionally, for much of the period of the Italian 'First Republic' (1948-92), the major channel Rai1 was under the patronage of the Christian Democrats, Rai2 of the Socialists, and Rai3 of the Communists.

2   Isimm Ricerche analyses television content for the Italian Authority for Communications. Its data are not collected using sampling methods. Isimm analyses all the editions of all national news programmes and political talk-shows.

3   In 2001 all Italian daily newspaper titles combined sold 6,017,564 copies per day on average. In 2011 this figure went down to 4,459,818. Source: data collected by several issues of the annual report of Fieg, the Italian federation of newspaper publishers (last issue: Fieg, 2012).

4   All the evaluations expressed here are based on secondary data collection and on interviews conducted with publishers, lawmakers, regulators, and media analysts. The data were collected by the author for the project *The Changing Business of Journalism and its Implications for Democracy*, coordinated by the Reuters Institute for the Study of Journalism and funded by the Open Society Foundations (Levy and Nielsen, 2010).

5   Source: author's elaboration on Auditel and Censis data.

6   The data provided by Auditel (the Italian audience measurement company) show that in July 2012 RaiNews had 0.61 per cent audience share. Auditel has not yet measured the viewing figures of TgCom and RepubblicaTV.

7   La7 strengthened its political news provision by also 'poaching' from Rai and Mediaset several managers (for example, Paolo Ruffini, former director of Rai3), renowned political satire comedians (notably Maurizio Crozza and Sabina Guzzanti), and well-known journalists and talk-show hosts (such as Lilli Gruber, Gad Lerner, Antonello Piroso, Serena Dandini, and Cristina Parodi).

8   Source: author's elaboration on Auditel data.

9   The data show a comparison between TgLa7's average audience share during the television season prior to Mentana's arrival (season 2009/10) and that of the season under his management (season 2010/11). Source: Palestini (2011).

10   In June 2012, for example, Luca Telese, a well-known journalist of *Il Fatto Quotiano*, criticised and left the newspaper because – in his view – its editorial policy had become much too close to the Five Stars Movement.

11   In July 2012, *Il Fatto Quotidiano* sold an average of 54,055 copies a day (source: ADS data). Its website attracted more viewers than better-established newspapers like *Il Giornale* and *Il Messaggero* (see Table 3.3) and it could count

on a higher proportion of subscriptions to both its online and paper versions than other Italian newspapers (Mazzoleni et al., 2011).

12 Minzolini was editor-in-chief of Tg1 from June 2009 until December 2011. In 2008, the average audience share of Tg1 was 30.7 per cent, while in 2011 it was 23.7 per cent (source: Auditel data published in AgCom, 2012 and Censis, 2010). As observed by the Italian social scientist Ilvo Diamanti – while commenting on an annual survey about trust in the Italian news media – in 2011, Tg1 was considered reliable by 50 per cent of the interviewees, whereas in 2007, when the public news programme had been managed by the previous editor-in-chief, this figure had been 69 per cent. Source: Diamanti (2011).

4

German Political Journalism Between Change and Stability

Carsten Reinemann and Philip Baugut

Introduction

Only rarely has the role of political journalism been discussed as intensively in postwar Germany as it has in the last two years. Outsiders may associate the Federal Republic with the sombre political style of Angela Merkel or Frank-Walter Steinmeier and quiet corporatist interest negotiation between unions, employers' associations, and other interest groups. But another, more flamboyant, side of German politics has been on display in recent years, a side that is deeply intertwined with the workings of contemporary German political journalism. Two cases in particular shed light on media power and the close relationships between journalists and politicians – the rise and fall of Karl-Theodor zu Guttenberg and Christian Wulff.

The first case concerns the unprecedented rise in 2009 and 2010 of a young politician who in just a year and a half went from being a largely unknown back-bencher to a nationally known figure considered by many as a possible future conservative candidate for chancellor. The rise of Karl-Theodor zu Guttenberg, who became minister of economic affairs in early 2009 and was promoted to minister of defence just a few months later, was made possible by a wave of exceptionally positive media coverage across virtually all news media, ranging from broadsheet newspapers and tabloids to the yellow press. In a very short period of time, the media hype made him the most popular German politician, and his popularity in turn fostered further positive portrayals. Only a few outlets criticised the coverage of Guttenberg as media hype, mostly focusing on the minister's relationship with the leading tabloid newspaper *Bild*. Guttenberg's unique career ended abruptly when the broadsheet *Süddeutsche Zeitung* in February 2011 broke the news that the minister had plagiarised his doctoral dissertation. The story immediately spread across the national news. Remarkably, Guttenberg's main media supporter, *Bild*, continued to support him throughout despite the scandal (Jansen and Maier, 2012). The intensity and ways in which *Bild* backed Guttenberg in turn sparked a heated public debate about how close relationships between politicians and media are and how they ought to be. The obvious nature of his misconduct and his handling of the allegations also forced Guttenberg to resign, illustrating the power of the media not only to propel politicians to prominence, but also to bring them down.

The second case also concerned close relations between news media and politicians, this time between the German president, Christian Wulff, and *Bild*. Though the tabloid had been very close to Wulff during much of his political career, and had promoted him in its coverage, the newspaper in December 2011 broke a story focusing on his questionable personal financial dealings with prominent businessmen in his home state of Lower Saxony when he served as a minister there. This story in turn transformed into a major scandal when it became clear that Wulff had – though he denied this at the time – contacted *Bild*'s chief editor to stop the story from being published. As is often the case, the cover-up became a bigger scandal than the original story itself, and enormous media hype led to Wulff's resignation in 2012. Again, the scandal provoked a protracted public debate of the President's misconduct, how he was covered, of his own attempts at handling the story, and especially of his long-running contacts with *Bild*. In this case, the tabloid was widely praised by other journalists for its investigative efforts and decisions to make public incriminating voicemails contradicting Wulff's public statements about what had been going on. Fewer focused on whether *Bild* had kept a proper professional distance to Wulff in the years before.

Both the Guttenberg case and the Wulff case have occasioned wide public debate about the autonomy and quality of political journalism and its role in democracy, an issue that has also been the subject of growing scientific interest in recent years. Political journalists have been included in representative surveys of German journalism as a whole (e.g. Meyen and Riesmeyer, 2009; Weischenberg et al., 2006) as well as studied on their own (Lünenborg and Berghofer, 2010). Further quantitative and qualitative surveys have focused specifically on correspondents based in the capital Berlin. Some studies have also included politicians and political spokespersons whose perspectives complement and sometimes contradict the views of journalists (Baugut and Grundler, 2009; Kepplinger, 2009; Kepplinger and Maurer, 2008; Lesmeister, 2008). In addition, German journalists have recently been included in several comparative studies of political journalists across Europe and the world, including the Worlds of Journalism project (Hanitzsch, 2011; Hanitzsch and Mellado, 2011), the *Political Communication Cultures in Western Europe* project (Pfetsch, 2013), and others (Dalen and Alest, 2012; Dalen et al., 2011; Deuze, 2002). Finally, analysts have examined the product of political journalism, both in a longitudinal perspective, studying news-making over time (Reinemann and Wilke, 2007) and in an international perspective, studying news-making across different countries (Esser, 2008; Esser et al., 2012).

Against this backdrop of studies of German political journalists, their relation to political sources, and the news that they produce, this chapter will summarise what we know about political journalism in Germany today. We will argue that it is characterised by a combination of stability and change. We first address some of the basic contextual factors that shape the work, performance, and impact of political journalism in Germany. We then focus on some of the key characteristics of German political journalists themselves. Afterwards we take a closer look at the most important changes in newsroom practices, in the relations between politicians and journalists, and in the resulting news coverage. Finally, we discuss the causes and consequences of the combination of change and stability that characterise German political journalism today.

Contextual factors

In recent years, internationally comparative political communication research has provided much evidence that variation in the national context can have a profound influence on journalists' values and working practices, including their interactions with politicians and PR professionals as well as the content of political media coverage itself (for an overview see Pfetsch and Esser, 2013). Therefore, we will briefly summarise here some of the most important contextual factors that condition political journalism in Germany.

Clearly, the historical development and structure of national media systems and media organisations provide a very important background for political journalism, its coverage, and its impact. Comparative researchers here generally categorise Germany as a representative of the democratic corporatist model of media and politics (Esser, 2008; Hallin and Mancini, 2004). The German media system has been characterised by the strong position of the regional press and by a system of public service broadcasting that also has a strong regional component. There are currently more than 340 regional newspapers and nine regional public service stations covering one or more German states. These public service stations have at least one regional TV programme as well as several terrestrial and even more digital radio channels (in addition to their online services). In terms of market shares, the TV market is about evenly split between public service and private stations. In terms of newspapers, the limited number of nationally distributed broadsheet newspapers only reaches a small portion of the German public, but at least some of them are regarded as opinion leaders that set an agenda across the media system and are important for political elites. In contrast to regional papers, which typically cater to audiences that are quite diverse politically, the national papers traditionally have had a more open political leaning – left-leaning for *Süddeutsche Zeitung*, more conservative for the *Frankfurter Allgemeine Zeitung*, and so on. The most successful newspaper in terms of circulation is *Bild*, the only nationally distributed tabloid. It reaches up to 11 million readers each day. Along with Spiegel Online, the website of the most important weekly political magazine *Der Spiegel, Bild* also publishes one of the most successful news websites. All in all, the German media system is very diverse and complex, in part because of its strong regional structure. This pronounced regional orientation and variation has to be taken into account when interpreting and generalising the results of studies, especially when they focus on specific groups of journalists like the correspondents in Berlin.

Beyond media structures, the political system is also an important influence on how relationships between media and politics develop and on how journalists covering politics work. In Germany, the most important structural features of the political system shaping political journalism include the strong role of parties, a multi-party system based on proportional representation, and the federal structure. This structure puts parties at the heart of the political process at both the national, regional, and local levels. Looking beyond the structure of the political system itself and considering citizens as voters, Germany is currently characterised by an increasing de-alignment of the electorate, an increasingly volatile public opinion, and a change in the way many people view politics and politicians. Although the intensity and effects of political alienation remain disputed issues in political science, it is at least clear that political journalists in Germany today are confronted with audiences less politically homogeneous and less likely to be strong partisans than they were 15 or 20 years ago.

Today, Germans have access to an unprecedented amount of material on politics. Despite the rise of online media, the majority of Germans still rely on traditional offline media as their primary sources of political information. In a 2011 survey, 60 per cent reported they had used TV to follow current affairs the day before, 49 per cent named print newspapers, 35 per cent radio, and only 18 per cent mentioned the internet (Köcher, 2011). In Germany as elsewhere, even those going online for political or campaign-related information also primarily end up relying on the websites of established offline media (Pape and Quandt, 2010). Despite the growth in social networking sites like Facebook, 2011 surveys suggest that online sites and social media still play a limited role in the political information habits of most Germans (Schneller, 2012). Only a narrow section of society makes extensive use of the unprecedented supply of political information available. Thus, predominantly regionally structured traditional, journalistic news media like broadcasters and newspapers remain the number one source of political information for most German citizens. (As we will discuss below, this does not mean that so-called web 2.0 media are without consequence for political journalism and political discourse. Though they play only a limited role in mass dissemination, social media do in fact influence journalists themselves and change the ways politicians, parties, NGOs, and social movements communicate.)

German political journalists and their characteristics

In Germany, political journalism has traditionally been a prestigious form of journalism. This is a contrast to some other European countries, where the political beat is just a stepping stone in a journalistic career. One result of this relatively high status is that German political journalists are older and better paid than their colleagues in other editorial departments (Dalen and Aelst, 2012: 517; Lünenborg and Berghofer, 2010: 10). Two-thirds of political journalists are men but in this part of journalism, as in the profession at large, the difference between younger and older journalists is stark. While only about 20 per cent of political journalists aged 56 and older are women, the share is twice as high in the group between 26 and 35. Looking at education, political journalism has become more and more academic. Today, more than 80 per cent of German political journalists hold a university degree (political science being the most common discipline). One in ten even has a doctorate, which is a much higher proportion than in other editorial departments. A university degree alone, however, is rarely enough. About 60 per cent of German political journalists also worked as a trainee reporter before or after their academic training (Lünenborg and Berghofer, 2010: 15; see also Weischenberg et al., 2006: 65–9).

Turning from the journalists themselves to the organisations they work for, surveys reveal both the diversity of the German media landscape and the relative importance of different media sectors as employers. In 2009, a third of political journalists worked for newspapers, almost a quarter for TV, meaning these 'old media' employ far more than any other kind of media. Seventeen per cent reported working for online media (Lünenborg and Berghofer, 2010: 16). It is important to note here that almost half of the journalists reporting political issues on a regular basis are not working in dedicated politics departments but are assigned to general news (18 per cent), economics (11 per cent), society/social issues, and other editorial departments. This means that a lot of journalists reporting politics are general assignment reporters or specialists from other fields for whom politics is just one of many issues they cover.

In Germany as elsewhere, the political attitudes of journalists have been subject to much debate and scrutiny. Some criticise the media for a supposed conservative bias, arguing that media owners and publishers naturally prefer right-wing viewpoints. Others focus on the attitudes of journalists themselves and accuse them of being too leftish or liberal. German political journalists have indeed consistently placed themselves on the left side of the political spectrum in surveys from the 1990s onwards, and the tendency is probably present throughout the postwar period (Weischenberg et al., 2006). When asked in 2009 what party they felt close to, 26 per cent of German political journalists mentioned the Green Party, 16 per cent the Social Democrats, and 4 per cent the former Communist Party Die Linke. On the other hand, only 9 per cent mentioned the conservative Christian Democracts (CDU) and 7 per cent the free-market liberal FDP. Although the rest of the journalists surveyed (36 per cent) said they did not feel close to any party whatsoever, this supports the view that German political journalists' individual political attitudes are to the left of the general population (Lünenborg and Berghofer, 2010).

Of course, the political preferences of individual journalists are not necessarily reflected in the media coverage they produce. Individual attitudes are countered by organisational rules requiring balanced reporting (in the case of private and public service broadcasters) and some news organisations have a specific political line that takes precedence over individual views. Indeed, several studies have documented differences between individual attitudes of journalists and the editorial lines of the media organisations they work for. Surveys suggest that political journalists typically perceive the media they work for as more to the right politically than they themselves are (Lünenborg and Berghofer, 2010; Reinemann, 2003; Weischenberg et al., 2006). Beyond this, there is also some evidence for a broader media de-alignment, a decline of press–party parallelism (where individual outlets take party-political sides) and the rise of a stronger across-the-board negative portrayal of politics combined with a tendency towards media populism (Reinemann, 2011).

Newsroom practices

Since the mid-1980s, Germany has seen an enormous expansion of the media sector, triggered first by the deregulation of broadcasting and since accelerated by the advent of the internet. Today, the German media market is regarded as amongst the most competitive in Europe, in sharp contrast to the relatively consolidated market of the early 1980s. As a result of the expansion of supply and the intensification of competition, media use has moved from being supply-driven to being interest-driven. An increasing individualisation of media use and a fragmentation of audiences and the public sphere has been the result. The divide between information- and entertainment-oriented audience segments – already apparent after the deregulation of broadcasting – is now accompanied by a gap in media use patterns between young and old generations driven by the emergence of online media in general and social media like Facebook and Twitter in particular (Köcher, 2011). All these changes directly impact newsroom practices.

For many media organisations, the expansion of the media sector has meant shrinking audiences and, especially for daily newspapers, a loss of advertising revenue. Public service TV news and regional newspapers in particular have seen their audiences decline and have lost large parts of their younger audiences to free online news services or to entertainment-oriented online content and social networks. Although many regional newspapers still have profit margins rarely seen in other sectors and although the papers differ in the extent to which they are affected, the consequences of cross-media competition cannot be overlooked. In 2012, *Financial Times Deutschland* closed down after years of losses and the *Frankfurter Rundschau* (a prestigious left-wing paper of national relevance for decades) declared insolvency. Moreover, various publishers of regional newspapers like the *Augsburger Allgemeine* and the *Westdeutsche Allgemeine Zeitung* announced financial cuts and newsroom layoffs in the autumn of 2012. The main changes in newsroom practices resulting from these pressures concern: (1) an increasing orientation towards commercial considerations and the imagined preferences of the audience, (2) a reduction in the resources available to journalists covering politics, (3) an accelerated news cycle, and (4) increased self-referentiality, including a greater tendency for a few prominent media organisations to set the agenda across the media sector. We will address each in turn.

Generally, increased competition and declining revenues have made economic arguments more and more important in media organisations. Scholars call this trend commercialisation. It means that financial considerations are becoming more important decision-making criteria for media managers and journalists and that public value-oriented considerations are receding. And because revenues are partly linked to audience success, audience orientation has become a major argument in a profession that for a long time did not seem to care too much about audience preferences. This has now changed. Today, market research and immediate online feedback have put the audience at the centre of both economic and journalistic considerations in news organisations. This can be clearly seen in studies of political journalists' role perceptions and how these have changed over time. From 1993 to 2005, for example, the share of journalists saying they want to cover only 'interesting' news rose sharply from 52 to 72 per cent. No other journalistic consideration had increased more in importance during that time (Weischenberg et al., 2006). A separate study shows that the average political journalist today spends almost 40 minutes a day with audience interaction – an activity that was quite uncommon two decades ago and that has been fostered lately by possibilities of online feedback. In fact, 43 per cent of the journalists surveyed say that they get feedback from their audience frequently or very frequently (Lünenborg and Berghofer, 2010: 22–3). These moves towards a greater degree of audience orientation have not translated into a more adversarial form of reporting or ambitions to act as advocates of disadvantaged groups. The above-mentioned survey clearly documents the decline in watchdog-type motivations since the 1990s. Whereas 77 per cent of the journalists surveyed in 1993 said that 'criticizing social or political grievances' was a major motive of their work, only 60 per cent of journalists agreed with this in 2005 (Weischenberg et al., 2006). A generational change in German newsrooms seems to be one of the reasons for this development. Growth across the media sector in the 1990s greatly increased the demand for a new generation of younger journalists, especially in privately owned media. This younger generation has been socialised into a more commercial and market-oriented kind of journalism and seems to be more detached and less political – reflecting a more general trend in German society.

For political journalists working for most privately owned media, economic pressures have led to a decline in the personnel, time, and money that can be invested in reporting most stories. In a 2009 survey, two thirds of political journalists said that work pressures had increased over the past five years, slightly more than half said that there were fewer staff, and half said that time for research had declined (Lünenborg and Berghofer, 2010). Political journalists in the important public service broadcasting sector have been affected more indirectly by rising competition. Since the deregulation of the mid-1980s, public service channels have lost large parts of their former audiences to private media. In light of their licence-fee funding, paid by every household, this decline in overall audiences has increased the pressures to compete for audiences and to justify their expenditures and the quality of the content produced.

Beyond commercial pressures, the newsroom practices of German political journalists have also been affected by the enormous changes brought about by the digitalisation of production processes and the emergence of new online possibilities. In 2009, about three-quarters of political journalists said that cross-media cooperation with the online departments of their organisation had grown significantly or very significantly (Lünenborg and Berghofer, 2010: 45). Digitalisation and commercial pressures also contributed to another trend: newspapers in particular, but other media too, have begun to restructure the organisation of their editorial work by establishing centralised newsrooms and newsdesks. Before that, such structures were quite unknown in Germany,

81

especially in newspapers. But by 2009, no less than 58 per cent of journalists surveyed said that their media organisation had a newsroom or similar centralised production units. It is important to note here that although the introduction of newsrooms sparked fears regarding the quality of journalism, only a minority of political journalists agree that quality has suffered (Lünenborg and Berghofer, 2010: 45). In addition, at least some media have come to the conclusion that reducing the resources for journalistic work might not be the best way to stop the loss of readers, viewers, and listeners or even to attract new audiences. Several media, such as the *Süddeutsche Zeitung*, Germany's largest national quality paper, have been installing special investigative reporting units crossing news departments in order to look for exclusive stories and scoops.

Technological change in the production and dissemination of news is intimately intertwined with another important development in newsroom practices – the acceleration of news cycles. This is a trend some political journalists say has changed their work most profoundly (Bruns, 2007; Lünenborg and Berghofer, 2010). The acceleration was triggered first by the spread of TV news from evenings to mornings and afternoons as well as the establishment of 24-hour rolling news programmes in the 1990s. With the advent of continuously updated news websites on the internet and the rise of new real-time web services like Twitter, the speed has only increased further. This trend is reflected in journalists' changing role perceptions. The share of political journalists who want to provide information 'as quickly as possible' rose from 73 to 86 per cent between 1993 and 2005 (Weischenberg et al., 2006: 284). The acceleration clearly also poses threats to the quality of journalistic work and political coverage, because information might no longer be double-checked and the fact that other media are covering an issue becomes a major criterion for decisions about what to cover. Moreover, some fear that the combination of commercialisation, acceleration, and increasing self-referentiality (where news organisations use each other as sources, especially online) will produce more homogeneous coverage across media as well as more media hypes for or against certain politicians or political projects (Hachmeister, 2007: 12; Reinemann, 2003). Although the media hypes around both the Guttenberg case and the Wulff case discussed at the outset of this chapter are not representative of daily political coverage in Germany, they are extreme and vivid illustrations of what such media hypes can look like and what the consequences are in terms of volatile public opinion and political fallout.

Paradoxically, growing audience orientation has also led to an increase of self-referentiality within the media system and political journalism. Because of the perceived risk of not getting a story or of getting it 'wrong', journalists tend to watch competitors and other media more closely than ever in order to justify and affirm their own news decisions (Reinemann, 2004). In fact, surveys suggest that political journalists most often use other journalistic media as sources (followed by news agencies, on-the-spot research, and interviews) (Lünenborg and Berghofer, 2010: 25). In addition, online sources have become very prominent in recent years. In 2009, nine out of ten journalists used search engines frequently or very frequently. In contrast, as of 2009, weblogs, social media, and Twitter were only used by a small minority of political journalists (Lünenborg and Berghofer, 2010: 27). Although social media have gained importance since then, more recent studies suggest that social media remain only moderately important for many journalists. For example, in their study of internet newsrooms conducted in 2010, Neuberger, vom Hofe, and Nuernbergk (2011) found that only a minority of journalists used Twitter on a regular basis. In addition, the importance of Twitter for journalistic work was rated much lower than the importance of Facebook. This might be traced back to the fact that an increasing amount of online traffic for news sites is generated via Facebook (Schmidt, 2011). All in all, however, the importance of Twitter for both media users and journalists in Germany has not yet reached the level of the US.

The changes described have also affected how inter-media agenda-setting works in political journalism. Due to its large circulation and a strong focus on socio-political issues since the late 1990s, the national tabloid *Bild* has become one of the most important opinion-leading media in political journalism (Reinemann, 2003). *Bild* was at the centre of both the Guttenberg and the Wulff scandals mentioned above, and its role and importance for both other media and the political system – demonstrated time and again in terms of catapulting individual politicians to fame, setting policy agendas, or bringing people down – are the subject of intense public controversies (there is even a *Bild*-blog, dedicated to critically covering the tabloid's coverage). Even more important in elite circles and in terms of setting the media agenda is *Spiegel Online*, the news website of Germany's most prestigious political magazine, *Der Spiegel*. No less than 88 per cent of political journalists said in 2009 that they use this website on a regular basis. Besides that, the weekly print version of the magazine (88 per cent), the daily *Süddeutsche Zeitung* newspaper (78 per cent), and the public service newscasts *heute* (73 per cent) and *Tagesschau* (65 per cent) are among the media most intensively followed by political journalists (Lünenborg and Berghofer, 2010).

Relationships between journalists and politicians

The above-outlined changes in newsroom practices, driven in part by commercial pressures and in part by new technologies, have changed the interactions between journalists and politicians. Many journalists feel they are working under more individual pressures, and yet politicians at the same time perceive the media as increasingly powerful and more and more important (Pontzen, 2006). Remarkably, surveys suggest that both politicians *and* journalists also think that the media are more important for politics than they ought to be (Kepplinger, 2009: 18). Clearly, the perceived influence of the media results in an actual impact on political processes and decisions as politicians act on their beliefs. In a survey of members of the federal and state parliaments, 45 per cent of the elected representatives said that complicated issues ill-suited for the media are less likely to even get into the legislative process today (Pontzen, 2006). This trend towards a growing impact of media and media logics on political processes and actors of course has to do with the expansion of the media system and the increasing importance of media in the life of citizens. But it is also the result of the growing volatility of public opinion and voting behaviour which effectively means that competition has also become stronger in electoral politics. As a result, media are regarded as more and more important, parties and governments have invested more resources in PR professionals in recent years, and politicians are dedicating more time and money to media training (Pontzen, 2006).

The trend can be seen as a change in Germany's 'political communication culture', defined by Barbara Pfetsch (2004: 348) as the shared orientations and regular interactions of various actors in media and politics that together produce political communication. Along these lines we can sketch key traits of the German political communication culture by examining: (1) how close journalists and politicians are, (2) how information flows from sources to reporters, (3) the degree to which their relationship is characterised by conflict or cooperation, and (4) how secluded and closed to the outside world interactions between political actors and journalists are.

Increasing competition in both the media system and the political system seems to have changed the relationships between journalists and politicians and reduced the distance between the two groups. Some authors argue that decreasing financial resources and personnel are making journalists more dependent on their political sources for new, potentially exclusive, stories or background information necessary to understand issues and decisions. This puts a premium on proximity, informal contacts, and intimate bonds of trust between journalists and politicians. This in turn may lead to journalists not keeping the appropriate distance from political actors, a development that would endanger the autonomy and independence of journalism because it raises the likelihood of journalists being instrumentalised for political purposes (Baugut and Grundler, 2009). (It is worth bearing in mind that it is hard to find an agreed-upon measure of what 'appropriate' proximity might mean, as journalists of course need relations to political sources to get access to information (Pfetsch, 2004: 352).) As political actors and journalists are expected to maintain distance in their formal contacts, closer relations are more likely to be cultivated behind the scenes in private settings allowing for more amicable contacts, mutual advice, and perhaps even the coordinated pursuit of shared goals. Qualitative interviews with politicians and journalists in Berlin suggest frequent close informal contacts at private meetings, background talks in exclusive circles in the federal capital, or contacts on politicians' journeys abroad (Baugut and Grundler, 2009: 254; Lesmeister, 2008). Numerous events organised by political and media organisations, lobbyists, and the like create room for more intimate talks and discussion. These informal contacts and the sense of proximity seem to be characteristic for all capitals where the paths of numerous politicians and journalists with long working experience intersect on a regular basis. Professional relations may sometimes also switch over to friendship, which is also well documented by qualitative and quantitative research. An experienced political journalist in Berlin noted: 'From my point of view, it is not alright to address each other with the casual *du* [you], to invite each other to family celebrations, for example birthdays, weddings, namely politicians inviting journalists and vice versa, as often occurs with these kinds of contacts. This is where bondage begins' (Baugut and Grundler, 2009: 201). The balance between formal distance and informal proximity is clearly not easy to strike. A 2006 survey of parliamentary correspondents in Berlin found that 44

85

per cent of them agreed with the statement 'there are more friendships between politicians and journalists than the public suspects' (Kepplinger and Maurer, 2008: 177). Obviously, these close interactions and intimate relationships between political correspondents and politicians in the capital are not without danger.

Informal ties with individual journalists are not the only way in which politicians try to influence the news. Another way to let information flow is through an increasing tendency to leak confidential information from political negotiations and background talks to journalists (Baugut and Grundler, 2009; Lesmeister, 2008). Many politicians criticise the growing tendency of even fellow party members to try to push their own political agenda and individual career interests by leaking information. At least some observers fear that this development may further a tendency towards informal political decision making in small and exclusive political circles, something that would in turn make the leaking of information from these circles even more attractive. The reasons for indiscretions are manifold. Both sides of a negotiation can arrange for leaks or they can be presented as a journalistic indiscretion originating from off-the-record briefings. In some cases, it might be unclear how journalists are expected to treat the information received. More than one in five German parliamentary correspondents say that they have been reproached for publishing information that was meant to remain secret (Kepplinger and Maurer, 2008: 175). Conversely, qualitative interviews with political actors and journalists suggest that confidentiality in fact often works (Baugut and Grundler, 2009: 228). These seemingly contradictory findings may be explained by different forms of background talks. Background circles comprised of numerous journalists searching for exclusive information are primarily regarded as the place for indiscretion. As a consequence, smaller groups or one-on-one conversations tend to become the real place for substantive information (Baugut and Grundler, 2009).

A third dimension of a political communication culture is whether it is dominated by conflict or cooperation. The scandal about former German president Christian Wulff in early 2012 has shed some light on this aspect of the journalist–politician relationship. In the course of the affair it became obvious that Wulff had over a long time cooperated intensively with certain media outlets including the leading tabloid *Bild*, ensuring favourable coverage during his divorce as well as during his candidacy and first term as president. Cooperation ended, however, when several media organisations started investigating charges of financial misconduct and subsequent false statements Wulff had made before the Lower Saxony state parliament denying these allegations. The conflict culminated in a phone-call in which Wulff supposedly threatened *Bild*'s editor-in-chief with legal action if *Bild* would not postpone a story focused on his personal financial dealings until Wulff got back from a trip abroad. Remarkably, the president left his message on the editor-in-chief's voicemail because he was not able to reach him personally. Not immediately released by *Bild* itself, this message finally made its way to other media that broke this part of the Wulff scandal. Generally, most of the German political actors and journalists perceive their relationship as 'partly harmonic and partly affected by conflict' (Pfetsch and Mayerhöffer, 2011: 54). However, there is a remarkable difference in perceptions: twice as many journalists as politicians say the relationship is 'affected by conflict'. It seems probable that journalists, who are expected to keep their distance from politicians, are more sensitive to conflict, while media relations are just one of many tasks for politicians who in Germany typically have professional spokespersons to settle their conflicts. Looking at the causes for conflict, almost half of the Berlin parliamentary correspondents say that conflicts result from being blamed 'for reporting wrong information about a politician or a political incident' (Kepplinger and Maurer, 2008: 175; Pfetsch and Mayerhöffer, 2011: 56). Another frequently mentioned source of conflicts is 'attempts of politicians to bring pressure to bear on me' (Kepplinger and Maurer, 2008: 175). Although empirical findings regarding the development of conflict and cooperation are not available, it seems likely that these kinds of conflicts may become more frequent to the extent that media and political competition increase. This does not mean, however, that cooperation between individual actors should not become closer as a result of the very same development.

As both politicians and journalists are supposed to work in the public interest, it may be seen as problematic if they constituted a secluded elite milieu lacking responsiveness to their audiences and citizens. Again, we do not know for certain whether the politics–media milieu has become more open or more secluded in recent years. What we do know from qualitative interviews with political actors and journalists in Berlin is that they do in fact have a critical view of their interactions and internal communication. Interviewees describe the Berlin microcosm as 'a spaceship' or 'a politics-media village' (Baugut and Grundler, 2009: 222), referring to the close informal relations and high level of self-referentiality discussed above. However, journalists' opinions about transparency differ. Some endorse transparency in terms of meta-coverage, some do not see efficient means of transparency, and there are also worries about the possible negative consequences of transparency. For example, a journalist with close contacts to politicians says: 'I find honourable the idea of telling recipients more about how the things they are being served have been made. But I would defend the opposite position: sometimes it may be better for the gourmet if he does not know how the sausage was made and what went into it' (Baugut and Grundler, 2009: 236). Besides the one group that basically supports the idea of more transparency, there is another one that opposes it. As many as one-quarter of German parliamentary correspondents agree with the statement that friendships between politicians and journalists are none of the public's business, that they are a private matter (Kepplinger and Maurer, 2008: 177). About another quarter are undecided, and one-half of the journalists do not agree – that is, they call for more transparency about private contacts. Taking into account that a social desirability bias may come into play here due to the democratic norm of transparency, the size of the anti-transparency group is remarkable. It probably mirrors the perceived importance of informal communication.

Structure and dynamics of political coverage

As made clear throughout, the German media system has been changing in recent decades, as have both newsroom practices and the relations between journalists and political actors. These changes have had a clear impact on the structure and dynamics of political news – although one should be wary of generalisations in this respect, as the German media landscape is, as outlined from the outset, characterised by great diversity nationally and considerable regional variations. Keeping this variation in mind, an overarching change is in the topics and the style of political coverage. What we have seen since the 1980s is more personalisation, more negativity, more strategic framing (focus on process), more interpretative journalism, more opinion polls, and more visuals, especially in the regional press but also in commercial and – with notable exceptions – public service TV. In addition, political documentaries and traditional news magazines have been pushed out of prime time and partly been replaced by talk shows that provide politicians with a platform to convey their own messages with less journalistic intervention. These changes can in part be traced back to the increasing commercial pressure on media organisations that have to meet the needs of audiences that are less likely to be strong partisans and interested in politics. These trends towards a trivialisation of large parts of political journalism are not only clear from content analysis, but are also highlighted by political journalists themselves. In a 2006 representative survey of Berlin correspondents, 63 per cent said that 'reporting events without any political substance has become part of my work' (Kepplinger and Maurer, 2008). Despite these worrying trends, it is important to keep in mind that the main edition of the most important and long-standing market leader in TV news, the public service programme *Tagesschau*, has by and large stuck to its traditional format, style, and criteria of news selection (Esser, 2008; for on overview of election coverage see Esser and Hemmer, 2008). All in all, several studies clearly show a trend towards a tabloidisation of political news. However, the evidence for an across-the-board tabloidisation is more mixed and the question of whether the trends actually found are a harm to political discourse has not yet been definitively answered (e.g. Reinemann et al., 2011; see also Lünenborg and Berghofer, 2010: 47). The enormous media attention on quite harmless private economic dealings of some German politicians suggests the ambivalence of tabloidisation. On the one hand, it positively illustrates the media's sensitivity to any semblance of political misconduct; on the other hand, such media coverage tends to be disproportionate to the degree of misconduct, thereby fostering political cynicism.

Interestingly, some of the trends identified are fostered by developments in which the interests of media organisations and certain political actors converge. This is especially true for the personalisation of news coverage in the context of national election campaigns. This trend was boosted by the introduction of one-on-one televised debates between the chancellor candidates of the two major parties. Although there are more than two parties represented in the German parliament, neither TV channels nor the two major parties have an interest in opening up the format to representatives of smaller parties (Reinemann and Wilke, 2007). Failures of political journalism such as the hype around the former minister of defence Karl-Theodor zu Guttenberg or the media's alleged blindness to the developments that led to the current financial crises have been attributed at least by some to the growing inability of journalists to see through political PR strategies and to act as a watchdog, or to the growing tendency to follow the pack (e.g. Hofmann, 2007).

Conclusion

This chapter set out to discuss the state of political journalism in Germany. As we have shown, several developments affecting political journalism in other countries are also present in Germany. In terms of context, we see trends towards commercialisation, audience fragmentation, digitisation, and the rise of online media. At the level of newsroom practices, we see an increasing tendency towards an audience orientation, reduced journalistic resources, the acceleration of news cycles, a growing importance of online sources, as well as an organisational restructuring of newsrooms. We also see signs of a move towards greater self-referentiality within the media system, the increased importance of inter-media agenda-setters including most notably *Spiegel Online* and the tabloid *Bild*, outlets that through the influence they exercise across the news media contribute to a relative homogenisation of coverage as well as to a greater frequency and intensity of media hype. Paradoxically, although media and journalists seem to be under more economic and time pressures than ever before, they are at the same time perceived as more and more important by many German politicians. All these trends resemble what is happening in other developed democracies.

But there are other trends found elsewhere that do not seem to be that prominent in Germany, for reasons having to do with the nature of its media system and its political system. For example, the political polarisation of cable television and talk radio seen in the US is absent in Germany where broadcasting regulation guarantees a minimum of diversity and balance on both commercial and public service channels. In addition, the commercial 24-hour news channels that have become so important in other countries are fighting hard for survival in Germany, mainly because of the strong position of public service television and radio stations that provide a number of news programmes throughout the day (Reinemann and Fawzi, 2010). In addition, online-only journalistic media have not been successful in Germany. Instead, the digital versions of traditional offline media dominate online news. Pure online journalistic media hardly play a role for the general public as a source of political information, which can also be traced back to the quite diverse media landscape and the strong position of public service broadcasters also on the web.

All in all, German political journalism today is under enormous pressures due to the worsening of economic conditions and the rapidly changing online environment, coupled with the increased resources ploughed into PR by many political actors. The future of political journalism – which is so vital for a flourishing democracy – depends not least on whether the media, politics, and citizens will find innovative ways to provide it with the necessary financial resources to fulfil its public role in the future.

5

The Emergence of an Increasingly Competitive News Regime in Denmark

Mark Blach-Ørsten

Introduction

The twentieth-century history of political journalism in Denmark is typically told as a story of a gradual transformation of a partisan press both personally and organisationally closely intertwined with the major political parties into relatively impartial news media central to most political processes but relatively independent of both political and economic pressures. In this chapter, I will argue that Danish political journalism from the late 1990s onwards has begun to move beyond the late twentieth-century independent news media towards a situation increasingly defined by a new and intensified competition for audiences, for advertising, and for privileged access to the authoritative sources that can generate journalistic scoops. With a term taken from institutional theory, we might think of this historical development as a change in the Danish 'news regime' (defined as a relatively stable set of rules and resources for the production of news) (Ryfe, 2006).

Using Ryfe's notion, we can speak in broad terms of a succession of distinct news regimes in Denmark. First was a 'partisan news regime' originating in the democratic revolution of 1848 and the late nineteenth-century development of what has been called the 'four-newspaper system', where each of the main national political parties was intertwined with a network of affiliated newspapers published across the country. This regime was in turn supplanted through the rise of broadcasting and the consolidation of the newspaper industry in the 1950s and 1960s and gradually transformed into an 'independent news regime' that combined an increasingly professionalised journalistic profession with a limited number of increasingly autonomous newspapers and broadcasters. In a development parallel with that observed in other Western democracies (Cook, 1998; Sparrow, 1999), these mass media organisations played an ever more important role in the political process as the political parties and their auxiliary organisations gradually lost their popular base, and more and more people got most of their information about politics from the news (Lund, 2002; Pedersen et al., 2000).

As I will show below, recent studies of political journalism in Denmark indicate that this independent news regime is now changing in important ways that do not displace the news media institution from its central position in political processes, but change the way it functions. In recent years, the proliferation of new media outlets (often extensions of existing media organisations, like the websites of newspapers and rolling-news channels associated with established broadcasters) and a significant growth in the volume of journalistic output have increased competition for audiences, advertising, and access to key sources. Everyday journalistic practices and indeed the journalistic product itself have changed in part as a consequence. In this emergent 'competitive news regime', journalists and media organisations retain the normative emphasis on independence and impartiality characteristic of the previous regime, but increasingly collaborate with more professionalised sources – especially top politicians and their advisers – to co-produce political news. This development has helped enable the enormous expansion in the amount of content produced by a relatively stable number of political journalists in Denmark but may also, as I will suggest at the end, be connected to the declining popular trust in political journalism itself.

In the first part of the chapter below, I provide an overview of developments in the twentieth-century Danish media system and its relations to the political system. In the second part, I elaborate on the notion of news regimes and briefly compare developments in Denmark to those observed elsewhere. In the third part, I detail the most important recent changes in Danish political journalism with reference to increased competition, increased coverage of political scandals, and increased co-production of news by journalists and political actors. In the final part, I summarise the main indicators for the emergence of a new competitive news regime in Denmark and discuss the drivers of this development, highlighting not only the political, economic, and technological factors behind this change, but also the important role of the competitive ethos of the journalistic profession itself. In the conclusion I discuss the democratic implications especially of the mounting evidence that many citizens trust the new, more competitive political journalism less than they trusted the independent news regime.

The Danish media system: an overview

The Danish media system has much in common with other Northern European (and especially Nordic) media systems. In their comparative analysis of Western media systems, Daniel C. Hallin and Paolo Mancini (2004) place Denmark in what they term the 'democratic corporatist' model as one of the European countries characterised by the early development of a large newspaper industry, active state involvement in the media sector, and an early focus on press freedom (Hallin and Mancini, 2004: 74).

Danish newspapers have historically been strongly linked to the political parties that grew out of the shift from absolutism to parliamentary democracy in the late nineteenth century. Today, the three most important nationally distributed broadsheet newspapers are all principally committed to impartial news coverage, but also retain their distinct ideological (though no longer party political) editorial profiles, being broadly associated with the Liberal Party (*Jyllands-Posten*), the Conservative Party (*Berlingske*), and the Social-Liberal Party (*Politiken*). (The last Social Democratic newspaper, *Aktuelt*, closed in 2001.) The party press reached its height at the beginning of the twentieth century, with newspaper penetration approximating 100 per cent and four titles (and sometimes more) published in most cities and much of the countryside. However, the party press began to erode after World War II with the rise of radio and later television, resulting in the consolidation of the newspaper industry in regional monopolies and a limited number of nationally distributed titles. Many titles closed, and the formal links between parties and papers withered as other publications were sold off or converted to independent trusts. The newspapers that survived this period of retrenchment continue to be among the most read titles in Denmark but, since the 1990s, print circulation, readership, and advertising revenues have all dropped dramatically as the traditional paid broadsheet and tabloid newspapers face challenges from newly launched free dailies and the rise of digital media (Esmark and Ørsten, 2008; Lund et al., 2009; Willig, 2011). The turbulence of recent years has led to a so far relatively minor reduction in the size of the newsrooms of the major Danish newspapers as well as a shift in focus from print to online where all legacy titles continue to reach large audiences. Despite the decline in print sales and advertising revenues, no established national or regional print newspaper has closed, though several of the free dailies launched in the early 2000s have disappeared and some smaller local newspapers have merged to cut costs.

In terms of broadcast media, 1926 saw the introduction of a state monopoly on the airwaves, initially in the form of the State Radio Broadcaster (Statsradiofonien). With the arrival of television and the creation of Denmark's Radio (DR) in 1959 as a national integrated public service provider funded by a licence fee levied on all receivers, both state monopoly and state regulation continued into the postwar period. Direct political control of DR and DR's monopoly on television and radio broadcasting were abolished in the early 1980s with the introduction of both local community and commercial radio and with the launch of TV2 as a competing, advertising-funded, state-owned public service broadcaster. With the development of satellite and cable television and a further liberalisation of broadcast regulation, several more commercial radio and television stations have entered the Danish market since, but they play no significant role in terms of news provision. Like the major newspapers, the two main broadcasters strive for impartial news coverage, and though the possibility that their journalism may be biased in one direction or another is a recurrent theme in public debate, empirical research has repeatedly found that political journalism remains by and large politically neutral (Albæk et al., 2010; Esmark and Ørsten, 2008). A study of news consumption in Denmark (Schrøder and Kobbernagle, 2012) shows that the two public service providers DR and TV2 still draw by far the greatest share of viewers and listeners and remain the main sources of news for many people. The same survey also reveals that though newspapers are losing print readers, newspaper websites play an increasingly important role for many Danish media users. Though a growing number of Danes access and share news via social networking sites like Facebook, stand-alone online media remain marginal. Legacy media continue to dominate news provision both online and offline.

Despite the disappearance of formal ties between parties and newspapers, the insulation of the two public service broadcasters from direct political control, and a further deregulation of broadcasting markets, state intervention still shapes the Danish media system in key ways, especially in terms of underpinning a diverse media scene. A report on media subsidies concluded that total subsidies across licence fees as well as direct and indirect subsidies for the newspaper industry in 2009 amounted to roughly 6.6 billion Danish kroner a year (just short of €1 billion). The report estimated that subsidies represented 39 per cent of total revenues in Danish television, 91 per cent in radio, and 10 per cent in the newspaper industry (Lund and Lindskow, 2011). The rationale for these subsidies rests upon the politically broadly shared view that media contribute to the greater good, and that the market alone cannot ensure a well-functioning democratic dialogue between politicians and citizens, especially in a small country like Denmark.

Though Hallin and Mancini stress the importance of the relationship between media and politics in understanding how media systems are shaped and develop over time, they have been criticised for paying insufficient attention to the political side of their equation (Esmark and Ørsten, 2008). Developments in Denmark clearly illustrate how intertwined media and politics remain, even as formal bonds have been cut and some forms of state intervention rolled back. In the twentieth century, the Danish political system was characterised by a combination of a fairly consensual multi-party parliamentary democracy and a strong corporatist tradition of interest mediation (as alluded to in the notion of a democratic corporatist system). As a paradigmatic example of a Nordic welfare state, Denmark has a strong tradition of state intervention and of strong union influence.

Especially since the 1970s and 1980s, however, the political system has changed in significant ways. Though turnout in national elections remains high (above 80 per cent), fewer and fewer voters retain a strong sense of party identification, and class-based voting has weakened in favour of issue voting. The previously firm and formally institutionalised alliance between the Social Democratic Party and the main labour federation (LO) came apart in the 1990s. Most parties have seen their membership organisations decline, especially rapidly from the 1980s onwards, but a broad majority has at the same time passed legislation in parliament to substantially increase the public funding of their professional secretariats. The money has to a large extent been invested in professionalised communications and campaign efforts aimed at appealing to an increasingly de-aligned and fluid electorate. Thus, the Danish democratic corporatist *political* system has changed at least as much as the democratic corporatist *media* system has in recent decades (Esmark and Ørsten, 2008).

Journalism and politics: an institutional perspective

In both their early partisan and their later more impartial iterations, the news media have been integral to political processes in Denmark. Though increasingly independent of political parties and today formally rooted in commercial (for privately owned newspapers) or public-interest (for state-owned broadcasters) logics, many scholars insist on seeing the news media as a political institution in its own right (Allern and Blach-Ørsten, 2011; Cook, 1998; Esmark and Ørsten, 2008; Ørsten, 2004; Ryfe, 2006; Sparrow, 1999). Clearly, the news media are not a formal political institution like the executive, legislative, and judiciary branches of government, but the metaphor of the 'fourth estate' suggests how they can be seen as an intermediary political institution akin to political parties and interest groups, a phenomenon that needs to be understood both as a disparate collection of individual organisations and as sharing certain social logics. Timothy Cook (1998: 64) lays out clearly the institutionalist perspective on news media in his *Governing with the News*:

> *The news media, despite different technologies, deadlines, and audiences, are structured similarly in their internal organisation, the way they interact with sources, the formats they use, and in the content they provide [...] This transorganizational agreement on news process and content suggests that we should think of the news media not as a set of diverse organizations, or even a batch of individual institutions, but collectively as a single social institution.*

Institutionalists interested in journalism have focused on the daily news practices of journalists, often seen as deeply embedded in historically developed norms, routines, and values shared across a range of organisations that thus, even when they compete, in key respects cover the news in a similar fashion. As suggested from the outset, a set of trans-organisational norms and routines for the production of news that remain stable and taken for granted over time can be seen as what David Ryfe (2006) has called a 'news regime'. In general the argument of an institutional approach is the assumption that intermediary institutions influence the impact of macro-level forces (like economic or technological change) on micro-level action (like the daily practices of journalists or politicians), but also that institutions develop over time, sometimes to an extent where one can talk about regime change, in part in response to these macro-level forces.

Some scholars, like Sparrow (1999), have highlighted the importance of economic forces in understanding how the news media institution develops. According to this view, concerns over revenue and the steady provision of content to audiences (sold in turn to advertisers) are the primary driving forces in the development of the norms, rules, and practices of journalism. Thus the rules may change in part in response to changes in the economic environment. Others, like Cook (1998), have highlighted political forces – most importantly the state – as the major exogenous force shaping the institutional norms and routines of news production. Cook argues that political legitimacy is of more immediate concern for journalists than the commercial preoccupations of their employers, and that in their daily work journalists find themselves in a complicated relationship with a large variety of political sources, and indeed with the (national) political culture itself.

The institutional approach has been highly influential in the study of political journalism in Denmark (Hjarvard, 2007; Lund, 2002; Ørsten, 2004). Most of these studies have shared Cook's (1998) focus on politics rather than Sparrow's (1999) focus on economics, although Danish researchers have generally acknowledged the importance of both political forces and market forces in shaping how news media develop (Allern and Blach-Ørsten, 2011; Hjarvard, 2007). Most of the Danish institutionalists argue that as a result of the combination of change in the Danish media system and the Danish political system from the 1970s onwards outlined above (the disappearance of the party press, the political independence given to public service broadcasters, changes in the parties and their relations to the electorate, etc.), the news media in Denmark can be viewed not simply as a political institution, but as an *independent* political institution playing an increasingly important mediating role between politicians and the wider population (Lund, 2002; Ørsten, 2004). In a fashion parallel to what had happened decades earlier in the very different setting of the United States (Cook, 1998; Ryfe, 2006; Sparrow, 1999), the emergence of the independent news regime involved not only the separation of political parties from newspapers (and broadcasters) that were increasingly run on a commercial or public interest rather than a partisan basis, but also the birth of an increasingly professionalised form of journalism that grew in importance as it provided the main independent sources of information about political issues and public affairs for most of the population. This regime became a defining part of the Danish political and media systems in the latter part of the twentieth century.

My contention in this chapter is that, at the beginning of the twenty-first century, this is changing, in part in response to political and economic (and indeed technological) forces, but also because of how these external forces interact with endogenous professional logics.

Evidence of a news regime in transition

In Denmark, the shift from a partisan news regime to a more independent news regime has affinities with similar developments elsewhere, but took place at a much later point than in, for example, the United States. Danish scholars typically date the reign of the party press from the late 1880s to the late 1950s and the age of the independent press (and later broadcasting) from the early 1960s to the late 1990s. During the partisan news regime, political journalism was mostly about the opinion of the party that a given newspaper supported. The editor was a party member and his editorial reflected party politics (Ørsten, 2004; Pedersen et al., 2000). The rest of the paper was largely made up of reports from different political meetings, again mostly reflecting the debate within the party. As late as 1958 this was still the way most Danish newspapers covered politics (Pedersen et al., 2000). However, during the 1960s and 1970s this changed, as the newspapers that survived the 'newspaper deaths' of the middle of the century separated themselves from their party ties and a new professional journalism emerged in both print and broadcasting organisations that emphasised tools like the inverted news triangle, talking to and quoting a diverse range of sources, and trying to live up to ideals of balanced reporting and the role of an independent fourth estate (Pedersen et al., 2000). The independent news regime of the latter half of the twentieth century was based on a consolidated media system with a limited number of generously staffed national titles and broadcasters that faced relatively limited competition for audiences' attention and for stories, a strong and trans-organisational sense of journalistic professionalism that, amongst other things, shied away from covering the private lives of politicians, and an emphasis on organisational and vocational independence that proscribed close links between reporters and politicians (though these were often still cultivated informally). All of these traits are under pressure today.

First of all, the total amount of journalistic output has been vastly increased since the late 1990s and competition amongst individual journalists for stories has increased too. Newsroom ethnographies have documented both an increased focus on scoops and exclusives in Danish news media in general (Willig, 2011) but also an increased tendency – because of time pressures – to rely more on other news outlets as sources as journalists continuously monitor their competitors and often use their stories as raw material for their own production, especially in online newsrooms (Hartley, 2013). One study by Lund, Willig, and Blach-Ørsten (2009), tracing changes in news production in Denmark from 1998 to 2008, shows that while the number of journalists working in the news media remained relatively stable, the overall production of news stories across print, television, and online almost tripled over this period. This huge increase in production is mostly attributed to the growth and demands of online journalism where there is a new deadline every minute, and the simultaneous rise of 24/7 news channels in Danish public broadcasting (both developments facilitated by new technologies). The study shows that, even in 2008, most news stories still originate with print media and their websites, and are then disseminated to a broader public via radio, television, and other media's websites, in large part through copying and re-use. Only a small number of original political news stories stem from radio and television, and even fewer from stand-alone websites. A parallel study documents the prominent place of political news in this vastly expanded news output. In 2008, as many as 88 per cent of the news articles in the main sections of the legacy broadsheet newspapers were concerned with politics. For front-page stories, the number was 91 per cent (Blach-Ørsten and Bro, 2009). Across the news institution, a 2010 study found that 31 per cent of all news items in Danish media concerned politics, making politics the single most covered subject in print, TV, and radio. (In the US, by contrast, 28 per cent of all print journalism is concerned with politics, but only 12 per cent of all television news focuses on politics (Who Makes the News?, 2010).[1] Not only politics but also politicians figure prominently in the news in Denmark. Of all the sources quoted in the main legacy broadsheet newspapers, 91 per cent were elite sources, and national politicians were the favourite sources in political stories (Blach-Ørsten and Bro, 2009).

Second, the vastly increased output and growing number of outlets have increased competition for attention. This has changed the approach to how politics and politicians are covered. One study focusing specifically on the critical case of public service broadcasting tracks a change towards political stories that are focused on conflict, stories that focus on politicians as personalities rather than as political figures or party representatives, and stories oriented towards process rather than policy (Binderkrantz and Green-Pedersen, 2009). In a general study of the personalisation of politics in nine European countries, Esmark and Mayerhöffer (2012) find the clearest example of increased personalisation in Denmark. Many studies have expressed concerns over sensationalism, tabloidisation, and the like, though these changes are not linear, nor inclusive to all media. A study of political scandals in Denmark suggests a change in political journalism in terms of the number and types of political scandals that are covered in the media (Blach-Ørsten, 2011). Tracking mediated scandals from 1980 to 2010, the study shows that the number of political scandals covered tripled in the ten years from 2000 to 2010. There are not only more mediated scandals today than in the late twentieth century. The scandals covered by political journalists are also different. In Denmark, political scandal coverage has moved closer and closer to the personal life of politicians. This has resulted in the emergence of the sex scandal in Danish media – a type of scandal that, despite the colourful personal lives of many prominent politicians typically only revealed in biographies published after their death, had not been common in Danish media before (in contrast to British and American media, see Thompson, 2000). It has also taken the form of increased focus on the private economy of politicians, including personal problems with debt, tax difficulties, etc. – issues that have rarely been covered in the past.

All in all, studies of political scandals in Denmark and the other Nordic countries show an increase in the number of scandals covered and in particular an increase in scandals concerned with the private life of politicians (as opposed to their political doings and/or wrongdoings). Thus, today, political scandals are no longer covered only by the tabloid press (as was largely the case in the 1960s and 1970s). Today any type of media may break a news story exposing a political scandal, and indeed many scandals are covered by all major news outlets, no matter how insubstantial the transgression involved may seem. Indeed, it seems that in Denmark as in the US (Entman, 2012), the more trivial the scandal is, the more coverage it gets (Blach-Ørsten, 2011). This increased focus on political scandals can be linked to both the question of the personalisation of Danish politics and the issue of increased competition and tabloidisation. From the personalisation perspective the increased focus on the personal lives of politicians can be seen as a 'natural' development from the side of voters, who increasingly focus on the personalities of politicians when casting their votes. Indeed a recent study argued that for voters with less factual knowledge of politics, political scandals, especially scandals related to the private lives of politicians, probably constituted one of the main ways in which they make sense of politics (Bhatti et al., 2013). However, the rise in the coverage of political scandals can also be linked to increased competition and production demands since political scandals are now part of all types of media, and no longer only the focus of the tabloid media.

Third, the increased competition and journalistic emphasis on scoops and unique stories combined with the professionalisation of the communications efforts of leading politicians and political parties have changed the relations between journalists and political sources. Danish political journalists have had their offices in the House of Parliament itself since 1918. Today around 180 journalists are registered as members of the parliamentary press corps, about equal to the number of elected representatives. All major media outlets thus have a significant number of journalists who spend the better part of their day working alongside politicians. These reporters and their sources are engaged in both adversarial and exchange-based relations, but as political journalists have to produce more and more content and leading politicians command more and more professional assistance, the balance of power changes. A nine-country comparative European study found Danish politicians more highly oriented towards the media than politicians in any other country and more likely to favour leaking news to select journalists than politicians in any other country (Esmark and Blach-Ørsten, 2011). As shown above, Danish journalists are highly focused on political news, and the interest is reciprocal, as Danish politicians are also highly focused on managing their media relations. The majority of the politicians also seem quite content with how things are working out. A longitudinal study of Danish members of parliament and their interactions with and attitudes toward the news media has shown that MPs not only appeared more in the news in 2000 than they did in 1980, but also they were generally more satisfied with their media coverage in 2000 than they were in 1980 (Elmelund-Præstekær et al., 2010). The authors of the study write (2010: 395) that 'with more competition among media outlets and an increasing demand for media appearances, MPs may – in spite of competition for media attention – be in a better position to exploit their privileged position as news suppliers in 2000 than in 1980.' The interaction between politicians and journalists is largely concerned with a trade in scoops where sources will offer reporters exclusive stories, expecting extensive and often mostly friendly coverage in exchange. Whereas as recently as in the late 1990s researchers found few signs that the phenomenon of 'spin doctors' played any significant role in Danish politics and political journalism (Pedersen et al., 2000), the 20 years since have seen the introduction of special advisers for all members of cabinet and an additional investment in PR by the major political parties, interest groups, and politically sensitive businesses. The relationship between spin doctors and journalists is a subject of much speculation and something tantamount to a theme in parts of popular culture (in television drama series like *Borgen*, for example) and has caused some concern and drawn some critical scrutiny from the news media themselves. The emergence of the 'spin scandal' is a powerful illustration of this, a sub-category of mediated political scandal concerned with exposing the – in a few cases outright illegal – machinations of special advisers and their political bosses.

The increased volume of output coupled with an emphasis on exclusivity, the changing nature of the content of political journalism, including an increased tendency to focus on politicians' personalities and their private lives (and scandals), and the changing daily interactions between ever more hard-pressed journalists and top politicians who have a growing number of staffers at their disposal are all changing the balance between the adversarial and the exchange models of journalist–source relations, and impacting the routines that define the everyday operations of the news institution as part of Danish politics.

The emergence of a new competitive news regime?

As made clear above, contemporary Danish political journalism has changed in several key aspects in recent years, suggesting a change away from the independent news regime of the latter half of the twentieth century towards a news regime defined more by increased competition for content, exclusive stories, and privileged access to politicians. This development does not represent a clean break with or a total abandoning of the aspirations associated with independent, impartial, professional journalism, but we see signs of the gradual emergence of a new regime that not only works in new ways (with routines that differ from the old regime) but also emphasises new values, in particular exclusivity even at the price of cultivating rather closer relations with political sources than was previously thought prudent (and thus also involves new norms). (One poignant example of this is the 'revolving door' that increasingly seems to exist between top editorial positions and jobs as special advisers. In recent years, several high-profile political reporters have moved to work for top politicians only to later return to journalistic jobs. Under the partisan news regime, this would have been routine. Under the independent news regime, such moves were largely one-way traffic from the media to politics.)

Just as the change from the partisan news regime towards the independent news regime was driven by a combination of political, economic, and technological factors, the ongoing change away from the independent news regime towards what we might tentatively call the competitive news regime is also driven by a combination of factors. They include the following:

- political factors, including de-alignment and decline in party membership combined with increased public funding for party organisations, which have increased the professionalisation of political communication and thus changed the relationship between journalists and political sources;
- economic factors, including commercial news organisations engaging in an ever more intense competition for attention and advertising and public service providers who need large audiences to justify their existence, thus changing the demands of news production; and
- technological factors, including technological convergence on digital platforms, meaning that previously separate media like newspapers, broadcasters, and new stand-alone websites now compete head-to-head and can monitor each other's news output in real time.

The emerging competitive news regime is, as institutional theory would predict, deeply shaped by the historical legacy of the partisan news regime and the independent news regime that preceded it in Denmark. The present-day Danish media system is formed by the legacy of the party-press parallelism of the four-party-press system and the politically controlled earlier public service broadcasting monopoly, just as it still bears the imprint of the aspirations to professional independence and impartiality of the consolidated late twentieth-century media system. But whereas in the 1990s many feared that political journalism had come to dictate political processes, it now seems clear that the relationships between journalists and politicians are changing. Research suggests that Danish politicians view the legacy media, especially television and the morning papers, as the most important agenda-setters for political debate in Denmark (Esmark and Blach-Ørsten, 2011). But top politicians and their aides in turn increasingly take the lead in the famous 'news tango' and set the media agenda because they, more than anyone, can offer the exclusive stories that are seen as so valuable in the competitive news regime. In the partisan news regime, politicians set the agenda insofar as they controlled news media organisations directly. In the independent news regime, politicians set the media agenda insofar as they convinced journalists that their ideas were newsworthy enough to be included in a fairly limited news hole. In the emerging competitive news regime, politicians set the media agenda insofar as they can offer individual journalists or media outlets exclusive scoops that in turn spread across the entire media landscape as other organisations repeat or copy the story. Even prominent politicians still get swept away by out-of-control media hypes. Scandal coverage or dedicated focus journalism by investigative reporters can be hard to influence even for well-assisted and highly placed sources. Individual back-bench members of parliament or aspiring candidates still struggle to attract media attention. Experienced journalists with time available to pursue a story can still proactively play sources against each other when different political actors have clearly conflicting interests. But in the routine coverage, top politicians and their aides generally take the lead in setting the media agenda (Green-Pedersen and Stubager, 2010).

Here it is important to highlight the role of professional norms and routines in the development of a new, competitive news regime driven by the pursuit of scoops (often provided by self-interested sources) and powered by widespread copying of others' content. While studies in the UK and the US (Brown, 2011; Davis, 2009) have often associated such tendencies with market forces (exclusives are assumed to drive sales, information subsidies from public relations personnel and copying from competitors make news production cheaper), the move towards a more competitive news regime in Denmark has happened without the kind of thorough commercialisation seen in some English-speaking countries, and seems to cut across the commercial media/public service media divide. So far, Danish commercial media continue to be subsidised by the state and have been spared the kind of economic crisis that has led to major downsizing in newsrooms in the UK and especially the US, and though the public service providers face many strategic challenges in a changing media environment, their revenue bases seem secure. And yet, even without the financial pressures so clear in the Anglophone countries, Denmark has seen some tendencies towards the kind of political news production coupling deliberately leaked scoops and exclusives with copy-paste 'churnalism' more often associated with cost-conscious and profit-oriented UK and US news organisations.

Part of the reason seems to be professional as much as political, economic, and technological. The emergence of a competitive news regime is in part driven by the political, economic, and technological developments discussed above – all external forces – but it is also shaped by professional norms and routines endogenous to the news institution and the journalistic profession, most notably what Rod Tiffen (1989: 59), in an evocative phrase, has called journalism's 'competitive ethos' – a norm that cultivates 'a war of all against all' (see Ehrlich, 1995, for a similar point). Danish journalism has long been competitive – competitive in a political sense as partisan papers faced off in every town; competitive in the independent news regime as a limited number of major news organisations competed to break the most interesting and important stories as part of their daily, limited news offering. But faced with a virtually unlimited supply of stories from self-interested political sources, an equally virtually unlimited news hole for publishing these stories especially across a growing number of continuously updated, 24/7 news sites, and the constant fear of losing a fickle audience to one of a growing number of competitors, the professional competition between individual journalists, their editors, and the news media organisations they work for has assumed a new importance.

In what Tiffin (1989) has termed an 'institutionally perverse' development, the continuous competitive race to break the news, to set the agenda, to be the dominant news medium pervades journalistic work even as the majority of news organisations lose money on their 24/7 rolling-news services and to a very large extent duplicate each other's efforts in terms of what is covered. As Willig (2011) has pointed out, there is nothing to indicate that the wider audience cares for or notices whether a news story is exclusive or not, and when exactly it is broken, nor is there any indication that competition produces more original journalism as much of the content is based on competitors' content more than original reporting. In terms of resource allocation, this is akin to what economists call 'competitive waste'. It weakens journalists by syphoning off time and money that could have been spent on independent reporting and strengthens top sources by allowing them to play on competing journalists' fear of missing out. The normative ideals of Danish political journalism still include the aspiration to be an independent fourth estate but, as especially the study of mediated political scandals and changing relations between reporters and sources suggest, this particular ideal clashes with an increased reliance on politicians in the routine co-production of news as political actors adroitly exploit journalists' hunger for exclusives and fear of being beaten to the story by the competition. Journalistic norms may thus combine with political and technological developments and contribute to the development of a more competitive news regime even when this makes little or no commercial sense.

Conclusion

Contemporary Danish political journalism is deeply formed by the independent news regime that developed in the second half of the twentieth century. The news institution continues to be defined by a set of norms and routines that cut across individual news media organisations. Mass media, most notably broadcasters but also newspapers (in part through their digital offerings), remain the single most important source of information about politics and public affairs for most of the population. Politicians continue to see the established news media as setting the agenda for public discussion and as an important way of reaching out to an increasingly volatile electorate that party organisations themselves can no longer mobilise as members. Journalists continue to see themselves as independent, impartial professionals reporting the news to, and for, the general public.

And yet, in some important ways, Danish political journalism is changing away from the late twentieth-century independent news regime, towards a new regime that seems defined by competition more than anything else. This new competitive news regime enables the production of much more content than was previously published, focuses on process and personalities more than policy, covers parts of politicians' lives that were previously thought to be private, and is increasingly dependent upon professional sources who can deliver much sought-after exclusives and scoops and help co-produce the news. What does this development mean for democracy? That depends in part on what the wider population think of the end product. Irrespective of what the journalists and politicians who animate its day-to-day operations think of it, surveys suggest that many ordinary Danes are very sceptical of the emerging competitive news regime and its constant flow of increasingly co-produced news. One comparative study found Denmark ranked only slightly above Spain and Great Britain – both countries with historically low levels of trust in political journalism – in terms of confidence in the press (Albæk et al., 2010). Another survey conducted in 2011 found that 84 per cent of the respondents felt journalists placed too strong a focus on sensational news (such as scandals), and 92 per cent felt that this focus on sensational news kept the media from publishing stories that focused more on political substance (Blach-Ørsten, 2012a). All in all, recent studies of trust in Danish news media indicate that the question of public trust in journalist and journalism is a delicate one. The surveys also indicate that the changes in the production of news may change political journalism's relationship with its audience. If indeed we are seeing the emergence of a new competitive news regime, then this news regime might lead political journalism to a crossroads that would bring it into conflict with the public understanding of journalism's role in society by aligning it too closely with elite sources, and too far from the general public it purports to serve.

From a media system point of view, the transition towards a competitive news regime may also be problematic. The political rationale behind the extensive direct and indirect media subsidies in place in Denmark remains based on the idea that state intervention is necessary to secure the media's role as an independent institution of democratic dialogue between politicians and citizens. The policies also stem from the view that the subsidies should help secure a diverse and pluralistic news outcome. The problem is that much research questions both how independent political journalism actually is and how diverse and pluralistic the news produced actually is. It is clear that increased competition may in fact both threaten journalism's independence vis-à-vis professionalised sources and lead to a more voluminous but also more homogenised news production. Taken together this indicates that the transition towards a competitive news regime in the future may lead to bigger and more fundamental questions on the nature and purpose of political news in the Danish media system.

In the general debate on changes in political journalism, commercialisation is often highlighted as a major catalyst of change. As is clear from this chapter, economic forces are amongst those driving developments in Danish political journalism, but so are political forces, technological forces, and professional norms internal to journalism itself.

The emergence of a new competitive news regime in Denmark is not driven simply by commercial news organisations searching for profit or new media platforms affording constant breaking news, but also by the way the journalistic competitive ethos has interacted with outside political and technological changes. Journalists themselves may not fully appreciate the importance of their own professional norms and values as drivers of current changes but, as this chapter has shown, the transition from an independent news regime towards a new competitive news regime in Denmark raises a number of questions that go beyond the market to touch on media policy, profession values, and the very role of journalism in a democracy.

Note

1 Politics here is primarily national politics. As a member of the EU, Denmark's politics is also in large part influenced by Brussels and the wider politics of Europe. The EU, however, is seldom at the centre of political coverage (Blach-Ørsten, 2012b).

6

The Impact of Market Forces, New Technologies, and Political PR on UK Journalism

Aeron Davis

Introduction

This chapter begins by setting UK political journalism in comparative context and looking at some of its key distinguishing features. In terms of its traditions of broadcasting regulation and its developed welfare state, the UK has much in common with many Northwestern European states. However, in its 'majoritarian' political system, its more recent history of neo-liberal economic policy making, and its free-market press business model, it has moved progressively closer to the US. The closeness of political journalists and politicians at Westminster, accentuated by a London-centred focus for reporting UK national politics generally, is also a distinguishing feature. As argued, this combination of extreme market pressures, majoritarian politics, and Westminster-centric features are key factors that have strongly steered UK political journalism during a time of rapid transformation.

Three particular areas of transition, noted in several recent overviews of UK political reporting (Fenton, 2010; Franklin, 2012; Lee-Wright et al., 2012; Leveson, 2012), are discussed in the chapter. These are: (1) the breakdown of the news business model, particularly in newspapers, (2) the impact of digital media, and (3) the increasing insularity of political source–journalist relations. The discussions draw on three periods of interview-based research with UK politicians and political journalists between 1997 and 2008 (Davis, 2002, 2007, 2010a). It is argued that the overall impact of these shifts has been to propel UK political journalism towards a sense of crisis, both financially and professionally. Many (although not all) of these trends are observable in public service media, such as the BBC, as well as in the commercial print and broadcast media. The political journalism emerging is more superficial and sensationalist, less informed and less investigative, more desk-bound, more cannibalistic, and generally prone to taking newsgathering short-cuts in its practices. Such trends are highlighted by the recent phone-hacking scandal and Leveson Inquiry that have dominated debates about the state of UK journalism since mid-2011.

Placing UK political journalism in context

In Hallin and Mancini's (2004) comparative work, the UK media are grouped together with 'liberal' or 'North Atlantic' nations, including the US, Canada, and Ireland. The features that distinguish the UK are the early development of an independent, mass-market news industry and a strong 'professional', 'Anglo-American' model of reporting that developed relatively early (see also Chalaby, 1996). Content traditionally intended to be 'neutral', 'objective', 'balanced', and fact-based. Unlike the 'polarised pluralist' nations of Southern Europe, or the 'democratic corporatist' states of North and Central Europe, newspapers have been more independent of political parties and organised interests. That said, today's UK national press is fairly partisan. Most papers, including the so-called 'quality press', ally themselves to particular political ideologies and policy directions that are associated with one of the major parties. For Curran and Park (2000) the UK media system is best classified as 'democratic neo-liberal'. Both typologies emphasise the role of the market in the development of the UK press in particular. Market competition is indeed fierce in the UK newsprint sector as 11 daily newspapers and 10 Sunday papers compete on a national basis.

However, in broadcasting, the UK is rather closer to the 'democratic corporatist' or 'democratic regulated' traditions of much of Western Europe. Unlike the US, the UK has a long history of public service broadcasting. The BBC, publicly financed and regulated but at arm's length from government, has dominated UK broadcasting since the 1920s. In 2006 in the UK, public service broadcaster (PSB) channels gained 51 per cent of audience share (Hardy, 2008), which was larger than in most other European countries. Regulation of ownership, content, balance, and political advertising in broadcasting is far closer to Europe than the US. Competition is less with only three real players dominating the news sector: the BBC, ITN, and News Corporation.

In terms of public engagement with political journalism, levels of newspaper readership, television ownership, and internet usage are better than average. Approximately a third of UK citizens read newspapers, above the European average but below many of the democratic corporatist countries. Confidence in the UK press, however, is extremely low, often being the lowest in European social surveys and near the bottom of the World Values Survey (2005–8). In the last survey only 13.8 per cent of the public trusted the press. Internet penetration levels and per capita television ownership are at the higher end in Europe. Faith in UK television news is far stronger than in its press and the BBC often draws international praise.

Looking at the political system, Lijphart (1999) classifies the UK as a 'majoritarian' democracy, as opposed to a more 'consensus'-based one. The UK, like the US, has a first-past-the-post electoral system which is dominated by two major parties, with one party taking control of government. Such a system, while directly linking individual politicians to their constituencies, does not reflect the overall voting intentions of the nation and discourages smaller parties. In the UK, from World War II until 2010, one party had always gained over 50 per cent of MPs, but never more than 43 per cent of the vote. The 2010 election bucked this trend and necessitated the forming of a coalition government. In Lijphart's schema (1999) the UK 'Westminster model' is regarded as the most majoritarian of the 36 democracies he looks at. Checks and balances on government are weaker. The executive has more power over the legislature and judiciary, as well as over local government. In each of these respects, the UK is less typical of Western European democracies, where there tend to be more multi-party systems and a greater balance of power between the pillars of the state.

UK politics itself has been more oriented towards neo-liberal economic and social policy making than much of Western Europe in recent decades. The US has been regarded as a greater source of inspiration for new political initiatives. Legislation on trade unions, welfare state support, public infrastructure, and regulation of the economy and finance has all been more favourable towards markets and large corporations. The UK also scores very highly on its business-friendly rating according to the World Bank (2009). It has more average or below average scores

113

when it comes to measures of equality, environmental per capita waste, and confidence in its governing institutions.

When it comes to public engagement with UK politics, recent indicators suggest weaker levels of support than in most comparable democracies. UK voting has moved between 59 and 84 per cent, one of the lower levels in Europe. New postwar lows were reached in 2001 and 2005. By 2002 only 1.5 per cent of the UK public were members of parties and only 16 per cent stated they felt strongly affiliated to a party (Heffernan, 2003), both below the Western European average. Hansard's (2009: 3–4) audit of political engagement found that only 53 per cent of the public said they would definitely vote in the next election. Only 9 per cent said they had contacted a politician and only 3 per cent had donated to or joined a political party in the 'last 2–3 years'. In September 2009, following the economic slump and a well-publicised MPs' expenses scandal, only 13 per cent of the public said they 'trusted' politicians to tell the truth (Ipsos-MORI, 2009).

Another feature of note is that UK national political news coverage is very focused on Westminster in London, where Parliament and the departments of government are. Here, the lobby system awards a limited number of passes to accredited political journalists. Most of these share cramped offices in Parliament. They are given access to MPs, press conferences, and briefing material but, in return, have to conform to a range of rules, both formal and informal. Within a couple of hundred metres of Parliament is Millbank Studios where the main news broadcasters are based. Political correspondents move between Millbank and Parliament throughout the day. This means that UK political reporters are very much part of the political environment they report on and, in addition, UK political reporting is extremely Westminster-centric. Elected MPs have to spend part of their time in their local constituencies, but political journalists rarely leave the metropolitan centre or look beyond Parliament when thinking about national politics. As one leading journalist commented:

> [T]he political system is very Westminster centred [...] you will be amazed how difficult it is to get stuff into the paper outside the template [...] I was the only political editor to go to the Blaenau Gwent by-election but I couldn't get it into the paper. I had to put it on the website [...] I sometimes say if the UK breaks up, the media broke up the UK before the political system did. (Michael White, Guardian)[1]

Consequently, the following features can be said to distinguish UK political journalism. Political news is highly commercial, competitive, and partisan in the newsprint sector. As in the US, market factors are very significant. Compared to other Western European nations, public trust in its content is extremely low. Broadcasting, on the other hand, is more in line with Northern Europe, being fairly strongly regulated, professional, balanced, and more trusted. UK politics, in terms of its majoritarian system and free-market bent, is closer to the US. It is a richer but less equal democracy with high levels of cynicism about political parties, politicians, the media, and state institutions. That said, many aspects of its culture and welfare state are closer to Europe (or were until the coalition government began dismantling at pace after 2010). Political journalism is very centralised and insular. Each of these elements of UK politics and media has influenced the ways in which UK political journalism has adapted to changing market conditions and new information and communication technologies over the past decade.

Transitions: the breakdown of the business model of UK news

A defining feature of UK print journalism in recent decades has been its struggle for profitability in an ultra-competitive environment. This has left it in a poor position to weather the current financial climate. Political reporting itself, like news journalism more generally, has suffered from the need to become more productive and market-oriented as consumption levels drop. Over the last quarter of a century, the following trends can be observed with some consistency: there is substantially more news space to fill and there are more producers, but also greater competition and fragmentation with fewer consumers per outlet (Curran and Seaton, 2003; Davies, 2008; Franklin, 1997, 2005; Tunstall, 1996). Global competition, market segmentation, and entertainment alternatives have meant a steady decline in audience figures and advertising revenues for most single news producers. In an effort to remain competitive and profitable, companies have raised prices well above inflation. They have also increased content output while simultaneously cutting back expenditure. Such market conditions have affected the publicly funded BBC as it has sought to justify its large news budget in the face of declining audiences. In December 2004, the then new director general of the BBC, Mark Thompson, announced cuts of 5,300 staff over three years. Again, in early 2005, 400 specific cuts were identified in the Corporation's news operations.

This has meant growing uncertainly and insecurity in the industry. In 2006, a year before the UK banking crisis began with the collapse of Northern Rock, 31 per cent of journalists were part-time or worked 'flexible hours' and 41 per cent were 'freelance' (NUJ, 2006; there is some overlap between these groups). It has also meant steadily increasing demands to produce more news copy in less time and with fewer journalists. In the UK, Tunstall (1996) estimated that, between the 1960s and 1990s, individual output had at least doubled. Franklin (2005) observed that modern news production had become almost factory-like in its practices, to the extent of becoming 'McDonaldised'. Davies (2008) concluded that journalists are now having to fill three times as much news space as they did in 1985, turning journalism into 'churnalism'. Such calculations may be over-estimates as it is difficult to work out how much the use of freelancers or new technologies has filled the gap. However, these and other accounts (e.g. Fenton, 2010; Lee-Wright et al., 2012) all agree with the general line of over-worked reporters producing more news under insecure working conditions. Such a message was frequently conveyed by journalists I have interviewed over the last 15 years. Several described personal experiences of job cuts and declining employment security, the hiring of cheaper junior replacements, an increase in output demands, and, above all, the relentless pace of the job:

> It has become more competitive and it's quicker. We are now in a 24 hours a day seven days a week news cycle. More instant analysis. The criticism is that it has become broader but shallower [...] Partly because of the speed we have to read things, there is far less time to follow up and assess the information. (George Jones, Daily Telegraph)

Long-term declines have been exacerbated significantly by two developments: the global recession and the advance of the internet. During economic downturns, advertising expenditure drops generally. The recession that began in 2008 potentially is as bad as or worse than the depression of the 1930s, with the UK, amongst others, unclear as to how to reverse several years of economic decline. At this point, the UK news industry is rather less healthy than it was then. In a time of high levels of UK government debt, the BBC too has been forced to further economise as part of the coalition government's austerity drive. In 2010, the BBC's licence fee was frozen for six years, amounting to a 16 per cent cut over the period. It was also forced to take on the funding of the BBC World Service. In 2012, another 800 staff cuts were announced across BBC news operations. Such staffing cuts were held to blame for recent, almost fatal reporting blunders by one of the BBC's flagship news programmes, *Newsnight*. The programme made some key editorial mistakes in its reporting of the Jimmy Savile scandal, which resulted in several senior resignations. As some pointed out, the programme had had to endure 15 per cent cuts in 2005, a further 20 per cent in 2010, with more announced in 2012 (Plunkett, 2012).

The internet's impact has been mixed (see the next section). However, there is no doubt that it has dealt a terrible blow to the long-term financial model which underpinned commercial UK news (see Freedman, 2010). This relied on a limited number of news producers and stable advertising. The internet has brought increased global competition as foreign news company outputs become easily and freely accessible. There has also been the flourishing of cheap, web-based news operations and news aggregators, such as Yahoo! and Google. Advertising has been moving from traditional news suppliers to online, predominantly non-news sites. At the same time, freely accessed online news is being funded out of traditional newsgathering resources. To date, the advertising generated in online news formats is a small fraction of that being lost to their offline versions. For example, the *Guardian*, which led the way in developing its online presence, had gained 60 million unique users by December 2011 but, at the same time, saw its pre-tax losses rise to £171 million for the year (Franklin, 2012: 668). In effect, according to Franklin (2012: 663) amongst others (see also Lee-Wright et al., 2012), UK journalism generally is reaching a state of financial crisis, with 'harshly competitive and fragmenting markets for audiences' and a 'collapse of the traditional business model'.

Such a crisis, in turn, has impacted on UK political reporting practices and content construction. For one, the nature of reporting is changing. It is likely that hard-pressed journalists have less in-depth understanding of political policy subjects and across fewer policy areas. With cuts to specialist news reporters, political lobby journalists have potentially to report on a greater range of policy areas. UK political reporting is likely to become even more Westminster-centric. With instant online publication and broadcasting there is also less time to develop stories or hold on to scoops. Thus, instead of covering unfolding events, the emphasis has moved to the politics behind the events, opinionated commentary, or second-guessing future developments:

> [T]he 24-hour news cycle means that we are all getting stories that we might have hoped to sit on, broken on television far, far earlier than they used to be [...] So newspapers have a pressure to go beyond the what's up for grabs for everybody and to tell the behind the scenes story [...] a big change for us in that the story is now often about what's going to happen tomorrow rather than what has happened during the day. (Philip Webster, The Times)

Second, it is likely that political journalism is, more than ever, becoming reliant on external source supply. Several past studies have observed that, as journalist resources become stretched, so dependency on source suppliers and 'information subsidies' rises (Fishman, 1980; Gandy, 1982; Sigal, 1973). UK news media generally have become more dependent on a variety of such subsidies in recent years. These include the use of news wire material, plagiarised copy already published by rivals, and unpaid pieces by public figures, experts, and 'citizen journalists'. Third, as many journalists admitted, political reporting has come to focus more on personalities, conflicts, and scandals, rather than policy or investigative journalism (see Davies, 2008; Davis, 2007; McLachlin and Golding, 2000). Such journalism not only requires less detailed investigation and knowledge, but is also considered more enticing to consumers:

> There's no doubt that the way politics is reported has changed. It's more obsessed with sensation and conflict [...] The tabloids haven't changed much but the broadsheets have. It's necessary to compete with the tabloids to make politics appear more vivid and exciting. The tendency began in the Sunday broadsheets and spilled over into the dailies – a general drive towards sensationalism. (Anonymous lobby journalist)

Such developments have propelled UK journalism towards a more urgent state of crisis. Leveson (2012: 7) comments, 'Competition (with its consequent pressures) has increased very dramatically [...] [and] contributed to a dramatic change to the cost base and economic model on which newspapers are based.' This all suggests that the future for political reporting, especially in print, is bleak. The choices appear to be eventual bankruptcy or a rather watered-down 'lite' version of what once existed.

This is likely to be less researched and policy-focused, more opinion-driven, sensationalist, and personality-obsessed, and more dependent on information subsidies.

Transitions: digital media and UK political journalism

Digital media undoubtedly have changed the way political news is sourced and constructed, both for good and for bad. On the positive side of the balance sheet, there is a new abundance of easily accessible information sources. When interviewing political journalists I asked how the internet had changed the way they did things (see Davis, 2010a: 105). The most common answers given related to its use as a research tool. The internet now enabled all journalists to spend rather less time in researching stories.

> I think the overwhelming importance of the internet is as the knee jerk and accessible information source. I mean you can access everything from government documents to chasing down a quote or whatever in a matter of seconds. Whereas before it would take you minutes if not hours. (Adam Boulton, Sky News)

Second, the emergence of high-profile political blogging, Twitter accounts, and chat-room sites in the UK, oriented around the major parties but not run by them, also seemed to be part of an important shift. Online sites were one increasingly useful means for getting and posting alternative information about party policy debates, wider party membership concerns, and the politics of parties themselves. Some, like Conservative Home or Labour List, were becoming recognised sources of detailed information, analysis, and debate. Others, such as Guido Fawkes, Left Foot Forward, or Political Betting, with strong political opinions and gossip, revealed anonymous insider accounts and more extreme views. Many politicians and journalists have followed suit to produce their own blogs. It was clear that MPs, journalists, and other Westminster insiders, both contributed to and took note of what came out of these many online sites:

> Blogs are the equivalent of going to the bar [...] 'Conservative Home' is terrific, I mean that really is a professional job, which you get quality information [...] on who's standing in constituencies for the selection processes. What used to be a really opaque process, has become

transparent, because of 'Conservative Home'. (Joe Murphy, Evening Standard)

Third, both reporters and bloggers argued that the internet had increased the available news space available to them when they wanted it. Established journalists, using online versions of offline outlets, could now file additional political reports, offer more background detail and opinion on those stories, and produce extra columns, in addition to running blogs. Thus they were free to cover more specialist topics, expand interviews and in-depth coverage, and pursue less newsworthy stories. In such ways, the internet has contributed to an expansion of politically significant information and interaction, offering something additional to what traditional institutions and news media provide.

However, at the same time, many journalists have noticed that the new digitalised news environment also brings distinct drawbacks. One of these relates to workload demands. Greater online research capacity brings greater expectations in production terms. There is a sense of information overload as the sheer volume of information sources to track and consult multiply. Most obviously, there is now the need for reporters to repackage news for multiple media platforms, including the internet, mobiles, and tablet computers:

> *[P]eople are under huge pressure, talk to anyone from the* Telegraph *[...] At the moment PMQs finishes, George Jones has got to go over and file stuff, and he may even have to do an iPod broadcast as well as something for the blog. And that's all time when you'd normally go straight downstairs and talk to MPs [...] and there he is stuck in front of his computer writing something that nobody's going to read. (Gary Gibbon, Channel 4 News)*

Second, as the pressures have mounted for greater productivity, so journalists have begun replacing conventional newsgathering routines with online news sourcing. Physical movement is time-consuming and general forays around Parliament, which do not have a direct story purpose, are risky. Several interviewees on both sides commented on how daily exchanges, a traditional means of newsgathering, were now much rarer. High-level meetings were still arranged, but the smaller, multiple, chance interactions were far less frequent. Instead, journalists pieced together politician-centred stories from quick mobile conversations and not always reliable websites:

I mean it's funny if you see a big story breaking on the telly, and you look at the presenter, let's say on a 24-hour news channel, yes you can see the presenters googling as they're broadcasting, because they're thinking you know 'shit Denis Healey, what did he do'. It gives you that thing, and that could be quite dangerous because the web is not a hundred per cent accurate [...] you could get something wrong from Wikipedia [...] a lot of the times people get things wrong, particularly on 24-hour news channels, it's because they're relying on the internet. (Daisy McAndrew, ITN News)

Equally significantly, the ease of accessing online news meant that news production was becoming increasingly cannibalistic in its activities. Political journalists often monitor each other and rival outputs as a means of keeping up with events and not losing out on a big story (Davis, 2007; Philips, 2010). When I asked journalists about how new media had changed their practices, the equal first most common answer I got was how it made monitoring other news outlets, as well as bloggers and tweeters, much easier (see similar findings in Allan, 2006; Reese et al., 2007). The picture emerging was one of increased journalist herd tendencies (see also Lee-Wright et al., 2012; Philips, 2010). Quotes, storylines, and whole story chunks are increasingly being cut and pasted with no concern for issues of copyright or plagiarism:

I had calls from Sky News, BBC News 24, Radio 5 Live, BBC Breakfast Show. Then, when I agreed [...] Before I got into the radio car I'd had BBC Radio Breakfast, BBC Radio Wales and BBC Radio Scotland all onto me [...] because through computers they can see the running order of various programmes and they hack into them and steal guests basically. And what happens is that one organisation will hear you on the radio and monitor it and think oh, that's good, we will have some of that [...] and what this is doing is it's generating more news for newspapers then because they pick up quotes. (Colin Brown, Independent)

Transitions: politician–journalist source relations in the UK

As explained earlier, UK national political reporting is very much centred on Parliament and government in London, and recent trends are only likely to have exacerbated this. Political journalism is almost entirely focused on parties, politicians, and Whitehall government departments around Westminster. Established lobby reporters may spend many years based in offices in Parliament, often being there longer than the average MP (see accounts in Barnett and Gaber, 2001; Tunstall, 1996). Such conditions mean that UK political journalists both report on politics and, at the same time, are very much part of the 'Westminster village' they report. This is by no means a phenomenon associated exclusively with the UK. However, it has been systematised and institutionalised far longer than in most comparative democracies. That, combined with the Westminster model of politics and the strong London bias of political news operations, adds to the insularity and incestuousness of politician–journalist relations.

My own interviews revealed MP–journalist levels of interaction to be extremely high. Just over two-thirds of MPs talked to journalists (local or national), on average at least once a day (at busy periods some, usually senior, politicians said they had between 10 and 20 conversations with journalists each day). The other one-third, with a couple of exceptions, talked to journalists once or several times a week. Politicians and reporters share the same spaces, restaurants, and bars around Westminster. They even play in organised sports matches together. Consequently, UK politician–reporter relations, regardless of their professional antagonisms, have evolved to become fairly institutionalised, socially integrated, and insular:

> *The great danger is that it becomes a small world of 2000 people. I was aware of it when I first came into Parliament. I realised a lot of bollocks was written, and written from the point of view of people in power. You get sucked into it because these are the people you mingle with and write for. [...] There's even a golfing mafia in Westminster. Journalists play with senior civil servants and advisors and other parliamentarians. (Kevin Maguire, Daily Mirror)*

Over time, and with such levels of personal interaction, politicians and journalists have become more attuned to each other. It is clear that the current generation of politicians are more likely to have had media training and/or previous occupational experience in journalism or public relations. Just over four-fifths of MPs I interviewed fell into this category. Indeed, when looking at the older and newer generations of the two front benches of the Conservative and Labour parties (Davis, 2010a), half of the younger generation had such experience. This includes the three main party leaders (David Cameron, Ed Miliband, and Nick Clegg). Consequently, many MPs appeared to have several journalist contacts as well as an extensive knowledge of specific publications, reporter routines, and news values. Conversely, political journalists had an extensive knowledge of how Westminster, the parties, and individual politicians operated:

> I've known them [Gordon Brown and Tony Blair] for 23 years [...] they know what to make of me, they know how to handle me, and also, vice versa [...] they know where I come from and all that. And over that period you learn about their strengths and weaknesses too. (Peter Riddell, The Times)

This closeness, in turn, has made politician–journalist relationships extremely intertwined and reflexive. The combination of journalist institutionalisation and positional longevity, as well as intense exchange and reflexivity, means that UK politicians and journalists have come to impact on each other's professions in a range of ways. On the one hand, there is clearly a 'tug of war' (Gans, 1979), with a general sense of suspicion and antagonism between the two professions often in evidence. On the other, the two sides make ample use of each other and do rather more than trade story information for media publicity. Politicians have used close journalist contacts to float stories, to influence political debate and government policy, and to undermine rivals, both in their own party and in the opposition.

They have also tried to gain advice on policy areas and presentation. Almost half the journalists asked said that (shadow) ministers had looked for policy advice from them. As also became clear in the interviews, politicians seek another significant type of 'expert' advice from journalists: knowledge of the micro-level politics of Westminster itself. In essence journalists spend much of their time collecting and exchanging information on 'the political', as opposed to policy, aspects of Parliament. Politicians then try to extract this during exchanges. A third of the political reporters spoke about MPs and ministers seeking information on some aspect of the political process itself. As such, they contributed to the rise and fall of political agendas, policies, individual politicians, and political factions within the parliamentary political sphere:

If X said 'how would it play in the media?' then I might well have an opinion on it in part because I'm probably trying to persuade them to give me the story [...] You know 'If we did this, how would it play?' and I'm saying, 'Well why don't you do it via me?'. (Nick Robinson, BBC political editor)

What this all suggests is that political reporting in the UK is far too insular. Political journalists spend all their time watching and interacting with politicians and other journalists. Consequently, they rarely look to outside sources to inform themselves of policy on the wider institutions, regions, and publics of the UK. Arguably, the combination of greater marketisation, increased media-orientation of politicians, and digitalisation has made UK political reporting even more insular and self-referential.

As already stated, greater marketisation has put more pressure on journalists to rely on external 'information subsidies' to fill space. A major source of such subsidies is public relations materials, supplied either directly by political sources or indirectly through wire services and news agencies. Lewis et al.'s study (2008) of 2,207 newsprint items and 402 broadcasts found that 19 per cent of UK press stories and 17 per cent of broadcasts were entirely or mainly reproduced PR material; 49 per cent of press stories were either entirely or mainly dependent on news wire agency copy, much of which itself had come from press releases. I have no hard data that demonstrates an increase in the use of such material in UK political journalism. However, all too often, political coverage now begins with a line such as 'Today the Prime Minister will say ...', or 'The Department will announce that ...'. The significant rise in public relations personnel and PR outputs is also notable. For example, in 1979 there were 27 'information officers' listed in the Home Office, 58 in the Ministry of Defence, and 6 in the Prime Minister's Office. By 2012, those figures had increased to 86 (Home Office), 237 (Defence) and 108 (now combined Cabinet and Prime Minister's Offices) (COI Directories, 1979, 2012).

Similarly, as also noted above, political reporters have been encouraged to stay close to their established parliamentary beats, if not their computers. Digital newsgathering has appeared to make the UK journalist beat even more Westminster-centric. As journalists and politicians described to me how they used the internet, it became clear that the web was more likely to increase their focus on, and communication with, others in the political centre. They increased exchanges with other parliamentarians substantially by using email.

They also were more likely to monitor each other's websites (see findings in Davis, 2010b). For both bloggers and blogging journalists there was a strong sense, based on experience of online responses, that their audience was primarily from a privileged, politically oriented demographic. Paul Staines's (Guido Fawkes) actual market data noted that his audience was from a very high social class with strong existing political connections (see similar results in Jensen, 2006). As he and other bloggers explained, they felt they were producing outputs for a relatively specialist group of political insiders:

> *Maybe during elections people read political blogs, but mostly it's activists and political junkies [...] I'm not aiming to write up a story that appeals to, you know, the same readers as the* Telegraph. *I mean, I'm more writing for political hacks and people obsessed with politics. Now I'm narrowcasting [...] about 3,000 hits a day on some of the politics blogs are from parliament.uk and gov.uk. (Paul Staines/Guido Fawkes, political blogger)*

Arguably, the same insular reporting networks and tendencies that existed prior to the current financial problems and digital age are likely to be intensifying now. Greater pressures for journalist productivity are increasing dependency on official and unofficial political source supplies. Digital media are linking those at the political centre as much as ever while, at the same time, distancing the mass of citizens at the periphery. As Leveson was recently led to comment (2012: 27): 'Taken as a whole, the evidence clearly demonstrates that [...] the political parties of the UK national Government and UK official Opposition have had or developed too close a relationship with the press in a way which has not been in the public interest.'

Consequences: pseudo news, News Corporation, and Leveson

Ultimately, these trends are not something political journalists draw public attention to. With a few exceptions, there is a reluctance to talk about the failings of UK political journalism, the insularity of its sourcing, the repercussions of the online revolution, or the breakdown of the traditional business model. Instead, there is a sense of public denial and/or an attempt to make sure the show goes on. News stories are still written and imparted with the same authoritative style as before; the same sense of an issue investigated, researched and sourced, and then 'expertly' presented. However, the production processes behind the presentation continue to change. The pseudo-expertise of the reporter is spread ever more thinly. The new ICTs have been utilised to paper over the ever-larger resource cracks that journalists struggle with, but offer quick, superficial knowledge rather than in-depth understanding. They have also encouraged slip-shod forms of newsgathering and plagiarism, thus further lowering the value of news content. The communicative ties between journalists themselves and between journalists and a limited number of Westminster political sources have become stronger and more internally facing. Following the fashionable story or the reporter herd, cutting and pasting parts of a rival's copy, and guessing the future are all too easy to do, as well as being more cost-efficient. So too is focusing on personalities and conflicts rather than policy matters and competence.

In many ways the scandal surrounding phone-hacking at News Corporation's *News of the World* newspaper in the UK and the Leveson Inquiry that followed illustrate many of the points made. News Corporation is a major international media conglomerate, primarily controlled by Rupert Murdoch, with extensive interests in news and entertainment in many countries. Murdoch's stable of newspapers (*Sun, News of the World (NotW), The Times*, and *Sunday Times*), has in recent decades been one of the more profitable in the UK, bucking the downward industry trend (see Currah, 2009). News Corporation also has a 39 per cent stake in BSkyB broadcasting, which has proved very profitable to the company. However, in mid-2011, after five years of rumours, secret court settlements, and stalled police investigations, it became clear that the *NotW*, had run an industrial-scale phone-hacking operation. To date, over 4,000 potential victims have been recorded, including a range of celebrities, politicians, and high-profile victims of crime. The scandal led to several senior resignations at News Corporation and the Metropolitan Police, as well as police investigations into phone-hacking and media bribery of public officials. At the end of October 2012, 90 people had been arrested and trials followed. Arrests included Rebekah Brooks and Andy Coulson, two former editors at News Corporation titles and both closely connected to David Cameron. It also led to the Leveson Inquiry, which in its report called for far stronger press regulation supported by statute and, among other things, greater transparency about media–politician relations (Leveson, 2012).

One way of analysing what happened at the *NotW* is through a closer look at its particular business model, its use of new media, and its over-close relations with its sources. Profitability was built on finding more cost-effective ways of producing populist celebrity and personality-focused news. Some of these were legitimate; others were less so. Among the latter, systematic phone-hacking of public figures and paying officials for information were far cheaper ways of finding regular news scoops than traditional, time-consuming, and costly forms of investigative newsgathering. Another aspect of this case was the extensive and close relations that had built up between journalists and media owners, particularly at News Corporation, on the one hand, and politicians and other public figures on the other. As leader of the opposition from 2005 to 2010, David Cameron had 1,404 meetings with journalists (*Daily Telegraph*, 14 July 2012). *NotW*'s editor, Andy Coulson, became the Conservative Party's head of communication, while Neil Wallis, a *NotW* deputy editor, became a PR consultant for the Metropolitan Police. During the Leveson Inquiry, it was revealed that Aidan Barclay, chairman of the Telegraph newspaper group, admitted that he had suggested to Cameron that he talk to the *Daily Telegraph* every day during the 2010 election (Watt et al., 2012). In the 15 months following the 2010 general election, Cameron had 76 meetings with news executives and editors, a third of which were with News Corporation. In the same period Ed Miliband had 48 meetings, 15 of which were with News Corporation (BBC, 25 July 2011). The more public focus of the Leveson Inquiry was on morality and regulation. However, such issues, while important, have distracted from the more fundamental story about the state of UK political journalism, its broken business model, levels of ownership concentration, and the questionable daily practices that keep it going.

Conclusion

In truth, UK political journalism, as in many countries, has never been as autonomous as it would like. The 'golden age' of British political reporting was never that golden. Reporters have rarely had the necessary resources of time, money, and knowledge that are required to fulfil all professional expectations. The presentation of professional autonomy and investigative priorities is, in part, a promotional confidence trick of the industry itself. It is a fairly small part of what constitutes 'the news'. However, in the case of the UK, the autonomy that did exist has been steadily eroded by market forces, digitalisation, and ever-closer relations with the political and institutional establishment in recent years. Such problems have intensified considerably in the past decade. Consequently, news is being reshaped in order to cut costs and supply multi-media platforms that usually do not pay. Pseudo-news and personality conflicts are replacing investigative news and informed analysis of policy. There is a growing dependency on information subsidies from sources, the internet, and rival publications. What is produced is increasingly watered-down, under-researched and under-checked, cannibalistic, rehashed, and highly dependent on PR materials. To the public it is presented in the same way, but what is left is a pale imitation of what it was (Lee-Wright et al., 2012). Critics have labelled the new end product 'newszak' (Franklin, 1997) and, most recently, 'churnalism' (Davies, 2008). Rather like a fake Rolex watch, it is not all it seems. In the difficult political and economic years that lie ahead, when journalism will need to be working well, such trends are of great concern.

Note

1   All journalists cited here were, at the time of the interview, senior political journalists and editors at the outlet stated.

Part II

Cross-National Themes

7

Reporting the European Union:
A Study in Journalistic Boredom

Olivier Baisnée

> I liked it [being an EU correspondent] a lot from the start. Because, if I turn to my past a little bit, why wasn't I interested in politics anymore, in political journalism as it is done in France or elsewhere, it's because [...] it's all about little political stories, it's about politicians' monkey business, things like that; but it's not about the background [of policies] [...] That's what I was upset with. Thus, here [in Brussels] I really discovered Nirvana: politics, but also some background, and I found it fascinating and, consequently, I've never wanted to leave. (French journalist, specialised media and regional press)

> To describe the developments of processes inside the EU is like describing paint drying. (Norwegian correspondent, AIM, 2007a: 113)

Introduction

This chapter aims to critically examine political journalism on the basis of a very particular case study: European Union (EU) news. As the two quotes above clearly show, EU news produces somewhat opposite reactions from journalists. The first journalist (who was a political journalist in France) discovered in Brussels a political system that initiated public policies, but was not surrounded by the usual political games. The second journalist emphasises one of the main obstacles to the newsworthiness of EU current affairs: the lengthy time-frame of the decision-making processes. While the first journalist appears enthusiastic about the fact that the EU stands apart from the usual political journalism, the second underlines how its functioning is problematic for journalists' professional standards. This contested nature of EU news and EU correspondence is challenging for journalists and their news organisations. Yet for the researcher it appears more as an opportunity.

On political journalism and EU news

Ten years ago I published a chapter entitled 'Can political journalism exist at the EU level?' (Baisnée, 2002). This current chapter is an opportunity to think again about the relationship between EU news and political journalism. Let us be clear from the outset: the question mark regarding political journalism at the EU level is still relevant. As I explained at the time, there were attempts by correspondents in the late 1990s and at the beginning of the 2000s to promote a professional model that was distinct from and an alternative to the traditional expert journalism that had been dominant until then. This new professional model was more critical towards the EU. These journalists were more interested in investigative journalism than their elders, whom they depicted as 'EU cheerleaders'. This new model of EU correspondence was closer to what we (and journalists) understand as political journalism. Did they succeed? In a way they did, as (at least in the French case) they are now dominant and the journalists representing the previous model of excellence in Brussels are now retired.

Yet EU news coverage did not become political journalism in the conventional sense. EU correspondence even faced a crisis, as in 2010 (for the first time in the history of the press corps in Brussels) the number of EU correspondents dropped – and dropped dramatically – from 1,300 in 2005 to 847 in 2010 (Raeymaeckers et al., 2007). As the *New York Times* summed it up in an article: 'As the EU does more, fewer tell about it' (Castle, 2010). If things have improved since then (probably thanks to the eurozone crisis), this situation is revealing of the uncertain nature of the EU when it comes to journalism. Put in a nutshell, the EU is still boring (for journalists) and as I will try to explain it is probably becoming even more boring. Indeed, the gap between what EU news has to offer and what political journalism has become in the last 15–20 years is now huge and the chances of bridging this gap are slim. These diverging trajectories offer an interesting field of investigation for media sociology. Indeed, if journalistic interests (usually called newsworthiness) are a legitimate field for sociological investigations (and a lot has been done in this respect), journalistic lack of interest is also an interesting point of departure. In a way, studying what journalists find boring tells us a lot about what they are interested in, since interest is a highly relational notion that needs to be unpacked (Davis, 1971).[1]

Indeed EU current affairs offer the potential to study the taken-for-granted basis of political journalism (understood as a specific specialised journalism). Is it political journalism because it deals with political actors? Because these specialised journalists cover a political system? Or is it political journalism because it is covered by political journalists writing for the politics section of their media outlet? To put it another way: is political journalism so labelled because it is defined as such by the actors covered or because editorial routines assign a current event to a specific section governed by specific interests (definitions of newsworthiness) and specific discourse registers? Put bluntly, political journalism refers to a specific framing of a specific social activity: politics. As the economic crisis developed (provoking a growing dissent in member states such as Greece and Spain) the political nature of the EU and of its decisions became more obvious. Yet, in journalistic routines and habits, EU coverage still does not belong to what is usually regarded as political journalism. This has consequences for the way these journalists see themselves, for the sections their reports will appear in, and for the actors and discourses they pay attention to.

When it comes to journalism, frames are 'principles of selection, emphasis, and presentation composed of little tacit theories about what exists, what happens, and what matters' or 'persistent patterns of cognition, interpretation, and presentation, of selection, emphasis, and exclusion, by which symbol-handlers organise discourse whether verbal or visual' (Gitlin, 1980: 6–7). Because journalism is based on unquestioned evidence, political journalists never wonder about whether what they are doing is political journalism. In this respect the EU, because of the unsure or hybrid nature of its political system, tends to challenge some of the basic (yet silent) assumptions political journalism is based on. It is a political system, populated by political actors who take political decisions (even if these are often presented as grounded in rationality alone). Yet EU correspondence differs greatly from political journalism in terms of outcomes.

In order to decipher this hiatus between the EU political system on the one hand and the media coverage it receives on the other, it is first necessary to confront EU correspondence with existing definitions of political journalism. Based on an extensive review of international literature on the subject, Erik Neveu (2002) emphasises three characteristics of political journalism in Western countries. First, it is a 'noble' journalism, since political journalists rub shoulders with supposedly powerful actors and cover an activity that is supposed to be able to change the destiny of societies. One indicator of this nobility can be found in the success of books written by political journalists that aim to give the readers access to the functioning of power. Another indicator, more internal to the profession, is the often fierce competition for political journalism positions within news media organisations. Second, it is an 'esoteric' journalism, since political journalists understand what most people do not. The professionalisation of politics has led to a growing feeling of incompetence but also of indifference among citizens. In this context, political journalists have access to a reality that most people do not understand and/or are not interested in. Third, political journalists differ from other journalists because of the proximity they enjoy with politicians. This proximity with power-holders both gratifies political journalists and leads them to share politicians' views and conceptions of politics. To these three common characteristics of political journalism Nicolas Kaciaf (2013: 19) adds a fourth: political journalists deal with discourses. This aspect is common to most journalists, but political discourses are also political acts in themselves and in this respect political discourses differ from other discourses.[2]

The contested nature of EU (news)

Does EU journalism meet these four criteria? One might certainly agree with the proposition that EU news (and, more generally, the functioning of the EU) is esoteric. Indeed, it is probably even more esoteric than national political news and processes. The proximity of EU correspondents and EU officials has been well documented (Baisnée, 2003; Cornia, 2010). In these respects, EU journalism much resembles political journalism. Yet by the other two criteria of political journalism ('nobility' and the inherently political nature of discourses) it diverges. EU journalism does not count among the noble positions of the journalistic profession.

One sign in this respect is the extremely low level of competition to be an EU correspondent, especially when compared with other foreign correspondence positions. In addition, the discourses EU journalists deal with are not political acts by nature. More specifically, most discourses they will have to deal with do not come from political actors (at least they do not see themselves as such) and are not intended to produce political reactions or to be political at all. Moreover, another element to be taken into account is the growing disconnection between what EU news is and the actual standards of political journalism characterised by personalisation, spectacular soundbites, and short time-frames. EU news does not encompass any of these apart from on exceptional occasions or in crisis periods.[3]

The EU and politics in general: some specificities

The point here is not to propose a piece on political theory that presents the general architecture and political mechanisms of the EU. It can be assumed (and all journalists/editors do so) that the EU is political by nature. The question when it comes to journalism is whether or not it involves politics. The ambiguous relationship that the EU and EU actors entertain with politics dates back to the origins of the European project (Cohen, 2012). In the 1920s and 1930s some intellectuals (mainly law professors and law practitioners) started to think and promote an alternative political model to parliamentary democracy. In this model, decisions should be based on expertise and rationality and not political agreement and support. At the core of the imagined political system were expert civil servants rather than parliamentarians. In the context of the crisis that European parliamentary regimes were undergoing during the 1930s, they promoted an efficiency legitimacy against the traditional political legitimacy (which 'obviously' was unable really to solve problems). This political system that they imagined materialised in the European Union.

When considering the EU, researchers (but also journalists) see a political system, a polity (all the political actors surrounding and involved in decision-making processes), and policies, but no political journalism as such (or only for very limited or microcosmic media – see below). The result of this ambiguous relationship to politics is that journalists in Brussels face actors who do not consider themselves as politicians, even though they are conducting politics. Since journalists cannot decide what or who is political and what or who is not (beginning with what a source accepts to say, the types of arguments they use, and so on) they face an intense political activity (including political actors, civil servants, and diplomats, but also interest groups and NGOs) that they cannot depict using the usual routines of political journalism. Some reasons for this situation are that, first, the traditional distinctions between politicians, civil servants, diplomats, activists, and experts are blurred at the EU level; second, there is nothing resembling a majority and an opposition (there are only short-lived coalitions on specific topics or issues); and, third, there are no actors with a political programme (except in a very limited manner regarding the rotating presidency of the Council of the EU) that would clearly explain what goals are to be achieved within a mandate and by what means (which in turn allows for judgements in terms of success or failure).

EU correspondence: the platypus of journalism

EU news is a specialised news beat, involving around 1,000 correspondents mostly from EU member states who practise a journalism that lies somewhere between foreign correspondence, economic journalism, and political journalism. At the same time, it does not easily fit into any of these traditional journalistic specialisations: it is the platypus of journalism.

At first sight, as these journalists are posted abroad, are usually institutionally attached to the foreign desk, and, for an important proportion of them, have had an internationally oriented career, it seems logical to assign them to the 'foreign correspondents' category. Yet both the peculiarities of the EU and their practices make this kind of categorisation nugatory. Their intermediary situation (neither really at the national nor at the international level) allows one to question this traditional (both historically and institutionally constructed) category of journalism that is called 'foreign correspondence'. A first differentiating indicator is that the significant proportion of EU correspondents who have experienced other postings abroad acknowledge that they are confronted in Brussels with a news beat that challenges their professional routines and constitutes a real 'calling into question'.

> First the level of information is a difficulty for someone who is not used to it. So, at first, it makes sense to take time, six months maybe, to get

to know Brussels. Because it's incredibly complicated how it works, the committee system for example, and to understand who actually decides what and who isn't important. [...] But it's the same as when I learned Russian. First, the alphabet is different, but after six months you get used to it and it's ok. [...] The press room, it's like your first day at school, you got to get to know people. You come in and they have a certain system, a certain way of doing things and [...] I think it's pretty difficult for someone coming from the outside. (British journalist, national daily newspaper)

If the Brussels posting challenges the habits of individual journalists, it is also problematic for newsrooms as they encounter major difficulties in assigning EU news to a section. If most articles end up in the international or foreign pages of most newspapers, one should not forget that this is simply a practical solution to problems that centre on the whole newsroom's organisation.[4] If the Brussels posting calls into question the traditional category of 'foreign correspondent' it is, above all, because EU news in itself renders obsolete the historically constituted division of current affairs. In contrast to their colleagues posted in foreign capital cities, EU correspondents do not cover a given territory but rather institutions which themselves face huge difficulties in referring to a specific geographic space (Smith, 1997, 2004). The European territory, institutionalised by successive enlargements, does not exist as such in journalism's division of labour. The difficulty that most media experience when it comes to covering Europe in general and the EU in particular is symptomatic of the impossibility of squeezing this object into the pre-constructed categories of journalism. Combining the political, diplomatic, economic, institutional, national, and supranational, EU news barely fits the logics of journalistic specialisation that assigns news to specific sections.

A (golden) niche journalism

If it is difficult to define EU journalism in terms of practices, discourses, sections, and place in the newsroom or in the newspaper, it is easier to define it in terms of audience. While it is clearly a niche journalism that is targeted at a very limited audience, it is a golden niche. If the EU is not interesting for journalists, then in contrast those who are interested in EU news are really interesting for the media, at least for some media.

For example, the readers of *European Voice* (the Economist Group) belong to an international elite. The newspaper has a very limited circulation (19,000 readers, 150,000 viewers on the internet) with a very specific profile. The readership of *European Voice* is not composed of the average layperson, as audience studies of the weekly show when describing the profile of its readers (as of 2000) as wealthy, bright, international, and potentially powerful: 30 per cent of them earn between €50,000, and €150,000 per year, 40 per cent between €20,000 and €50,000, and only 10 per cent earn less than €20,000; 43 per cent have published a book or an article; 64 per cent have participated in a conference or have given a speech; 39 per cent have given an interview; and 42 per cent have been consulted by their governments.[5] Readers of *European Voice* spend €30,000 on their first car and have travelled abroad more than 12 times in the past year. What is interesting about *European Voice* is that it is probably the media outlet that conforms most closely to the common understanding of political journalism, but in this case applied to the EU: personality portraits, interviews, undercover information, gossip, and rumours. How can a weekly survive with such a low circulation? Thanks to its audience. One might note that, among the sample in Table 7.1, *European Voice* is the print media outlet that charges the highest advertising rate per reader. This example is of course very limited, but as a case study of editorial and

Table 7.1   Circulation and advertising costs of selected print outlets

	Circulation	Full page of advertising (in euros)	Euros/reader
Le Monde	366,356	146,000	0.39
Libération	160,799	54,500	0.34
Voici (celebrity press)	521,684	15,900	0.03
Daily Telegraph	545,283	54,000	0.09
Financial Times	273,047	115,701	0.42
European Voice	19,000	9,950	0.52

The information presented in Table 7.1 was accessed in April 2013.
Sources for circulation figures: www.ojd.com for France; www.abc.org.uk for the UK. Advertising rates figures were retrieved from www.tarifspresse.com for France and relevant individual newspapers' websites for the UK. Circulation figures and advertising rates for *European Voice* were obtained from the weekly's website: www.europeanvoice.com.

commercial strategies in this field, it sheds some light on the more general incentives to cover (or not) EU news on a regular basis.

In a sense, EU news might challenge journalistic routines and categories, but it remains a potentially relevant area of coverage given the sociological profile of the audience who are interested in it. That explains why the most mass market-oriented media tend to be absent from Brussels (for example, tabloids and mid-market newspapers in the UK; television;[6] and the regional press in France) while media that attract an audience with a high social profile are prepared to invest in EU coverage. The probability of a media outlet having one (or more) EU correspondents is strongly linked to its readership or audience profile. As we will see below, while the need to cover EU current affairs is not questioned in elite media, the situation is often more complicated for correspondents from other types of media. In turn, this has consequences for the work of these journalists and for their relationship with their newsrooms.

The ubiquitous position of EU correspondents[7]

Given the problematic nature of their position, it is now necessary to focus on these EU correspondents with the aim of trying to understand their employment situation and in particular the fact that they work for media outlets in national journalistic fields (Benson, 1999; Benson and Neveu, 2005).[8] The situation of EU correspondents is specific in the sense that they are posted to a place which is a point of contact (that they, in a way, embody) for different national media systems and journalistic cultures. This contact point is governed by principles that differ from their national equivalents and, as such, correspond (or not) with the needs and practices to which the journalists are accustomed. In this respect EU correspondents are at the heart of a tension between where they are ('here', in Brussels) and the media organisation that they work for which operates in a national context ('there'). Since these national contexts differ from each other, EU correspondents, while covering a common current affairs agenda, have to deal with different expectations from their editorial offices. Resolving the conflict between what is happening 'here' and what is wanted 'there' is a central aspect of the job of EU correspondents and, thus, also of the logic of EU news production.

To echo the title of one of David Lodge's best-selling novels, the Brussels of EU correspondents represents a 'small world', a microcosm

139

with its own rules, rhythms, 'places to be', and 'ways of doing things'. It is a world quite closed in upon itself and out of touch with ordinary people – a self-sustaining working environment. The press corps has a history that has produced specific arrangements and a peculiar hierarchy of sources, but also a tone and a way of covering the EU which no individual journalist can fundamentally alter. In theoretical terms this local arrangement can be considered as a social institution that provides journalists with specific sets of rules and norms deeply embedded in daily practices. These provide individuals with expected social behaviours or what Berger and Luckmann (1989) call social roles (see also Blumler and Gurevitch, 1995; Lagroye, 1997). They offer a set of norms, rules, and beliefs that the newly arrived correspondent will have to deal with. The latter's individual characteristics and journalistic position (with respect to the media they belong to) might or might not fit with the role as it is locally institutionalised. This might engender moral, professional, or even ethical dilemmas.

At a more general level this fit/misfit dimension influences the nature of the coverage for different media outputs. Due to the national context regarding the EU and to the structure of each national media field, what correspondents report about a common set of events and processes will differ greatly from one country to another and, within the same national context, from one media outlet to another. This is a situation that EU civil servants experience every morning when they open the press reviews prepared by the official communication services. While all correspondents cover the same events, go to the same news places, and attend (more or less) the same press conferences, the journalistic outcomes are significantly different.

If one analyses, as the AIM consortium did (AIM, 2007b), the coverage of EU-related topics over a particular time period, the journalistic image of the EU varies in terms of both general attention devoted to these topics and what is given editorial space. Over a selected three-week period, for instance, the British media chosen for analysis devoted 74 news items to the EU, compared with 478 in the case of the French media, 419 for the German, and 219 for the Norwegian (and Norway is not even an EU member state). When it comes to what was reported, significant differences are also evident (see Table 7.2).[9]

These differences in the coverage of a common set of events and processes have been extensively documented. For example, in their study of four national newspapers (of Austria, France, Germany, and the UK), Brüggemann and Kleinen-von Königslöw (2009) distinguish four patterns

Table 7.2 Multiple response cross-tabulation between recorded themes of news items and participating countries (%)

	Internal affairs	External affairs	Economics and finance	Social affairs	Human-itarian	Culture and communi-cations
Belgium	17	11.9	50	**8.5**	6.3	6.3
Estonia	15.5	**31**	38.4	5.6	*2.6*	6.9
Finland	25.2	13	54.8	2.2	3	1.7
France	**53.3**	9.2	32.1	1.9	2.6	*0.9*
Germany	15.8	20.5	50.3	4.5	3	5.7
Great Britain	22.1	8.1	54.7	1.2	**11.6**	2.3
Ireland	14.9	15.6	51.7	5.9	5	6.9
Italy	*10.7*	*5.3*	**79.1**	*0.5*	2.9	1.5
Lithuania	13.6	23.1	43.6	5.8	4.7	**9.2**
Norway	27.4	30.6	*31.9*	2.9	3.6	3.6

Based on a content analysis over three consecutive weeks (7–28 March 2005) of one national newspaper, one regional newspaper, one popular title, and the main news programme of public and commercial television in each country.

Source: Raeymaeckers and Golding (2007). The highest score in each category is in bold, the lowest in italics.

of Europeanisation in coverage that related to four different editorial strategies institutionalised in procedures and allocation of resources. The attitude of *The Times*, for instance, is characterised as a 'relatively parochial public sphere': no editorial space devoted to the EU and a single 'super-stringer' in Brussels. *Le Monde* is described as representing a 'segmented Europeanisation' with a lot of attention devoted to EU institutions (the specific EU page is now defunct) and a lot of resources devoted to this news beat with four full-time correspondents (currently two).

The second aspect that has to be addressed relates to the constraints associated with the EU correspondent's particular media outlet. The latter might have specific needs and expectations that do not fit with the journalist's working environment (some areas, institutions, and individuals might be out of reach) and/or the 'reality' of the EU information the correspondents have discovered (which might differ significantly from what editors-in-chief and desk editors think is happening). In some cases this might provoke a deep moral dilemma for the correspondent. They might decide to give up on their own judgements and beliefs so as to adapt their production to what is expected 'back home'. On other occasions they might resist pressures and so be accused of misbehaving or exhibiting an unfriendly and selfish attitude. They might even be accused of not being a 'good professional' when the articles and news reports they send differ greatly from what was expected. Newsroom expectations might heavily rely on misperceptions or biased understandings, based on readings (of what peers and competitors are producing about the area) and contacts with national sources (such as diplomats, for example). This might result in EU correspondents being asked to report about aspects that appear to them to be of minor importance, odd, or even false.

EU news between Brussels and the nation state

Individual situations of EU correspondents are in this sense a projection of a wider phenomenon. Difficulties encountered are a reflection of different dominant national frameworks across the EU. These dominant frameworks greatly differ from one country to another and, within the same country, from one media outlet to another.

First, the importance of the EU in the media organisation correlates with the tradition of national EU policies and the relative power position of a given country within the EU. If the EU is deeply embedded in domestic politics, the way of considering the news coming from Brussels will differ significantly from that in a country where the EU has no (or almost no) political importance. In the first situation, news about the EU will make sense for national newsrooms only if it has some political implication for domestic politics. In terms of organisation this will mean a stronger link between the correspondent and the politics desk. In the second situation, the EU will remain out of the range of political topics. It will not make sense to frame EU news in political terms. Obviously, these processes are beyond the control of most of the actors (journalists or spokespersons) since they depend on developments taking place in the national political field. Yet this does not mean that no evolution is possible. It simply implies that attention needs to be paid to the political dynamics regarding the EU at the national level. The central element to be taken into account in understanding dominant national frameworks is the political configuration regarding the EU. Is it a political issue at all within the national political field and, if so, what kind of political issue is it? For instance, the fact that the UK holds significant power within the EU but does not ascribe high relevance to European politics is reflected in news policies as well.[10] Conversely, other older member states (such as Belgium, France, and Germany) tend to invest most in EU news; French and German journalists in particular assume that the status of EU news will be strengthened in the future. Italy represents a special case in this respect. In Italian news organisations, EU topics are intimately connected to national politics. Insofar as national politics are deemed central for news, this holds true for EU politics as well.

Second, we may elaborate our understanding about news flows by making distinctions between different types of media outlets, notably their degree of specialisation on the one hand and their relationship with the target audience (the general public or a specialised audience) on the other. A well-known distinction in this respect is drawn between popular and elite news media. What is noteworthy is that the news policies of elite and popular media represent two distinct ways of conceiving the newsworthiness of the EU. In the elite media there is no controversy about the importance of creating a functional surveillance system of the EU and national EU politics. In this sense, elite newspapers and public service broadcasters constitute a particular media structure for a European level of political communication. Outside this structure, attention to EU topics is more selective and sporadic; and in the popular press the newsworthiness of the EU is often seen through the lenses of particular local stereotypes and dramatic, personified news values.

Third, the ways in which newsrooms go about reporting on EU topics tend to reflect two different strategies for the selection of news. In one, the EU is treated as just another news beat that deserves no special organisation or news policy. In contrast, there is another professional attitude that suggests that the EU is a special case that needs to be addressed by specific means. According to a more contextual understanding of journalism, EU news is either given a special status due to its presumed importance or degraded due to a news policy adopted by a given news organisation. An obvious token of special attention paid to the EU is the assignment of correspondents to Brussels.

Depending on what they represent (in terms of media, country, etc.) and in what context they have to work, reciprocal influences of the personal status and of the local working environment might vary considerably. For EU correspondents, a way to solve the above-mentioned dilemma between being 'here' (in Brussels) and 'there' (member of a media organisation) is in fact to switch between one aspect of the role and the other. When among peers, they will endorse the 'expert' role by letting others know that they understand what it is all about. When negotiating their articles with the newsroom they switch to the 'good professional' role, where the correspondent shows an understanding of the logics of the media organisation they belong to and also knows what EU news represents in their home country. In this respect, being an efficient EU correspondent requires a certain degree of split personality.

EU news and political journalism in the French context

Political journalism has evolved in the opposite direction to what the EU has to offer in terms of information. It is now more about politicians than about policies or even politics (in terms of ideological debate). A Republican member of the US Congress quoted by Michael Schudson explained: 'The press thinks it can only report events. Congress is not an event, it is a process. Either the press doesn't understand that, or it assumes the public doesn't understand it'. And Schudson elaborates: 'Political reporters tend to be politics wonks rather than policy wonks, absorbed by "inside baseball" analysis rather than fascinated by the question of how the government should run the country' (Schudson, 2003: 48–52). The congressman's quote perfectly describes the situation of the EU. In contrast, what Schudson underlines about political journalists does *not* apply to EU correspondents: they are policy, not politics, wonks. More generally, the EU remains foreign (even remote), institutional (bureaucratic, technocratic), incredibly dry in terms of information provided, and (desperately) slow.[11]

To understand the logics of news production about the EU it is now necessary to turn to the evolution of political journalism. As it would be extremely difficult to give an account of universal trends in political journalism, I will contextualise what has been said about EU news with reference to developments in political journalism in France.[12] French political journalism has changed dramatically in the past 15–20 years (Kaciaf, 2013). The dominant actors within the field are now television channels, and television journalism is imposing its news values and news formats. This has had an impact on all political journalists, who have adapted to the way television covers politics: short news, entertaining news, exclusive news, and events-driven news. This new way of covering politics has been implemented (and largely promoted) by a new generation of journalists who are quite distinctive from their elders in terms of educational and political backgrounds. The current generation of political journalists are more professional (they have been trained as journalists in journalism schools), less 'political' (in terms of background and trajectories), and less interested in politics in general (they do not intend to spend their whole career as political journalists).

More and more, journalistic coverage of politics in France resembles a telenovela. A season lasts for five years (the length of a presidential term) and the casting is partly renewed at the end of it. Coverage of politics also tends to revolve around the individual political actors. What is now central in journalists' understanding of politics is the psychology of the characters: their biography, their childhood, and their background are supposed to explain what they are as political actors. The consequence of this new way of covering politics has been the loss of the centrality of what used to be regarded as key arenas of politics: parliament and political parties. The central scene of politics is now televison and the performances of political actors when appearing on it. To this development in political journalism one has to add the transformation of the coverage of foreign affairs (since most correspondents depend on their foreign desk). In foreign news too there has been a decline in the coverage of institutional and political events (Marchetti, 2005). All of this makes the current situation of EU news and Brussels correspondents extremely difficult. What they have to offer would have been perfectly acceptable 40 or 50 years ago, but it is now completely out of kilter with what is considered as valuable (political) news today. EU news is about institutions, not individuals; EU news is about processes, not events. All of these elements tend to relegate what is happening in the EU outside the scope of political journalism.

Conclusion: an Orléanist European public sphere?

Paul Magnette, a Belgian political scientist, summed up the situation by saying that the EU has an Orléanist public sphere (Magnette, 2000). This is a reference to the French political situation after 1814 when Napoleon left power: a monarchy was restored with some elements of a parliamentary regime. There were elections, but the vote was reserved for the wealthiest in society. Politics during this period was confined to an elite.

145

In the EU politics is not the privilege of a minority (after all there are European parliamentary elections) and a lot of information is available about what the EU is doing. Yet when it comes to being involved in EU debates (the EU public sphere) where media and news play a role, then the exclusion of the vast majority of EU citizens is obvious. The question then is whether citizens have an appetite for news about the EU. In professional discourses, especially among editors-in-chief, the answer is clear and unequivocal: absolutely not. Two elements then need to be addressed. First, the idea that journalists have to provide information about things that interest their audience is questionable in terms of both professional standards (what journalism is about) and, above all, actual practices. After all, television news programmes and newspapers give a lot of time and space to information that is doomed to be irrelevant for a large part (sometimes even a majority) of their audiences. Two examples in this context are football results and stock exchange indices. These forms of specialised news, while excluding a priori a vast proportion of the audience, are reported on a daily basis, yet the question of their interest for the public is never raised. Thus the issue of newsworthiness and of 'what interests the audience' remains both tricky and, what is more interesting for the sociologist, unquestioned.

Second, is news about the EU so clearly of no interest to the public? The issue here is not to fuel a long-lasting and more political than scientific debate about the so-called 'EU communication deficit'. Thinking in these terms implies that if communication were better achieved then all political problems would be solved. This is surely debatable. Rather, the question is whether citizens are indeed less interested in these issues than, for example, in news about their domestic politics. The gap between what journalists find interesting and what the audience finds interesting is in fact often considerable. For example, every year an opinion poll company publishes a survey about the confidence of French people in the media. One of the questions posed concerns those issues that respondents thought that the media had over- or under-reported. In 2006, the year following the referendum vote on the European constitution, the results were of particular interest for our purpose. After a period where Europe had probably never been so debated and reported in the French media, only 28 per cent of respondents considered that the media had over-reported the issue, with just as many (27 per cent) saying that the topic had been under-reported and 39 per cent considering that it had been fairly reported. In contrast, the two topics that the respondents ranked as being the most over-reported in 2005 were, first, the relationship problems of the Sarkozy couple and, second, the return of retired players to the national football team. In short, the confrontation between the interests and disinterests of journalists on the one hand and of those of the audience on the other leads one to wonder about the origins of the exclusion of citizens from European debates. The journalistic 'theory' is one based on self-exclusion – people are not interested in these issues. The EU institutions 'theory' is one based on exclusion – the media do not adequately report about EU news. Obviously neither of these theories is wholly satisfactory. If the sociology of journalism has brought anything to our understanding of the social world, it is that what is central to the work of journalists is the set of 'little tacit theories' about what is interesting and what is not (as mentioned at the beginning of this chapter). The current conventional wisdom about EU news is to see it as irrelevant to the general public. As previously mentioned, the development of political journalism at the national level (at least in France but probably in other countries too) tends to take EU news away from mediation in the public sphere. The point here is not to wonder whether the public wants more news about the EU. It is rather to underline that when it receives more, as was the case in France in 2005, the public does not complain.

The eurozone crisis of the past few years has been the subject of intense media coverage that might appear to contradict the above developments. Yet, this very peculiar period is not just an exception to the rule or an indication that things will never be the same again. In a way it confirms the rule. Indeed, the whole crisis offers characteristics that are usually absent from EU news: the main national political actors were involved in face-to-face meetings, conflicts escalated, dramatic tension was heightened, and the tempo of decision-making processes accelerated. All these elements enhanced the newsworthiness of EU decisions.[13] The crisis also brought out in a particularly crude manner the political nature of the decisions that had been made in Brussels or Frankfurt over the previous two decades (for instance, on bank and stock exchange regulation, interest rates policy, and budgetary rules). Yet at the time these decisions were made (or not made) most of them were considered too 'technical' to be reported by most newsrooms. In short, this intense period of journalistic interest should not overshadow the decades of journalistic boredom that preceded it.

Notes

1   Sobieraj (2010: 514) rightly points out, when emphasising the need for ethnographic accounts of journalists' work: 'Looking at the news, we are unable to see what goes unreported, what is unnoticed, and what is dismissed. In order to fully understand what becomes news we must also be able to see what does not.'

2   To give an example: a football player commenting on the game he has just finished playing in is producing a discourse, but his discourse does not change anything about the game. In contrast, a parliamentarian commenting on a speech that has just been given in Parliament is still performing a discursive political act.

3   Such as in 1988 during a European summit when French Prime Minister Jacques Chirac (thinking that his microphone was off) said about Margaret Thatcher: 'But what more does this housewife want from me, my balls on a plate?' The ongoing eurozone crisis, but also the resignation of the Santer Commission in 1999 or the referendums on the European constitution, are good (but rare) examples of periods of intense politicisation.

4   The creation of an EU page in *Le Monde*, ultimately abandoned, is revealing in this respect.

5   *European Voice*, reader profile and circulation data (2000) and *European Voice*, subscriber study (Total Press Search, 1997).

6   At the start of the 2000s there was only one (France 3) correspondent for all French television outlets. With some notable exceptions (the large regional daily *Ouest France* has a long tradition of EU correspondence motivated by its pro-European commitment), the French regional press (which has a large readership) is scarcely represented in Brussels.

7   This section is based on the findings of the AIM project (AIM, 2007c). The AIM project investigated the logics of EU news production in ten countries (Belgium, Estonia, France, Germany, Ireland, Italy, Lithuania, Norway, Romania, and the UK). The project included content analysis of EU coverage in national press systems and interviews with journalists and news editors in national newsrooms, with EU correspondents from the ten countries, and with communication officers of the EU. It also included observations of journalists' work in Brussels and of the editorial routines in national newsrooms. The following analysis is based on these results and aims to provide a general framework of analysis of EU correspondence. Details about national specificities are to be found in the working papers of the AIM project (AIM, 2007a, 2007c).

8   With the minor exceptions of those media dedicated to the EU microcosm, such as *European Voice*.

9   The chosen period heavily influenced the results for France, since the EU referendum campaign was developing at this time.

10 Given the high level of politicisation of EU topics in British domestic politics, these are frequently debated in the British press. Yet what is central to understanding the British coverage of the EU is the national political agenda and the structure of the national political field partly structured by these issues. Put in a nutshell, what matters in terms of newsworthiness relies on political developments in London (domestic political news) much more than what goes on in Brussels (EU news). Since our focus is on EU news, that explains the rather paradoxical evaluation of coverage of the EU by British media outlets.

11 On slowness, just to provide a comparative point with contemporary French politics: more than 250 laws were voted on by parliament during Nicolas Sarkozy's presidency (2007–12). That makes one law voted on per week; in fact the average is even higher, since parliament sits for only eight months in the year.

12 Apart from the fact that this is 'the country I know best' (to use the ritual expression used by EU commissioners when they refer to the country they come from), France is also a *bizarre* country at the crossroads of different journalistic traditions and cultures. This uneasy qualification of France in terms of journalism has been underlined by Hallin and Mancini (2004), who recognised that it challenges their threefold model of media systems, even if they included France in their 'Mediterranean model'.

13 Just the very fact that heads of states were involved would have made it newsworthy in journalists' eyes.

8

Do Public Service Media (Still) Matter? Evaluating the Supply, Quality, and Impact of Television News in Western Europe

Stephen Cushion

Introduction

In Aaron Sorkin's 2012 HBO drama series *The Newsroom*, viewers are invited to suspend their disbelief by imagining a US cable news television channel that abandons its ratings-driven agenda with a pledge to better inform the electorate about public affairs. The mostly young and idealistic characters in the drama are editorially driven by stories that have informative value, operating under journalistic conventions that objectively convey what is happening in the world without partisan or commercial influence. While the series is injected with the same pace and liberal optimism that defined the success of Sorkin's previous drama, *The West Wing*, underlying much of the plot is a wider disapproval of contemporary US television journalism and the increasingly corrosive influence the advertising industry has had on news-making for many decades.

For many US liberal pay-per-viewers, *The Newsroom* represents only a fantasy utopia in television news-making, a temporary respite from the competitive market-driven system that is largely preoccupied with satisfying advertisers and obtaining maximum ratings. But for the many nations that make up Western Europe, the fictional yearning for the type of journalistic values being championed has been a reality for several decades. Whereas the US media system was driven by a free-market model throughout the twentieth century, in Western Europe many nations (notably in Northern Europe, such as the UK, Germany, and the Scandinavian countries) pioneered public service broadcasting models

151

that operated to prevent excessive market power or political interference from shaping the delivery of news. Of course, it is important not to generalise – or romanticise – the past and present freedoms enjoyed by Western European broadcasters. The relative political autonomy of many Northern European countries contrasts starkly with the governance structures and journalistic and political traditions of some Southern European states (such as France, Italy, and Spain). Nevertheless, according to Blumler (1992: 1): 'For more than half a century assurance and pride were hallmarks of Western European broadcasting. The appropriateness of public service principles, as legitimating creed and policy guide, was unquestioned.' The values of Western European public service broadcasters subsequently spread around the world, with not just their philosophical aims emulated but funding models and editorial processes structurally replicated to countenance any state influence or commercial pressure.

However, at the tail end of the twentieth century many of the public service values and structures long maintained by European broadcasters were threatened by wider cultural, technological, and commercial trends. As in the US media system, competition between channels increased dramatically in the 1980s and 1990s and, for many European policy makers, public service broadcasters came to be viewed as somewhat antiquated organisations, distorting the free market and constraining commercial innovation. As more commercial channels have come to co-exist with public service outlets, the precise characteristics of public service broadcasting have also become difficult to define, since the funding, regulation, and content of competing broadcasters can vary not just cross-nationally but also within countries (Cushion, 2012a; Moe and Syvertsen, 2009). This situation is further complicated by digital, online technologies that shape a new era of public service *media* as opposed to broadcasting (Iosifidis, 2010). In short, many Western European broadcasters have been historically well served by non-market-driven broadcasting systems – the type only fictionalised for US audiences in *The Newsroom* – but today they face intense pressure in a more competitive multimedia environment.

This chapter explores whether Western European broadcasters are generally living up to their historic reputation by asking if they continue to supply high-quality television news in an increasingly commercialised twenty-first-century media landscape. Before outlining the more specific questions posed, a brief introduction to previous research into comparative media systems is necessary.

In trying to understand comparative media systems and regulatory cultures cross-nationally, scholars have generated typologies that broadly characterise countries or regions around the world. Siebert et al.'s *Four Theories of the Press* (1956) is often attributed as the first attempt to classify media systems according to their political identity, but their largely normative appraisal examined just three countries. Since then prominent scholars in political communication research have sought more empirical understanding of comparative media systems (Blumler and Gurevitch, 1995; Curran and Park, 2000; McQuail, 1987). The most influential comparative study is arguably Hallin and Mancini's (2004) *Comparing Media Systems*, which drew on a range of relevant empirical data sources in Western European/North American countries to develop three models – 'liberal', 'democratic corporatist', and 'polarised pluralist' – that characterised the political and news media structures generally in 18 countries. In doing so, they assessed the attributes of different media markets, the linkages political parties have with media systems, the professionalism of journalists, and how far media regulation is shaped by the state (Hallin and Mancini, 2004: 21).

While the Hallin and Mancini book has rightly been hailed as a landmark study, scholars have questioned grouping certain countries together. For example, Curran (2011) suggests that placing the US, UK, Canada, and Ireland within the liberal model – a media system primarily defined by a reliance on market power and influence – fails to take into account the US's hyper-commercial forces and its status as a political superpower, both of which help shape its journalism. Furthermore, Curran views the three models as failing 'to recognise the underlying commonality between Western European countries' (2011: 44). Curran's comparative analysis of US and Western European media systems is worth quoting at length:

> *Western European countries do not constitute a superpower. To a greater extent than the US, they are welfare democracies that redress inequality through redistributive politics. [...] They also have media systems shaped by a conception of the public interest realised through the state. Thus, apart from Luxembourg, all Western European countries have significant public TV and radio channels, charged with serving the public interest. Most regulate major commercial TV channels for the public good much more extensively than the US. (Curran, 2011: 44)*

In other words, the values inherent in public service broadcasting across Western European countries can often be marginalised in attempts to generally interpret cross-national media systems. In more recent years, there has been some attempt to empirically isolate the comparative differences between public and market-driven news media cross-nationally. While comparative assessments of media systems around the world had relied primarily on gathering secondary data sources or large edited collections (Blumler and Gurevitch, 1995; Curran and Park, 2000; Dobek-Ostrowska et al., 2010; Hallin and Mancini, 2004), collaborative cross-national empirical studies have increased within the discipline of political communication.

The intention of this chapter is to draw on the latest empirical studies to generate an evidence-based account of the supply and quality of public and market-driven news among Western European broadcasters as well as the impact they have on audiences cross-nationally. Since it has been suggested that Western media systems increasingly resemble Hallin and Mancini's liberal model, the chapter will compare evidence relating to Western Europe with the US. While broadcasters increasingly supply online output also, the focus will primarily be on television news. Television, of course, remains the dominant source of information in most Western European countries and has been the subject of several recent cross-national and longitudinal empirical studies.

Yet while the intention of this chapter is to broadly represent the media systems of Western Europe, it is worth emphasising that many of the comparative content-driven news studies published – and drawn upon in this chapter – are based largely or solely on the experience of Northern European countries. This is partly a limitation of my own reliance on only English-language publications. While a wider set of studies from other European nations is unpacked in greater detail elsewhere (Cushion, 2012a), more cross-national studies from Southern Europe would shed further empirical light on the comparative differences between public and market-driven news media throughout Western Europe.

Funding, regulating, and scheduling television news programming: the US vs Europe

In Western Europe the BBC is the model of public service broadcasting that many other countries have broadly replicated. While the BBC began broadcasting in 1922, it was not until 1 January 1927 that the British Broadcasting Corporation was recognised under royal charter and a system of public ownership via a licence fee was established (see Cushion, 2012b). With one eye on the US's commercial approach to regulating the fast-growing radio sector, a 1923 Broadcasting Committee report warned that a funding model based on advertising would 'risk lowering the standard of broadcasting'. This view was widely shared across Western Europe and, just a few years on, national radio broadcast stations were launched around this region broadly based on the BBC's funding model and wider mission to deliver high-quality programming not debased by market priorities. For example, the mission statement of Sweden's Radiotjänst in 1925 read: 'Broadcasting shall be undertaken in such a manner as promotes the enlightenment and education of the public' (cited in Findahl, 1999: 14). In other words, public service broadcasting should be viewed as a shared public good for 'the nation'. This has become a core principle of public service broadcasting – providing programming of universal appeal to all citizens it serves, while at the same time satisfying niche or minority tastes often neglected by wholly commercial competitors (Tracey, 1998). The commitment towards public service broadcasting in Western Europe is reflected by the high level of funding many national broadcasters receive relative to other countries around the world (see Table 8.1).

Although public service broadcasters have long supplied a wide range of programming, central to their identity is the provision of news and current affairs. After all, while entertainment-driven programmes such as sport, soap operas, and comedies have tended to appeal to mass audiences and are typically well stocked on commercial television channels, the genre of news does not always contain the market incentive to satisfy advertising demands or deliver high ratings. Moreover, news is recognised as playing a decisive part in informing – and educating – citizens about key democratic institutions and public affairs. Underpinning the mission statements of public service broadcasters established in the 1920s and 1930s was the stipulation that news should be reported impartially without political interference. Having experienced the power of German propaganda in the lead-up to and during World War II, fears about the influence of television – which overtook radio in the 1950s and 1960s as the most popular medium – reinforced the importance placed on maintaining impartiality in broadcasting. As Humphreys observed (1996: 14–15), 'European broadcasters came typically to be subjected to strict regulation according to principles of impartiality and political pluralism.

Table 8.1 Funding public media in leading advanced democracies

Country	Year	Public funding ($ million)	Non-public funding ($ million)	Total revenue ($ million)	Per capita public funding ($)	Per capita total revenue ($)
Australia (ABC)	2008	728.9 (82.3%)	157.0 (17.7%)	885.9	34.01	41.34
Belgium (VRT/RTBF)	2008	805.1 (77.8%)	229.8 (22.2%)	1,034.9	74.62	95.92
Denmark (DR)	2008	717 (91%)	70.9 (9%)	787.9	130.52	143.42
Finland (YLE)	2007	526 (95%)	27.7 (5%)	553.7	99.00	104.21
France[1] (Fr2/Fr3)	2008	3,211.1 (74%)	1,128.2 (26%)	4,339.3	51.56	69.68
Germany (ARD/ZDF)	2008	10,778.5 (86.2%)	1,721.5 (13.8%)	12,500	131.27	152.23
Ireland (RTE)	2008	317.1 (45.6%)	378.3 (54.4%)	695.4	71.65	157.30
Japan (NHK)	2009	6,900 (100%)	–	6,900	54.03	54.03
Netherlands (NPO)	2007	822.3 (68%)	386.9 (32%)	1,209.2	50.00	73.53
New Zealand (TVNZ/NZoA)	2008	126.5 (38.5%)	202.4 (61.5%)	328.9	29.63	77.05
Norway (NRK)	2007	636.9 (95%)	33.6 (5%)	670.5	133.57	140.62
Sweden (SVT)	2008	533.5 (93%)	40.1 (7%)	573.6	57.87	62.22
United Kingdom[2] (BBC)	2009	5,608.8 (77.9%)	1,593.4 (22.1%)	7,202.2	90.70	116.43
United States[3] (PBS/NPR)	2008	1,139.3 (40%)	1,710 (60%)	2,849.3	3.75	9.37

[1] For France this included France Télévisions and Radio France.
[2] For the UK this included the licence fee and government grants.
[3] For the US this included federal, state, and local government funding.

Source: adapted from Benson and Powers (2010: 61).

It became a fundamental ideal of public broadcasting that democratic pluralism should be upheld: that the public service broadcasters should reflect a range of democratic viewpoints.

The broadly interventionist tradition of Western European broadcasting policy contrasts with the US's minimalist approach (Moe and Syvertsen, 2009). Generally speaking, the US's media regulator, the Federal Communications Commission (FCC), has operated as a 'light touch' body, encouraging self-regulation. The most vigorous regulatory intervention in the provision of news and current affairs programming was arguably in the 1960s. Under the auspices of the Fairness Doctrine, the FCC attempted to enhance the level of news programming and instructed all broadcasters to be impartial in the reporting of politics and public affairs.

In the 1980s, however, the US witnessed a period of rampant deregulation, driven by new technologies and relaxed media ownership laws (McChesney, 2000). The broadcast environment changed dramatically, allowing the launch of many cable and then digital channels. For example, in 1987 the legal requirement to be impartial was abolished, since free-market politicians and policy-makers successfully argued that viewers had the choice of many different broadcast outlets, which delivered, so it was claimed, a pluralistic culture of news. Western Europe was not immune from these wider technological, commercial, and deregulatory changes. Its broadcast ecologies also expanded as television moved into the multi-channel era and by the end of the decade the monopoly of public service broadcasters was broadly over. Yet the strong tradition of public service broadcasting in Western Europe was reflected in the kinds of regulations policing the new commercial television channels that launched in the decades after World War II. The dual system of public and private broadcasting produced commercial public service channels in many countries in Western Europe. And despite considerable commercial lobbying to relax impartiality requirements – with the exception of some countries such as Italy – most Western European broadcasters continue to abide by robust regulations about accuracy and balance (Cushion, 2012a).

Nonetheless, the liberalisation of the broadcast airwaves and convergence with new media throughout the 1980s and 1990s created a far more competitive and commercialised media landscape across Europe in the twenty-first century. Many scholars have argued that this was reinforced by EU policy-making that created a market-friendly environment with fewer imposed regulations (Wheeler, 2004). As Meier (2011: 157) has noted, European media policy-making has moved from a phase of top-down government rule-making to a lighter approach defined by 'soft' governance where co- or self-regulation are ways of policing content management. In doing so, while 'the main rationale for PSB [public service broadcasting] has been that it serves the public interest', according to Jakubowicz (2010: 9) 'it has been dethroned by commercial and individual interests'. Of course, with more commercial choice, public service broadcasters have had to respond to a more competitive environment and appeal to increasingly diverse tastes and expectations within 'a nation'. Yet although many scholars have lamented the deterioration of standards among public service broadcasters, these can often be impressionistic rather than something more empirically verifiable. Within news and current affairs programming, for instance, has public broadcast journalism succumbed to market-driven news values or maintained a serious agenda? Since television news is not typically the most popular programme or advertising-friendly genre, has it slipped down the scheduling order as commercial competition has increased?

A range of news studies comparing US and Western European media systems helps shed some empirical light on these questions. Content analysis studies by Iyengar et al. (2009) and Curran et al. (2009) compared the supply of hard and soft news on US television with that of some Western European countries. In doing so, they interpreted the significance of the overall nature of news by carrying out representative national surveys that examined people's knowledge about politics and public affairs. Broadly speaking, the authors found that in market-dominated systems – most strikingly the US – citizens had less knowledge than in countries where public service television news was well funded and widely watched. Moreover, each study concluded by emphasising the influence the ready supply of public service news programming had on maintaining levels of political interest, despite increasing competition for viewers in the multi-channel television age.

Aalberg et al.'s (2010) detailed schedule analysis of peak-time television news programming between 1987 and 2007 in the US, UK, Belgium, Norway, Sweden, and the Netherlands was able to trace longitudinally the availability of news on public and market-driven channels (see Table 8.2). In every year (when comparisons could be made) public service broadcasters supplied a higher volume of news in peak-time hours. The scheduling of news and current affairs at US peak-time hours stood out. Not only was there a low overall supply on both media systems, but the US public broadcaster (PBS) aired – proportionally speaking – the lowest amount of hours when

Table 8.2 News and current affairs programming scheduled on public and commercial television channels (1987–2007) (average minutes per day)

	Public			Commercial		
	1987	1997	2007	1987	1997	2007
Belgium	43	72	84	–	29	42
Netherlands	56	47	54	–	31	20
UK	93	90	93	29	47	37
Norway	37	63	84	–	46	19
Sweden	88	89	76	–	25	27
US	11	33	47	9	9	6

Source: adapted from Aalberg et al. (2010).

compared to Western European public service broadcasters. Since PBS is less well funded (see Table 8.1) and watched by a minuscule share of the market (approximately 2–3 per cent of total viewers), the influence of public service broadcasting in the US appears extremely limited.

To date, however, Esser et al.'s (2012) 30-year (1977–2007) cross-national schedule analysis of television news programming is arguably the most comprehensive interpretation of the provision of news between media systems. While the US's hyper-commercial exceptionalism is often used as a counterpoint to other countries around the world, their study sampled public and market-driven television news bulletins in 12 (primarily Western) European countries (Austria, Belgium, Germany, the UK, Greece, Italy, the Netherlands, Norway, Portugal, Spain, Sweden, and Switzerland) as well as Israel. The research split news programming into four different genres and, as Tables 8.3 and 8.4 indicate, it is the public service programming that dedicates more airtime than more commercially driven channels.

However, compared to limited peak-time programming aired on US television news (see Table 8.2), it is also apparent that the arrival of commercial channels has enhanced the political information supply overall. While it is important to interpret this within a national context (since funding levels, regulatory rules, and journalistic cultures differ cross-nationally), it could be concluded that the historically strong commitment to public service broadcasting has influenced the provision of news on commercial television in Europe generally. In the UK and Norway,

Table 8.3 Changing news supply of news programming on public service television bulletins (in minutes per week)

	1977	*1987*	*1997*	*2007*
News in brief	509	497	675	826
Main newscasts	5,772	6,302	7,460	7,454
News magazine	2,170	2,122	2,528	2,304
Interview/ discussion/talk	540	1,090	1,188	1,769

Table 8.4 Changing news supply of news programming on commercial bulletins (in minutes per week)

	1977	*1987*	*1997*	*2007*
News in brief	0	79	327	281
Main newscasts	336	621	5,154	6,100
News magazine	27	530	904	926
Interview/ discussion/talk	0	0	825	746

Source: Tables 8.3 and 8.4 adapted from Esser et al. (2012).

for example, ITV and TV2 respectively operate as commercial public service broadcasters and are obliged to carry certain news programming irrespective of their reliance on advertising. This has not necessarily been achieved out of regulatory pressure alone: Sjovaag's (2012) document analysis of TV2's public service licence renewal indicated a willingness to retain its status as a public broadcaster despite the regulatory obligations. In doing so, the station believed it would distinguish itself from the multitude of entirely market-driven channels and would be better placed to forge a closer relationship with audiences who appear to engage with mixed genre programming, including regular news bulletins.

Rather than classifying media systems by their shared political, legal, or cultural similarities, the strength of these recently published collaborative cross-national studies has been to compare directly the political news environments of competing public and market-driven channels nationally. This approach, according to Esser et al. (2012: 269), has 'the advantage of being less abstract, closer to actual news providers and news consumers, and easier to operationalise and measure' than generating normative media models. Put another way, cross-national empirical studies can more accurately link *national* regulatory requirements, editorial motives, and journalism conventions – such as the commitment towards impartiality in the reporting of politics and public affairs – with the *specific* media model that helped produce and police television news content.

Making sense of cross-national empirical studies: comparing the democratic value of news in public and market-driven media systems

Longitudinal trends of television news programming can help generate a broad quantitative picture of the political information environment in recent decades. However, the breadth of analysis can limit a deeper understanding of the nature of journalism produced. To achieve this, an assessment of more comparative micro-empirical studies is required as well as making value judgements about the relative merits of information supplied and the wider impact different news media can have. It is a point conceded in Esser et al.'s study (2012: 269): 'Since our analysis tells us little about the quality of information provided, it may be the positive effect of the growing amount of information is at least partly wiped out by rising levels of soft news that are of little democratic value [...] only a large-scale content analysis of news over time across different countries could address these concerns.' In this section a more critical appreciation of the democratic value of news between competing media systems is developed not by drawing on one cross-national quantitative study, but by analysing a wide range of empirical studies to generate an overall interpretation of news in different areas.

Of course, in interpreting the democratic value of news, difficult judgements about what constitutes 'value' or 'quality' are needed. In the supply and reception of news and current affairs on public service broadcasters – the focus of this chapter – general assessments of delivering 'public value' (editors being committed to achieving impartiality or television scheduling peak-time news output) only scratch at the surface of what the concept represents. If value judgements about the relative merits of particular news issues or stories are not made in the interests of citizens, it can encourage an almost relativistic assessment of journalism where all news is celebrated irrespective of its impact. The public value of news, in other words, needs to be operationalised and empirically assessed in order to meaningfully interpret which media system produces news of democratic value for citizens.

This was the intention of my book, *The Democratic Value of News: Why Public Service Media Matter*. In it a comprehensive review was undertaken of empirical news studies that compared cross-nationally the quality of journalism on public and market-driven news media (Cushion, 2012a). While a single longitudinal, cross-national, quantitative study (as suggested by Esser et al., 2012) of broadcast news in a wide range of countries would have been the ideal research design and sample, this is logistically very challenging and costly to establish. Instead, my aim was to take advantage of the internationalisation of journalism studies and political communication studies in recent years (Esser and Pfetsch, 2004; Löffelholz and Weaver, 2008) by carrying out a review of more than 250 empirical news studies. These focused primarily on US and Western European media systems, since this is where most scholarship is produced and evidence (in English) is available. As previously conceded, however, many of the cross-national studies drawn upon in this chapter are made up of Northern rather than Southern European nations.

Four areas of journalism were selected in order to develop a focused comparative assessment of output (during routine news agendas, election campaigns, wars and conflicts, and the medium of 24-hour television news). In each case the democratic value of news was interpreted as having informative quality, conveying news that can enhance people's understanding of the world on issues likely to empower them as citizens in a democracy.[1] While it is not possible to fully unpack the level of detail contained in the many empirical studies reviewed in the book (Cushion, 2012a), the broad thrust of the identified dominant trends related principally to Western European countries is as follows:

- In routine output, several longitudinal studies found evidence in both public and market-driven systems of news agendas more generally becoming 'soft' in focus and style. However, the shift was more striking in market-driven media, which many studies linked to the pressure to relegate serious, public-affairs-orientated or international news in favour of 'lighter' agendas. In contemporary cross-national studies, public service media were shown to supply a harder news agenda, providing more local or international affairs, policy, or analytical information.

- During election campaigns, longitudinal trends demonstrated that public service media reported more campaign news than their commercial competitors. Moreover, publicly funded election news generally had less emphasis on game-type coverage and the personalisation of reporting than market-driven media and spent more time on matters of policy significance. Most strikingly, Western European countries tended to cover more serious election news including policy differences than US broadcasters, many of which spent a great deal of time on campaign tactics.

- In understanding wars and conflicts, the review focused on empirical studies exploring the events surrounding the 2003 war in Iraq. Several studies concluded that the US's largely market-driven news media did not robustly scrutinise government decisions in the post-9/11 environment, nor explain why military action was being taken in Iraq. During the war there was explicit pro-war bias in both US network and cable news. However, while the BBC was praised for challenging the UK government over the existence of weapons of mass destruction (WMD) months after the war had already begun, several empirical studies suggested public and market-driven news was broadly similar in Western European countries.

- The commercial broadcaster CNN held a monopoly on 24-hour television news until the late 1980s. In the decades that followed, a rise in market-driven national and localised news channels led to an enhanced use of news-breaking or 'live' conventions on commercial stations and to a lesser extent on public service channels. Several studies suggested that this potentially compromised the accuracy or context of journalism produced. Since rolling-news channels were launched in a more lightly regulated environment in the US (with the abolition of the Fairness Doctrine in 1987) compared to Western European broadcasters, more partisan channels such as Fox News have been launched. Yet robust regulation has so far restrained the import of a full-blown Fox-style journalism into Western Europe.

Overall, the comprehensive review of empirical studies found that the democratic value of news was more likely to be enhanced when produced by public service media. At the same time, the very presence of public service broadcasting in Western European countries was viewed as elevating the standards of journalism more widely in either commercial public service broadcasters or wholesale commercial media.

163

For example, ZDF, the well-resourced German public service broadcaster (see Table 8.1), has historically devoted considerable attention to foreign news reporting in its news programming. As a consequence, it has been observed that market-driven competitors have been reluctant to editorially marginalise international news – despite having no formal legal obligation to cover foreign affairs – because this has become a familiar part of German television news agendas (Kolmer and Semetko, 2010). Similar observations have been made about the BBC's influence on the wider journalistic culture in the UK. Even though Sky News in the UK has no regulatory obligations to maintain a hard or foreign news agenda, it has followed a relatively broadsheet agenda and its editorial team has dismissed any pressure to make the channel more opinionated along the lines of its US sister channel, Fox News (Cushion and Lewis, 2009).

Indeed, in the UK's dual system of broadcasting – where public and commercial broadcasters have co-existed since the 1950s with varying levels of regulatory commitments – empirical studies have shown that commercial public broadcasters have contributed to news of democratic value by maintaining a relatively hard news agenda over successive decades (Barnett et al., 2000; Hargreaves and Thomas, 2002). Barnett et al.'s (2012) updated longitudinal study (see also Barnett et al., 2000) of the routine agenda of UK national television news confirmed the hard news agenda of commercial public service broadcasters (notably Channel 4), with a sizeable proportion of stories covering international affairs (see Tables 8.5–8.7).

Of course, it is difficult to define what 'sizeable' represents. Yet when compared to a wholly market-driven system, such as the US, the

Table 8.5   Percentage of broadsheet news on UK television news nightly bulletins (1975–2009)

	1975	1980	1985	1990	1995	1999	2004	2009	Difference over time
BBC 6pm	59.5	49.8	45.2	59.8	60.7	44.6	51.9	55.1	−4.4
ITV early evening	59.5	49.8	44.3	55.8	51.4	43	47	44.3	−15.2
BBC 9pm/10pm	59.7	39.2	44.6	56	56.3	43	42.3	46.4	−13.3
ITV late evening	55.5	46.9	45	53.3	48.3	29.8	35.8	40.8	−14.7
Channel 4 7pm	–	–	49	54.8	54.8	51.9	50	50.5	+1.5

Table 8.6 Percentage of tabloid news on UK television news nightly bulletins (1975–2009)

	1975	1980	1985	1990	1995	1999	2004	2009	Difference over time
BBC 6pm	18.4	18.8	25.9	6.5	17	28.9	20.1	23.2	+4.8
ITV early evening	15.4	22.6	32.2	18.7	29.5	33	32.9	34.4	+19
BBC 9pm/10pm	16.2	17.1	22.6	4.9	13.2	13.3	14.3	19.2	+3
ITV late evening	14.8	18.9	24.9	10.9	26.1	42.1	33.1	34.1	+19.3
Channel 4 7pm	–	–	11.1	5.1	4.8	10.6	16.9	18.8	+7.7

Table 8.7 Percentage of foreign news on UK television news nightly bulletins (1975–2009)

	1975	1980	1985	1990	1995	1999	2004	2009	Difference over time
BBC 6pm	21.7	31.2	28.9	33.7	21.6	26.5	28	21.8	+0.1
ITV early evening	24.2	28.5	23.5	25.6	19	25.6	20.1	21.4	−2.8
BBC 9pm/10pm	24	43.6	32.9	39.2	29.7	42.8	43.5	34.4	+10.4
ITV late evening	29.4	34.7	28.9	35.9	25.6	28	31.2	26.2	−3.2
Channel 4 7pm	–	–	39.4	40.7	39.3	37.5	33.1	30.6	-8.8

Source: Tables 8.5, 8.6 and 8.7 adapted from Barnett et al. (2012).

difference is striking: empirical news studies in the US confirm that news programmes tend to spend less time on foreign news reporting and place a greater emphasis on softer stories than Western European commercial broadcasters (Curran et al., 2009; Patterson, 2000; Pew Research Center's Project for Excellence in Journalism, 1998; Scott and Gobetz, 1992).

The impact of public and market-driven news media systems on people's knowledge and understanding of the world was also assessed in the review of empirical studies (Cushion, 2012a). Several cross-national representative surveys of people's general knowledge of politics and public affairs have been carried out in the US and Western European countries. They broadly found that in countries with a well-resourced and robustly regulated public service media system (such as Switzerland, Finland, and Denmark) people's knowledge about the world was higher than in dual public–private systems (the UK) and significantly higher than in dominant market-led systems (the US) (Curran et al., 2009; Iyengar et al., 2009). Even when controlling for external variables that clearly help shape public knowledge, the dominant media culture in each country was considered a significant influence alongside people's level of education, income, interest in politics, or sense of civic duty.

Soroka et al. (2012) updated previous studies exploring the impact of public and market-driven news on people's knowledge by extending the sample of countries to six – Canada, Italy, Japan, Norway, the UK, and South Korea – thus including nations with long public service histories beyond Europe. Developing a questionnaire about people's knowledge of current affairs (with some questions tailored for individual countries), they found – after, once again, controlling for external variables (age, education, political interest) – that exposure to public service media was likely to increase the likelihood of answering questions correctly.

While their findings did not convey a wholesale endorsement of public over private media systems, they did provide qualified evidence that the core principles of public service broadcasting are more likely to lead to an increase in people's knowledge about current affairs. In Italy and Korea, for example, commercial television news was more positively correlated with raising overall knowledge. In the remaining countries the impact of public service television was noticeable and – in the case of the UK and Norway particularly and to a lesser extent Japan – the effect was interpreted as being much stronger than that of their commercial competitors. In each of these countries, Soroka et al. (2012) suggested, the reliance on high levels of direct public funding rather than via advertising, greater overall audience share of the television market, and a relatively high level of legal independence all contributed to the production of high-quality journalism that could enhance people's knowledge of current affairs.

In contrast, Italy's public broadcaster has to rely somewhat on commercial activities to fund its journalism, does not attract such high audience ratings as other countries in the sample, and does not have the same level of legal autonomy (nor, as previously outlined, does it have the same commitment to impartiality in news coverage as many other

Western European broadcasters). Consequently, Italy's main commercial broadcaster was found to enhance people's knowledge about current affairs far more than the leading public television channel. In their final appraisal of the study, Soroka et al. (2012: 14) suggest that 'given that public affairs knowledge appears to be significantly improved through the publicly-funded provision of news [...] then governments' decisions about funding for public broadcasters seem in many cases to be very much like decisions about just how well informed their citizens will be'. A brief discussion about the future funding of public service media will now conclude this chapter.

Public service media in austere times: commercial challenges and financial threats

The chapter began with a contrast: on the one hand, a US fictional drama of a television news channel (HBO's *The Newsroom*) becoming less reliant on ratings and advertising and enhancing its commitment to report serious and balanced news and, on the other hand, the history of Western European broadcasters, where the funding of non-market journalism and impartiality of news coverage have long been a reality in many countries' media systems. In the corporately controlled and market-driven media system of the US, *The Newsroom* offers a fantasy version of what viewers in Western Europe have ostensibly enjoyed for many decades. Since recent observations about changing media systems have suggested that many are replicating US trends or have hypothesised that editorial standards in public service broadcasters are deteriorating, this chapter asked whether public service media still matter to Western European audiences.

Drawing on a wide range of cross-national comparative studies and a comprehensive review of academic literature, the broad conclusion reached was that Western European public broadcasters more regularly scheduled peak-time news than their commercial competitors, that their news was of higher democratic value, and that such news appeared to generally enhance public knowledge about current affairs to a greater degree. Or, put more succinctly, the supply and viewing of public service journalism was the media system most likely to generate informed citizenship.

Yet while the evidence amassed suggested that public service media play a significant role in democratic life, their influence is under threat. The continuing penetration of commercial media and the financial

167

uncertainty surrounding the funding of public service media pose serious concerns to the latter's long-term sustainability. At present, many Western European public broadcasters continue to enjoy a large share of television news audiences. For instance, a recent study found that the evening news bulletins on public service channels in Belgium, the Netherlands, Norway, Sweden, and the UK attracted larger audiences than their main commercial competitors (Aalberg et al., 2010). However, according to a detailed audience study of public service television news output between 2006 and 2010, the main nightly bulletins in Germany, Spain, France, Italy, and the UK failed to increase their audience share (EBU, 2011). On average, this was 21.8 per cent of the audience share, a drop of 2.8 per cent since 2006. In six other public service television evening bulletins across Western Europe – Austria, Belgium, Greece, Ireland, the Netherlands, and Portugal – a similar average size (21.3 per cent) was identified. The Nordic countries had the highest combined average nightly audience (29 per cent).

Of course, dwindling audiences for news programming is a familiar story not just on television but in journalism more generally. In the digital and online environment, commercial competition has delivered far more entertainment-based genres, potentially distracting citizens from the supply of news (Prior, 2007). However, for public rather than commercial broadcasters fewer people watching their flagship news bulletins can trigger existential questions about their role and relevance in an increasingly commercialised landscape, since most public service broadcasters rely on the popular support of citizens for financial sustainability. If commercial choice is seen as an alternative to publicly funded stations, public service broadcasters appear more susceptible to attack from governments tinkering with the public purse.

Indeed, since the financial crisis rocked much of Western Europe in 2008, some public service broadcasters have experienced a considerable downsizing of their resources. According to the EBU (2012), the Portuguese government has halved the total income of its public broadcaster, RTP, in recent years. In the Netherlands, an estimated €200 million was cut (Henning, 2011), as was the case in Spain (Penty, 2011). Meanwhile the BBC planned in 2010 to cut 16 per cent of its budget over six years, amounting to a reduction (via a freeze in the licence fee) of £340 million (Spanier, 2010). Funding reductions are not the only means to downsize public service broadcasters: some governments have recently changed funding mechanisms. For example, Spanish and French public service broadcasters banned advertising (in 2010 and 2012 respectively) to fund programming and instead moved to a tax (set by the government of the day). While this might inject more investment in the short term (since advertising revenue has declined in recent years) or make programming less attentive to the needs of advertisers, it can also mean governments have greater freedom more directly to influence the funding of public service broadcasters according to the current economic environment. As Nikoltchev and Blázquez (2011: 89–90) have noted:

> Broadcasters that are recipients of direct state payments rather than beneficiaries of licences and commercial revenue – such as advertising and sponsorship – have less protection again potential state interference [...] Only when the level of funding is determined in accordance with actual needs – and not as a consequence of political decisions possibly unrelated to the mandate of public service media – are broadcasters guarded against funding cuts based on economic crises such as we are currently facing in Europe and many other parts of the world.

In other words, licence fees are the best buffer (although by no means entirely immune, considering that the BBC's freeze amounts to a significant reduction in revenue over time) from the prevailing political and economic winds. As was recently observed in the Netherlands and Iceland, 'The government declared that they would put financing of public service under the state budgets, with a guarantee of the level of financing [...] And a few years later, with a change of government, or a change of political and economical context, there were grave cuts' (Moring cited in Kirchner, 2012). Comparatively speaking, however, many countries in Western Europe are arguably in good shape to resist threats to government funding and absorb pressure from commercial rivals. The licence fee is the most widely used funding model among Western European media and public consumption of and support for public service broadcasting generally remain high. By comparison, the future of PBS in the US seems remarkably more perilous. During the run-up to the 2012 presidential election, leading Republicans proposed entirely abolishing public funding for PBS to reduce public expenditure (Bond, 2011) despite the federal government investing far less proportionately than most European countries (see Table 8.1). Moreover, the ratings of PBS's flagship programme, *NewsHour*, typically amount to 0.7 per cent of total viewers, a sixth of the figure the evening network news bulletins average (Pew

Research Center's Project for Excellence in Journalism, 2012). The number of viewers watching *NewsHour* (1.1 million) is roughly half the average proportion of people tuning into HBO's fictional portrayal of non-market television journalism in *The Newsroom*.[2]

This contrast between fact and fiction is an instructive reminder of the striking difference that distinguishes the US's media system from that of many European countries. While Western European public service media continue to face hazardous challenges in a more commercialised media landscape with increasing pressure on public expenditure, it is perhaps easy to forget that – unlike in the US – most citizens have access to a regular supply of well-resourced and impartial journalism. As the overwhelming evidence drawn upon in this chapter has demonstrated, public service media still profoundly matter in much of Western Europe and their influence on the wider culture of news should not be underestimated as the twenty-first century evolves.

Notes

1   Of course, understanding what the democratic value of news represents for all citizens cannot easily be categorised and understood. However, to compare the quality of information supplied by competing media systems, general value judgements or criteria had to be established (see Cushion, 2012a).

2   This is based on ratings of the first few episodes aired in the US.

9

Americanisation Revisited: Political Journalism in Transition in the United States and Western Europe

Rasmus Kleis Nielsen

Introduction

American journalism, American forms of political communication, and the specific relations that have developed between the media system and the political system in the United States are not, have never been, and probably will never be the global standard. And yet there is no question that developments in American journalism, American campaign practices, and relations between journalists and politicians in the United States have historically influenced many other countries through the invention of new discursive practices like 'reporting' and 'interviewing' in the nineteenth century, through outsiders' fascination with the spectacle of American politics and media coverage in the twentieth century, and through the selective adaptation of professional practices, managerial strategies, and organisational forms originating in the United States across the world. America fascinates the world in ways few other countries do, and this applies to media and politics too. Journalists all over the world have heard of Watergate and know of Bob Woodward and Carl Bernstein. Few outside France know of the *affaire Bettencourt* and Mediapart; few outside Germany of the *Spiegel* affair and Rudolf Augstein.

The diffusion of practices, strategies, and organisational forms associated with the United States has often led to claims of the 'Americanisation' of political communication or the media in other countries. In public debate, the term is usually used as a critique of what is, at least in Western Europe, typically taken to mean trends towards more

171

sensational, superficial, and market-driven journalism, towards more crass and instrumental campaign communications. Scholars mostly use the term in a less prejudiced fashion to capture the global influence of American programming especially in television, the partial dissemination of the norms of American journalism across the world, the gradual expansion of commercial media partly at the expense of state-owned public service media in much of Europe, and the increased tendency to use outside consultants in political campaigns (see for instance Blumler and Gurevitch, 2001; Hallin and Mancini, 2004). The purpose of this chapter is to compare recent developments in political journalism in the United States with trends in select Western European countries to revisit the Americanisation thesis and identify key similarities and differences during a time of transition.[1]

Political journalism is no one thing, not in the United States, and certainly not across all of Western Europe. The United States is a continental-scale country of 50 states that vary in important ways in terms of media system and political culture, and indeed in terms of demographics and economic structure. Western Europe is much smaller geographically, but in terms of media, politics, and culture arguably even more diverse. Here, I will focus on the most important general developments in the United States – recognising that there is substantial variation across the country and its more than 2,000 television broadcasters, almost 1,400 daily newspapers, and countless websites – with trends in France and Germany (both discussed in detail elsewhere in the book). These three countries produce a useful, strategic sample for comparison as the United States is often taken as the most important example of what has been called the 'liberal' media model, dominated by commercial media and characterised by relatively high levels of journalistic independence, whereas France and Germany are important examples of the two models seen as most common in Western Europe: the 'polarised pluralist' or 'Mediterranean' model (France) with relatively weakly developed commercial news media, considerable state intervention in media markets, and high levels of interpenetration between media and politics, and the 'democratic corporatist' or Northern European model (Germany) characterised by the co-existence of commercial media, media tied to civil society and political groups, and public service media (Hallin and Mancini, 2004). All three countries are affluent, established democracies with similarly high levels of internet use, where politicians, journalists, and ordinary citizens have begun to supplement their existing (mass) media habits with a growing range of digital and networked communication technologies. In terms of political journalism and the possible Americanisation of political communication and the media, I will argue that the three countries have been characterised by persistent systemic differences over the last decades, but that there are also some important similarities in terms of the most important changes in how political journalism functions.

Political journalism in the United States

To understand the state of political journalism in early twenty-first-century United States, it is necessary to know where it comes from. In a thumbnail sketch, one could summarise what Daniel C. Hallin (1992) has called the 'high modernism' of American journalism in the 1970s and 1980s as a period in which the journalistic profession could see itself as increasingly independent of both political parties and the state, more inclusive and open to a changing world, and yet safely ensconced symbolically as a trustworthy and socially acceptable part of the establishment.

Though newspapers like the *New York Times* and the *Washington Post* published some of the most outstanding examples of political journalism during these years, it was, in a broader perspective, an era of what Bruce A. Williams and Michael X. Delli Carpini (2011) call 'broadcast news'. By the 1970s, television had conclusively been established as the dominant mass medium and the most important source of news for most Americans – nationally from the three competing networks ABC, CBS, and NBC, and locally from (usually) one or at most a few stations covering a particular area. Newspapers still dominated news production, often set the news agenda across print and broadcasting, continued to provide most of the news at the local level, and, after a period of market consolidation and newspaper deaths in the 1960s, enjoyed strong economic foundations due to their monopoly on many kinds of advertising. But it was nonetheless television that provided for what 'common knowledge' Americans shared, raised the salience of certain issues, informed the general population about public affairs, and made it possible – indeed routine – for millions of ordinary people to follow politics (Neuman et al., 1992). Other media mattered but, for most Americans, the political information environment of the 1970s and 1980s was dominated by a few mass media – the national networks, local television, and the local daily newspaper.

While journalists may in retrospect romanticise the period, it was no uncomplicated 'Golden Age' – as many studies have shown, news coverage during these years often focused on process at the expense of policy substance, reporters routinely let a narrow range of official, often government, sources dominate the news, and a wide range of minorities and social movements were routinely misrepresented and vilified in public debate (Bennett, 1990; Gitlin, 1980; Patterson, 1993). Due to the pioneering work of a small group of scholars who did extensive ethnographic fieldwork in newsrooms during these years (Gans, 1979; Sigal, 1973; Tuchman, 1978), we know a great deal about the work routines and professional norms that produced this coverage. Fastening onto the similarities in how different news media covered politics, the political scientist Timothy E. Cook (1998) suggested that the news media in the United States should be seen as constituting a *political institution* despite their firm roots in the private sector. Cook argued that the newsroom ethnographers had uncovered a shared set of trans-organisational routines and norms that governed the co-production of (political) news by journalists and their sources, and that these routines and norms, when combined with the centrality of news media as the most important intermediaries between people and politicians (documented by surveys), made political journalism integral to how politics functioned in an increasingly mediated democracy. The ongoing and institutionalised negotiation of newsworthiness, a process that Herbert J. Gans (1979) described as a 'tug of war' between reporters and their sources, thus suggested that journalism may have become more independent than it had been in the early postwar years – and was arguably more independent than state-owned public service television and politically affiliated newspapers in much of Europe (Hallin and Mancini, 2004) – but was far from autonomous from political and governmental pressures.

The 1970s and 1980s thus were, simplifying greatly, a period dominated by a daily news cycle built around the morning papers and the evening television news, produced by news organisations that aimed at impartiality and objectivity (for both editorial and commercial reasons) and strove for independence even as they remained highly dependent on official sources. It was a time when most Americans who followed the news followed basically the same news as everyone else in their community (and had little else to choose from), and an era in which those – the majority – who felt part of mainstream society and of the political and cultural currents that dominated the news also felt that political journalism was relatively fair, thought that one could have confidence in the press, and saw journalists as amongst the most trustworthy professions (Ladd, 2012). It is also a period of American political journalism that is over, because of changes in American society, American politics, and in the American media system itself.

American political journalism in transition

Especially from the early 1990s onward, many of the defining features of the era of high modern journalism, dominant daily newspapers, and broadcast news have been under pressure (Hallin, 1992; Neuman, 1991). There is a deep, underlying continuity in key aspects of American journalism and the American media system in the form of a journalistic profession strongly oriented towards ideals of objectivity and impartiality (especially in political coverage), in the predominantly regional rather than national orientation of much of the media system (most importantly the newspaper industry), and in the virtually complete dominance of commercial media when it comes to news provision (with non-profit and public media as small though sometimes significant supplements). The constitutional framework and many basic social and political fault-lines also remain the same. But political journalism in America, as elsewhere, is in a period of transition, as both the political world that journalists cover as well as the news media that they work for have changed.

American politics has, first of all, become increasingly polarised and confrontational in recent years, especially at the national level. Using standardised measures of partisanship calculated on the basis of voting patterns in Congress, one team of political scientists has shown that the distance between the two parties has increased rapidly since the 1980s and is today greater than it has been at any point since the Civil War (McCarty et al., 2006). Republicans tend to attribute the polarisation to what they perceive to be the divisive politics of the Clinton administration, and Democrats often to the conservative movement that propelled Ronald Reagan to office, to the aggressively negative George H.W. Bush presidential campaign in 1988, and to the high-charged right-wing rhetoric of the congressional freshman class of the 1994 'Gingrich revolution'. It is important to note that this trend towards political polarisation is much more pronounced at the level of elected officials than the general population. While commentators have often talked about a 'Red America' and a 'Blue America', most political scientists contest the idea that the electorate is deeply divided and argue that while partisan supporters of both parties have indeed moved apart, both politically and geographically, the more important popular political divide in America is between a politically engaged (and often highly partisan) minority and a disengaged and frequently disenchanted majority (Abramowitz, 2010).

In this increasingly partisan climate and faced with a sceptical citizenry, political parties and elected officials have stepped up their fundraising efforts and their investments in communications and campaign efforts. Even before the 2010 'Citizen United' Supreme Court decision dismantled much of the regulatory framework around campaign finance, the cost of competing for office in the United States had increased dramatically. The Campaign Finance Institute has calculated that the average expenditure in congressional campaigns almost tripled from 1994 to 2010.[2] The Center for Responsive Politics estimates that the 2012 elections cost a combined $6 billion, more than twice the $3 billion total cost of the 2000 elections (Alexander, 1996; Center for Responsive Politics, 2012). Part of this money, as well as parts of the daily operating budget of the two national parties and of individual executives and legislators' own staff, is used to fund day-to-day communications as top politicians go toe-to-toe with one another and with journalists in what has been called the 'permanent campaign'. Martha Joynt Kumar (2007) describes the gradual expansion of the White House communications operation to a point where by the mid-2000s, more full-time staffers work with communications than with domestic and economic policy combined, and where President Bush's chief *political* strategist, Karl Rove, was, in a highly symbolic move, made deputy chief of staff for *policy* after the 2004 election. Part of the money is invested in hiring a growing number of campaign staffers and consultants and in television advertising, direct mail, online communications, and door-to-door canvassing efforts that all allow political actors to circumvent journalists and the news media and reach citizens in other ways (Herrnson, 2004; Nielsen, 2012b).

While it is clear that politicians and political parties in much of Europe have strategically adopted key parts of the campaign and communication strategies of American politicians (Plasser and Plasser, 2002) and a growing body of work suggests that many political actors have increased their investments in ongoing media relations and PR (Davis, 2002), it is not clear that the more fundamental trends of increased partisanship and massively increased campaign budgets that have shaped so much of American politics over the last decades are present in Western European countries like France and Germany. The 2012 French presidential elections were contentious, but in the German Bundestag broad political coalitions are still common. Electoral campaigns in both countries have grown more expensive but, as noted in Chapter 1, not nearly as expensive as those in the United States.

American news media have, meanwhile, lost much of their institutional capacity even as politicians and political organisations have increased theirs. The newspaper industry that throughout the twentieth century employed the majority of American journalists has in the early twenty-first century suffered through a painful adjustment to a new media environment. From 2000 to 2009, paid printed newspaper circulation per capita declined by 25 per cent in the United States, newspaper industry revenues fell by 36 per cent, and the total number of journalists employed by the industry declined by 17 per cent – a net reduction of almost 10,000 reporters in an industry the US Bureau of Labor Statistics in 2011 still estimated employs 60 per cent of all journalists in the United States (Nielsen, 2012a). Overall, the television industry did well financially during the same period, but it has been gradually backing away from its commitment to invest in news since the 1980s.[3] The growing ecosystem of journalistic online start-ups and non-profit news initiatives offers many interesting, innovative, and important complements to legacy media coverage of politics, but nothing like the institutional resources lost in the newspaper and television industries. One report estimates that the 'new journalism ecosystem' employs around 600 full-time reporters, compared to the roughly 40,000 journalists still working for the struggling newspaper industry (Lewis et al., 2012). Across the United States, news organisations ranging from the most prestigious newspapers, over major television and cable channels, to metropolitan and local newspapers, are struggling to reinvent themselves – their social role, their professional practices, and their business models – as part of a new media environment (Anderson, 2013; Ryfe, 2012).

This reduction in the reportorial workforce has had direct consequences for political journalism in the United States. High-profile events like presidential elections, the daily churn around the White House, as well as key battles in Congress are still covered in detail and at length by a multitude of media, including legacy brand-name news media and new online-only entrants. A variety of televised talk shows, talk-radio hosts, and political blogs provide both a steady stream of political stories and much commentary and opinion. Specialised niche outlets and information services like Bloomberg Government and various newsletters provide in-depth reporting on the minutiae of policy processes that may impact particular businesses or other organised interests. But large swaths of American politics are no longer covered by journalists on a routine basis. As of 2009, 27 states no longer had a single reporter covering their congressional delegation in Washington. The same year, the *American Journalism Review* (2009) estimated that only 355 newspaper reporters covered state capitols full-time (more than 7,000 state legislators serve in the 50 state legislatures and billions of tax dollars are raised and spent by state governments).

France and Germany, by contrast, have seen no comparable reduction in news media's capacity to cover politics. Public service broadcasters in both countries face a variety of strategic challenges and pressures, but remain broadly speaking financially robust. French newspapers never grew to the size and strength of their American counterparts, but have not suffered the same decline either. The German newspaper industry has so far fared better during the digital transition than virtually any other newspaper industry in the Western world (Nielsen, 2012a).

In the American context of increased political polarisation, political actors investing increasing amounts of money and efforts in their communication strategies, and news media institutions cutting back on their investments in journalism, researchers have identified five facets of contemporary changes that are particularly important for understanding how contemporary American political journalism functions. These are: (1) increased audience fragmentation, (2) an accelerated news cycle, (3) some tendencies towards partisan polarisation in the media and in media use, (4) the increased importance of non-journalistic actors in shaping and disseminating news and information, and (5) low levels of public trust in traditional sources of political news – the so-called 'mainstream media'. It is worth going through each of these points in some detail and briefly comparing American developments to trends in France and Germany.

Audience fragmentation

Across the Western world, recent decades have seen an explosive growth in the number of places people can access news and political discussion, first in the form of multi-channel television from cable and satellite, which took off in the United States in the 1980s, then the growth of political talk radio on the AM band in the early 1990s, and the rise of the internet especially from the mid-1990s onwards. In his book *Post-broadcast Democracy*, Markus Prior (2007) captures the trend clearly. He describes a change from a situation in 1970 where television was universally available and widely watched, predominantly in the form of network programming – the average US household had about half a dozen channels to choose from, and ABC, CBS, and NBC and their affiliates captured 80 per cent of all viewing – to a situation in 2005 when the average household has multiple TV sets, access to cable or satellite television, a choice of over 100 channels, and internet access, and ABC, CBS, and NBC with their affiliates drew less than 20 per cent of all viewing.

Prior's analysis has demonstrated how the move from the 'low choice' media environment of the 1970s to the 'high choice' media environment of the early 2000s has vastly increased the importance of individuals' relative interest in public affairs for how much they know about politics. He has also shown concretely how differences in both levels of political knowledge, levels of political involvement, and levels of party identification have increased between an interested and engaged minority, who have enthusiastically embraced many of the new ways of learning about politics on offer, and a larger majority, many of whom are drifting away as they no longer learn from the 'incidental exposure' that broadcast television offered when there was little to choose from as all networks scheduled the evening news to coincide with dinner time. All these trends are likely to be even more pronounced online (Tewksbury and Rittenberg, 2012). The long-term implications are likely to be a more unequal democracy, as the common knowledge of yesteryear becomes uncommon, and some have speculated that fragmentation over time may imperil the very social cohesion, political integration, and imagined sense of shared community that underlie modern nation states Katz, 1996).

It is clear that some of the trends towards audience fragmentation seen in the United States and discussed by Prior and others are also present across Western Europe as the number of television channels available increases and more and more households get access to broadband internet connections. Competition for media users' attention has never been as fierce as today. And yet, audiences are not as fragmented, even in large and heterogeneous Western European countries like France and Germany, as they are in the United States. Retaining a focus on the largest television channels in light of the importance assigned to broadcast news as the provider of common knowledge, a sense of imagined community, and accessible information about public affairs, one can compare the degrees of audience fragmentation in different countries by comparing the combined share of the three most widely watched television channels respectively. Figure 9.1 presents developments from 2000 to 2009 in this regard in the United States, France, and Germany.

As is clear from Figure 9.1, audience fragmentation is not only far more pronounced in the United States, where the three networks together commanded a modest 16 per cent audience share by 2009. Fragmentation has also *increased* more rapidly in the United States than in France or Germany as the three largest channels have lost a third of their combined share from 2000 to 2009. France has a far less fragmented television audience, especially because of the strength of the private commercial broadcaster TF1, but also because of the relative popularity of the two most widely watched public service channels, France 2 and France 3. In 2000, the combined share of these three channels was not far from that enjoyed by ABC, CBS, and NBC combined in the United States in 1970. Fragmentation in France has increased from 2000 to 2009 as each of the major channels has lost about a quarter of its audience share, but less rapidly than in the United States. Germany, in contrast, seems more stable. In 2000, it was, with its high proportion of multi-channel households with cable or satellite

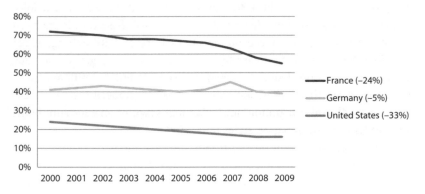

Figure in parentheses is the change in combined audience share.

Source: European Audiovisual Observatory and the Project for Excellence in Journalism.

Figure 9.1 Combined audience of top three channels (2000–9) in France, Germany, and the US

access, a good deal more fragmented than France (though less so than the United States). But both of the public service broadcasters (ARD and ZDF) and the main private commercial broadcaster (RTL) in Germany, accustomed to competition, retained most of their audience share over the decade, losing on average only about 5 per cent of their share from 2000 to 2009. Astonishingly, though the American population is almost four times the German population, the most widely watched German newscast, ARD's *Tagesschau*, draws more viewers in absolute numbers than any television news programme in the United States. While TF1 *News* in France falls behind both the ABC and NBC evening newscasts in terms of average audience, its approximately 7 million regular viewers is still more than the regular viewership of the CBS *Evening News*, available to a population more than five times that of France. (These patterns are not limited to television. Local newspapers outstrip national ones in circulation and reach in both France and Germany, but both countries have a far more widely circulated national press than the United States. This is also clear online, where the websites of the most important broadcasters and national newspapers reach significant parts of the French and German populations on a routine basis whereas online news in the United States is somewhat less centralised.)

An accelerated news cycle

Since the 1980 launch of CNN as the first 24-hour television news channel, American political journalism has moved at a faster and faster pace. Online publication, first on the websites of legacy media like broadcasters and newspapers, then increasingly also from stand-alone news websites, and now additionally also by individual journalists (and sometimes citizens and political actors) breaking news via blogs, Twitter and Facebook, has further accelerated the news cycle.

From the outset, CNN stood out from the orderly packaged news provided by the morning newspaper and the evening news programme with its rolling, round-the-clock, steady stream of stories. Often derided by print reporters as well as network news competitors as breathless in its reporting of inconsequential events marked more by their 'now-ness' than their newsworthiness, the cable channel gradually established itself and drew larger audiences during times of heightened interest, like the 1991 Gulf War. Today, CNN itself sometimes seems staid when compared to the market-leading cable news channel, the conservative Fox News, as well as

181

to the liberal-leaning MSNBC – both of which have overtaken it in terms of prime-time viewership.

Despite their rise to prominence over the last 30 years, it is important to keep in mind that all-news channels still reach only a relatively limited number of Americans directly on a regular basis. Cable news is a widely used source of information about politics as people dip in and out to sample the rolling news, but the median prime-time viewership of Fox News in 2011 was under 2 million, a fraction of what ABC, CBS, and NBC News drew; and, on the basis of detailed audience data, James G. Webster (2008) has shown that the average Fox News viewer still spends more time watching network news than watching the ideologically charged cable channel. Similarly, continually updated news websites draw impressive audiences, but most Americans continue to spend more time with offline news sources than with online ones.[4]

But even without dominating news provision to the broader public, rolling news on dedicated cable channels and a growing number of increasingly important news websites (both free-standing and those associated with legacy media) still change the way in which American political journalism functions as they speed up the production cycle itself, influencing how stories evolve and spread across platforms as well as changing the relationship between journalists and their sources. From the outset, the immediacy of rolling news has increased the tension between the two parts of the journalistic dictum 'get it first, but get it right' (Tuggle et al., 2010). The Pulitzer Prize-winning reporter Dean Starkman has decried what he calls the 'hamster wheel' of contemporary journalism, the constant churning out of an ever-growing number of stories by a reduced number of reporters who are ever more dependent on their increasingly professional sources feeding the bottomless editorial and managerial demand for breaking news (Starkman, 2010).

The rise of rolling news and of the accelerated news cycle has forced politicians to respond to ever more inquiries from ever more media at an ever faster pace, or risk that others beat them to it and 'take control of the narrative.' The White House communications team can no longer limit its focus to the television networks, the Associated Press, and the most prestigious big-city newspapers, or even to these 'high modern' news media plus the cable news channels. They also have to contend with a growing number of all-news, politics-only news sites tailored to an inside-the-beltway DC-oriented audience. The most important is arguably *Politico*, launched in 2007, and widely seen as an important influence on conversations in the capital. Mark Leibovich (2010) captures the site's new-found centrality well in a profile published in the *New York Times Magazine*: 'Before he goes to sleep, between 11 and midnight, Dan Pfeiffer, the White House communications director, typically checks in by e-mail with the same reporter: Mike Allen of *Politico*, who is also the first reporter Pfeiffer corresponds with after he wakes up at 4:20.' By contrast, the Bush White House press secretary, Scott McClellan (2008), describes how as late as 2006 he would still begin his morning routine with the print editions of the *New York Times*, the *Wall Street Journal*, and the *Washington Post*.

The increasing pressures on politicians to respond immediately to everything and the increased investment made by political actors keen to shape news coverage suggest that the news media have in some ways become more important as an institution. But at the same time the accelerated news cycle and the increased demand for content seem to have given at least some political sources more power to pressure individual reporters and influence news coverage that, even as it is voluminous and sometimes overwhelming, is also mostly reactive. President Obama's top political adviser, David Axelrod, has captured the situation clearly in an interview with Ken Auletta of the *New Yorker*: 'There are some really good journalists there, really superb ones. But the volume of material they have to produce just doesn't leave [them with] a whole lot of time for reflection.' In the same article, Auletta (2010) goes on to describe the typical daily workload of Chuck Todd, chief White House correspondent for NBC *Nightly News* (the most widely watched evening newscast) – in a typical day in 2010, Todd would do eight to sixteen stand-up interviews for NBC or MSNBC, host his show, the *Daily Rundown*, appear on other programmes including *Today* and *Morning Joe*, tweet or post to Facebook eight to ten times, and write three to five blog posts. Obviously, this is very different from focusing on just one daily evening newscast.

Trends towards acceleration are also pronounced in much of Western Europe, though not necessarily in the form of rolling-news television channels (which have not always taken off to the same extent). In Germany, for example, the most popular news channels, n-tv and N24, are both commercial channels with limited journalistic resources. They serve more as 'documentary channels' than round-the-clock news services (Reinemann and Fawzi, 2010). There, as Carsten Reinemann and Philip Baugut describe in Chapter 4 of this book, the accelerated news cycle is driven more by the constantly updated websites of major news organisations like the tabloid *Bild* and the news magazine *Spiegel* and the spread of social media like Twitter amongst journalists and politicians.

Partisan polarisation

American political journalism has not only become more fragmented and more accelerated in recent years. It has also become more partisan, partly in response to the political polarisation discussed above. The ideologically differentiated cable news channels, Fox News and MSNBC, arguably remain the most prominent examples of the growing number of American news media that reject the traditional professional journalistic aspirations of objectivity, detachment, and impartiality and embrace a clearer position. Other important examples include talk radio on the AM band (from national celebrity hosts like Rush Limbaugh and Sean Hannity to their local equivalents, overwhelmingly from the right), individual brand-name media personalities like the conservatives Andrew Breitbart, Glenn Beck, and Tucker Carlson, self-styled 'guerrilla journalists' like James O'Keefe, and a number of important political blogs dominated by the progressive community blog Daily Kos and the liberal-leaning news aggregator and opinion site the Huffington Post as well as less popular but still significant right-wing sites like Little Green Footballs and Townhall. com. Though most Americans still rely on mainstream news media (in a 2011 Pew survey, 63 per cent of respondents said they prefer news with no particular point of view), elected officials and other political actors have had to contend with the rise of these new, more explicitly partisan and increasingly widely used media (Pew Research Center, 2011).

The ongoing tensions between some conservative politicians and the news media were on display throughout the George W. Bush presidency, where the White House explicitly regarded the national news media as 'just another special interest group' (McClellan, 2008). The conflict between liberal politicians and more conservative media outlets in turn flared in a very public fashion after the election of President Obama in 2008. The incoming Democratic administration manoeuvered to marginalise Fox News by limiting access and excluding it from some briefings it had had routine access to under the Bush administration. In October 2009, things came to a head after months of tensions. White House communications director Anita Dunn dismissed Fox News as 'opinion journalism masquerading as news' in an interview with the news magazine *Time* and later said in a live interview on CNN that it often 'operates almost as either the research arm or the communications arm of the Republican Party'. Things further escalated in late October as the Obama administration apparently sought to exclude Fox News from an interview while admitting the rest of the press pool. The Washington bureau chiefs of ABC, CBS, NBC, and CNN announced they would refuse the invitation unless Fox News was also included. The administration subsequently invited all five channels. (The whole episode caused some debate and Dunn left her position soon after.)

The 2009 controversy illustrates some re-emergent tensions between the majority of American political journalists and the news media organisations who still aim for objectivity, detachment, and impartiality, their more partisan competitor-compatriots, and the politicians they cover. It is clear that things are changing in parts of the media landscape. While former *Washington Post* executive editor Len Downie and the well-known PBS *NewsHour* anchor Jim Lehrer famously did not even vote, lest they imperil their political impartiality, the former MSNBC *Countdown* host Keith Olberman donated thousands of dollars to several Democratic candidates for Congress (and was suspended for this violation of NBC rules) and Fox News president and former Republican political consultant Roger Ailes apparently actively tried to recruit General David Petraeus to run for the Republican nomination for president (even as his channel assiduously covered the very same primary election).

So far partisan polarisation in the news media has probably changed politics and politically engaged partisan minorities more than it has impacted the less politically interested popular majority, but the consequences can be felt beyond the beltway bubble. Faced as they are with a growing number of available sources of news, Natalie Stroud (2011) has shown how 'partisan selective exposure' – people choosing media that match their own views – is a growing phenomenon for Americans. (In terms of online media use, various commentators have expressed parallel concerns over 'cyber-Balkanisation' or the emergence of 'filter bubbles'.) Stroud argues that partisan news consumption has no adverse effects on how much people know about politics, and tends to keep them more informed than more impartial news consumption does, but also contributes to a further political polarisation of the electorate. Other researchers have suggested this latter phenomenon is particularly pronounced on the right side of the political spectrum, where a veritable 'echo chamber' encompassing the editorial pages of the *Wall Street Journal*,

Fox News with its rolling news and many high-profile conservative hosts, as well as the wildly popular talk-radio programmes hosted by Rush Limbaugh, Sean Hannity, and others (plus the web editions of each and a growing number of conservative political blogs) has created an 'enclave hospitable to conservative beliefs' where a growing number of like-minded audience members are reinforced in their beliefs, encouraged to regard mainstream news organisations with suspicion, drawn closer to the Republican Party, and distanced from their more moderate or liberal fellow Americans (Jamieson and Capella, 2008).

The re-emergence of significant partisan media is a relatively recent phenomenon in the United States, only really taking off from the 1990s onwards. In much of Western Europe, by contrast, partisan media have been a staple of the media environment throughout the postwar period. While television news has often been dominated by state-owned public service broadcasters and commercial channels subject to impartiality rules, national newspaper markets have long been far more ideologically diverse and polarised than even cable television is in contemporary America. France has titles with editorial lines ranging from communist (*L'Humanité*), left-leaning and liberal (*Le Monde* and *Libération*), and moderately conservative (*Le Figaro*) to a paper closely aligned with Roman Catholic values (*La Croix*). Germany has no far-right national newspapers but still offers a wide range stretching from the new left TAZ (*Die Tageszeitung*) to the more conservative FAZ (*Frankfurter Allgemeine Zeitung*) – all of course compete with a full range of digital offerings too. Partisanship in the media is thus nothing new in Western Europe, and many researchers suggest that recent years have seen more media de-alignment than increased political polarisation (see for instance Chapter 4 on Germany).

The increased importance of non-journalistic actors

Whereas American political journalism in the 1970s and 1980s was dominated by the institutionalised interplay between reporters and their (mostly official) sources, with almost everyone else excluded or consigned to a passive role as spectators, in recent years a growing range of non-journalistic actors has played an increasingly important role in shaping and disseminating news and information about public affairs. Two lines that defined 'high modern' journalism have become more blurred: first, the line between news and entertainment; second, the line between mass communication and mediated interpersonal sharing of news.

The first development, the rise of so-called 'infotainment', is often traced back to Bill Clinton playing the saxophone on MTV's *Arsenio Hall* show in the run-up to the 1992 presidential election. There had of course been an undercurrent of sensationalised and tabloid media content accompanying mainstream news and political journalism long before that, but it is striking that politicians increasingly seem to seek out entertainment programmes as part of their communication strategies, and that a growing number especially of young Americans report that they got much of their information about public affairs from these shows (Williams and Delli Carpini, 2011). The *Tonight Show with Jay Leno* on NBC and the *Late Night Show with David Letterman* on CBS have become frequent stops for prominent politicians and, in October 2012, President Obama made a priority of appearing on Jon Stewart's *Daily Show* on the cable channel Comedy Central in the run-up to the election. Some politicians do not stop at being guests of the infotainment industry, but take a step further to become permanent parts of it – including most prominently the former Republican vice-presidential candidate Sarah Palin, who not only started a political action committee (SarahPAC) after the 2008 election and kept toying publicly with running for office again, but also published a best-selling campaign memoir, embarked on a lucrative speaking tour, served as the anchor of the Fox News series *Real American Stories*, and starred in her own reality programme *Sarah Palin's Alaska* on the cable channel TLC. No one seems to challenge the fact that various soft news, 'infotainment', and all-out entertainment genres have become more important parts of American political communications since the 1990s, though researchers disagree over the implications. Some argue that these genres mean that otherwise politically inattentive people are exposed to useful information about public affairs, somewhat countering the knowledge gaps that result from audience fragmentation (Baum, 2002), but others suggest there is only limited evidence that people actually learn much from this exposure (Prior, 2003). (The rise of infotainment and politicians' involvement in entertainment programmes is a hotly discussed issue in Europe too, though some researchers suggest the line between politics and entertainment may be less blurred in, for instance, France (Kuhn, 2004).)

The second development, the blurring between mass and inter-personal communication, is a more recent phenomenon and is more closely tied to the spread of digital and networked technologies. Especially easy-to-use web 2.0 tools like blogs, comment and share functions of websites, and social networking sites like Facebook seem to facilitate rapid change in how people engage with news and politics (Tewksbury and Rittenberg, 2012). Elected officials, journalists, and other professional opinion-makers use these tools to comment on the issues of the day, but a growing number of individual bloggers from outside the traditional DC circles have also managed to establish themselves as active parts of what Andrew Chadwick (2011) suggests we call the 'political information cycle' (because it is no longer simply about the news). Individual entrepreneurs like Matt Drudge of the Drudge Report, Joshua Marshall of Talking Points Memo, Markos Moulitsas of Daily Kos, and Charles Johnson of Little Green Footballs have not only built sizeable audiences of their own and sometimes lively communities around their sites without having to maintain the kind of organisational overhead traditionally associated with, say, a political monthly magazine. They have also at key moments influenced mainstream news coverage of politics and public affairs either on their own or through what Lucas Graves (2007) has called 'distributed news analysis', where networks of mutually sympathetic bloggers and their users have broken stories or shed new light on existing storylines. So far, France and Germany have seen fewer bloggers and online-only sites establish themselves as important parts of the news and information cycle, though the investigative journalism site Mediapart has broken important political stories in France and media-watch blogs like BildBlog.de guard the guardians in the German media system (Bruno and Nielsen, 2012).

Potentially more profound than various forms of elite use of digital and networked technologies, however, is the role played by what Jay Rosen (2006) has dubbed the 'people formerly known as the audience', the sizeable minority of ordinary people who actively share news content, comment on it, and mix it using internet tools like email and the functionality of news organisations' own websites where these allow for commenting and forwarding of information, as well as easily accessible blogging platforms like Blogger, Livejournal, or Wordpress and widely used social networking sites like Facebook and Twitter. These more web-native and social ways of accessing news are increasingly widespread in all countries with high levels of internet access, but a recent 2012 Reuters Institute survey of the media habits of online news users in a range of Western democracies suggests they are more developed in the United States than elsewhere. Using online-only sources like aggregators and accessing news via social networking sites like Facebook is significantly

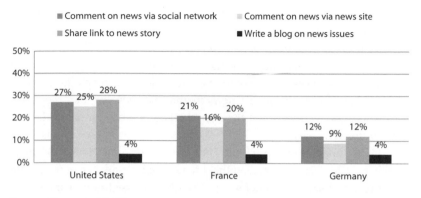

Source: Newman (2012).

Figure 9.2 Participatory news use (2012) in France, Germany, and the US

more widespread amongst American online news users than amongst their counterparts in France and Germany, though all three countries have similar levels of internet access and use. The same trends apply for more 'participatory' forms of news use, like commenting on news via either social media platforms or news websites, as well as sharing links to stories. Figure 9.2 shows the percentage of online news users in the United States, France, and Germany that report they engage in these activities as well as blogging. In general, more American online news users actively comment on and share news content than amongst French and German online news users. In all three countries, only a small minority of 4 per cent engage in more time-consuming participatory forms of news use like blogging.

Declining trust in news

Since the end of journalistic 'high modernism' and the 'age of broadcast news', America has seen a dramatically reduced public trust in the traditional mainstays of political news, including national broadcasting networks, daily newspapers, and the journalistic profession itself. The Pew Research Center for the People and the Press has time series going back to the mid-1980s suggesting a substantial increase in the percentage of Americans who think that news stories are often inaccurate (from 34 per cent in 1985 to 66 per cent in 2011), that the news tends to favour one political party over another (from 53 to 77 per cent), and that news media are often influenced by powerful people and organisations (53 to 80 per cent) (Pew Research Center, 2011). News media can find some solace in the fact that the American population still trusts both local and national news media more than they trust the federal government, state and local government, or business corporations, and that most people have much higher regard for the particular news media that *they* use than they have for media more generally, but the overall trend is a substantial decline in trust in the news over time.

In his book *Why Americans Hate the Media and How It Matters*, Jonathan Ladd (2012) has argued that the reduced confidence in the media is the result of several developments already discussed here, namely: (1) increasingly polarised national politics leading to increased partisan elite criticism of the media and (2) increased competition between financially pressured commercial news organisations leading to some tendencies towards tabloidisation, especially in television news. (One can speculate that recent plagiarism scandals like Jayson Blair's years of serial fabrication at the *New York Times* and Jonah Lehrer's self-plagiarism at the *New Yorker* have done little to increase confidence.) Ladd argues that the reduced trust in mainstream news organisations means that people are less likely to let their views be influenced by news coverage and makes them more likely to seek out media outlets that confirm their pre-existing views, self-selecting along the lines already discussed above.

The international World Values Survey includes cross-national data on confidence in the press specifically that puts the American experience into perspective. Figure 9.3 includes data on the percentage of respondents who expressed 'a great deal' or 'quite a lot' of confidence in the press in France, Germany, and the United States in the four survey waves of 1981/1982, 1990, 1999/2000 and 2005/2006.

The trend in the World Values Survey data clearly corresponds to the Pew studies and other American studies suggesting a substantially reduced confidence in the press in the United States, especially from the early to the late 1990s – coinciding with the growth of increasingly partisan cable news, the emergence of various online-only news sites, and increased political polarisation, especially at the national level. Developments in France and Germany are much more stable, with moderate trust in the press throughout the period and no dramatic changes.

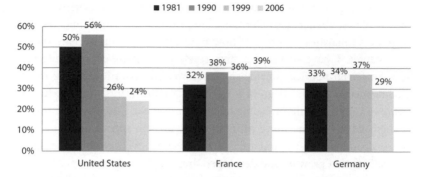

Source: World Values Survey 1981/1982, 1990, 1999/2000, and 2005/2006, respondents answering 'a great deal' or 'quite a lot' of confidence in the press. US data from 1982, 1990, 1999, and 2006, France and Germany from 1981, 1990, 2000, and 2006. Data for Germany for 1981 and 1990 are for West Germany only, 2000 and 2006 for the reunified Germany. France was not part of the 1995/1996 survey wave so that year is excluded here.

Figure 9.3   Confidence in the press (1981–2006) in France, Germany and the US

Conclusion

As made clear from the outset, American political journalism differs from political journalism in Western Europe – here exemplified by France and Germany – in important, persistent, and systemic ways. Political journalism is a highly endogenous institution, deeply shaped by the structure of and developments in political systems and media systems. At these systemic levels, the United States remains very different from most Western European countries, both in terms of its increasingly polarised political scene and the massive growth in the resources available to political actors as they wrangle over public support and their various policy agendas in a permanent campaign and in terms of the severity of the crisis facing news media organisations in what remains a commercially dominated media system amongst major Western democracies. It is not clear that there has been any substantial 'Americanisation' of Western European political or media systems at these levels over the last decade, even as individual Western European politicians and media organisations have often strategically adopted practices, strategies, and organisational forms originally developed in America for their own purposes (Nielsen, 2012a).

191

But deep and durable as the systemic differences are between the United States, France, and Germany, there do at the same time seem to be some similarities in terms of how political journalism is changing. In this chapter, I have focused on five facets of contemporary changes in how American political journalism functions. All five pre-date the rise of the internet to various degrees – Daniel C. Hallin (1992) and W. Russell Neuman (1991) pointed to some of them in the early 1990s – but several of them have become more pronounced with the spread of digital and networked technologies, and are likely to become even more important as generations that grew up and developed their media habits in a mass media environment gradually give way to so-called 'digital natives' (Tewksbury and Rittenberg, 2012). The five facets are: (1) increased audience fragmentation, (2) an accelerated news cycle, (3) some tendencies towards partisan polarisation in the media, (4) the increased importance of non-journalistic actors in shaping and sharing news, and (5) declining trust in traditional sources of political news. The full impact of these trends on political journalism in America and elsewhere is yet to be understood, but from the evidence and research available so far it seems that though developments differ in some important ways, the trends towards audience fragmentation, an accelerated news cycle, and the increasing importance of non-journalistic actors are also to be found in France and Germany. Partisan polarisation in the media, in contrast, is nothing new in Western Europe, where national newspaper markets have long been ideologically diverse and differentiated, and the marked decline in confidence in the press seen in the United States is not to be found in France and Germany, where people never trusted newspapers as much as Americans did as recently as in the 1980s.

Broad generalisations like 'Americanisation' (or 'Europeanisation') are probably more rhetorically attractive than analytically useful when it comes to understanding developments in media, journalism, and communications around the world. However, if we stick to the question lurking behind them, this chapter argues that the systemic differences – even within the world of similarly affluent, Western democracies – remain pronounced and persistent, and that the similarities in terms of contemporary changes represent a mixed picture where a number of developments that first became apparent in the United States are also increasingly found in Western Europe, but where facets that have long been features of Western European media systems are also becoming apparent in the United States. In all three countries considered here, political journalism remains an important, integral, and institutionalised part of politics and the media. It is also changing in all three countries: in France and Germany in ways discussed elsewhere in this book, and in the United States in ways that leave media and communication no less central to politics but do pit weakened news media and a reduced number of often overworked journalists against increasingly polarised and powerful political actors even as large parts of the public seem to have turned away and lost confidence in both sides.

Notes

1 As Blumler and Gurevich, who have written extensively about differences and similarities between political communication in the United States and Western Europe, rightly commented more than ten years ago (2001: 381), such cross-national analysis has to be regularly updated.

2 www.cfinst.org/pdf/vital/VitalStats_t2.pdf (accessed 11 February 2013).

3 http:/stateofthemedia.org/2004/overview/news-investment(accessed 11 February 2013).

4 Television remains the main source of political information for most people, and in 2012 the combined number of daily unique visitors to newspaper websites was 25 million according to the Newspaper Association of America, but the total readership of newspaper content across all platforms, including print, web, and mobile, was more than 100 million adults. See Hendricks (2012) and Newspaper Association of America (2013).

10

Changing Political News? Long-Term Trends in American, British, French, Italian, German, and Swiss Print Media Reporting

Andrea Umbricht and Frank Esser

Introduction

Two opposing perspectives are prevalent in international comparative journalism research. The first assumes that political journalism in Western media systems has undergone a slow but definite standardisation since the 1960s – driven by the diffusion of Anglo-American professional standards, the influence of global news leaders such as the BBC, the *New York Times*, Reuters, and the Associated Press, and the imitation of reporting techniques proved to be professionally (journalism prizes) or commercially (audience responses) successful in the Anglo-American world. In addition, the emergence of global media markets and technological standards as well as European integration and the Americanisation of popular culture are seen as further forces driving the homogenisation of media. The opposite perspective does not deny these tendencies but argues that these processes will not eradicate deep-seated differences in national media structures and news cultures. These systemic differences have led Daniel C. Hallin and Paolo Mancini (2004) to develop three 'models' of Western media systems which, according to them, have shown their distinct contours most clearly in the 1960s and 1970s. Since then, they argue, Western media systems have become partially more similar without losing their different identities. The authors support their thesis of the continued relevance of the three models with evidence gathered mainly at the institutional level of media systems. What they do not examine, however, is the content produced by news media. In this chapter, we aim to fill this gap by examining systematically whether the political news coverage produced by print media in six Western media systems has retained its characteristic differences over time or whether the content produced in different systems has become gradually more alike.

The comparative approach: three models of media and politics

The field of comparative political communication research has steadily grown during the last decades. Several scholars have theorised about and investigated empirically the influences of national media systems and political and cultural contexts (e.g. Blumler and Gurevitch, 2001; Pfetsch, 2001; Semetko et al., 1991), and identified different models of journalism after comparing historical roots and contemporary practices (e.g. Mancini, 2005; Williams, 2005). These works are consistent with a framework developed by Hallin and Mancini (2004) that uses four media-related and five politics-related dimensions to differentiate types of political communication systems. The media-related dimensions are the development of an audience-oriented and commercialised mass press; parallelism between party lines and newspaper lines; journalistic professionalism and independence; and the degree of state intervention in the regulation of media. The five politics-related dimensions concern the role of the state in society; majoritarian or consensus character of the political system; patterns of interest group organisation; distinction between moderate and polarised pluralism; and development of rational–legal authority in contrast to clientelist forms of social organisation.

On this basis, Hallin and Mancini establish three ideal typical models that form the theoretical backbone of our analysis: the liberal model, the democratic corporatist model, and the polarised pluralist model. They categorise as *liberal* those countries where press freedom and mass-circulation press developed early, where state interference in the media sector is low, and where parallelism between political parties and editorial preferences of newspapers is also low. On the other hand, internal pluralism in newspapers is high, as is the professional status and political independence of journalists. The established textbook history argues that news organisations in this model gained independence from party-political bonds in the middle of the nineteenth century when commercial pressures began to push partisanship out of newspapers (Chalaby, 1996:

320). The US press is often presented as a case in point. Here, newspapers became prosperous in the 1880s because they increased their readership by reducing one-sided propaganda (Fengler and Russ-Mohl, 2008: 679). The fact that newspapers supplanted commentaries by news reports facilitated the spread of the objectivity norm and boosted revenues from sales and advertising (Chalaby, 1996: 303). Canada and Ireland are other countries grouped as liberal, as is, with some restrictions, Great Britain.

The *polarised pluralist* model features an elite-oriented press with limited overall circulation. Journalism here originates as an extension of the worlds of literature and politics and has historically been an elite occupation. The literary and political roots can be seen in the strong presence of commentaries, intellectual analysis, political judgement, and ideological tendencies (Benson and Hallin, 2007: 35). Newspapers are largely focused on politics and distinguished by relatively strong external pluralism and advocacy journalism. Political parallelism dominated for most of the twentieth century, and the tradition of partisan newspapers overlapped with the practice of instrumentalisation. Many newspapers did not become financially independent and stayed reliant on the goodwill and support of political parties, the state, and/or influence-seeking owners (Hallin and Mancini, 2004: 114; Hallin and Papathanassopoulos, 2002: 18). Press freedom developed late, professionalisation was weak, and the autonomy of journalists was limited. At the national level of polarised pluralist systems, formal accountability systems like press councils are absent, professional organisations and journalists' unions are generally weak, and there is little consensus on ethical standards in the media (Rieffel, 1984). Spain, Portugal, and Italy are classified in this model, as is, with some restrictions, France.

The *democratic corporatist* model includes countries with an early development of press freedom, high newspaper circulation, and strong journalistic professionalisation. The historically strong political parallelism in the media bears traces of external pluralism and slightly partisan and advocate opinion journalism. Partisan journalism is rooted in the close ties to politics through corporatist bargaining and interest negotiations. It coexists with a high level of professionalism which is evident in the widespread recognition of ethical norms regardless of journalists' political affiliations (Williams, 2005: 66). Systems belonging to this model include Belgium, the Netherlands, Denmark, and the other Nordic countries, as well as Germany and Switzerland.

Naturally these models represent theoretical ideal types, and some real-world cases cannot be categorised easily. For instance, the liberal model suggests a professional emphasis on neutrality but much British newspaper journalism shows remarkable degrees of political parallelism and is more adequately assigned a mid-position between US professionalism and continental European partisan tendencies (Schudson, 2001: 167). The notion 'Anglo-American' refers to the numerous commonalities between the British and US media and political systems (liberal democracies with little state intervention in the press, majoritarian political systems, two large catch-all parties, many catch-all newspapers, etc.), but obscures some very important differences (the greater role of public broadcasting, press partisanship, tabloid news culture, and competition in Britain). It is thus necessary to ask whether such an Anglo-American model really exists (Mancini, 2005: 78). France is another mixed case, falling between the polarised pluralist and democratic corporatist models. It is characterised by a strong role of the state, polarised pluralism, and a history of strong political parallelism, but also by a relatively strong mass-oriented regional press and a more developed tradition of rational-legal authority that favour a more fact-oriented news style.

Our study examines how relevant Hallin and Mancini's typology of media systems is in terms of explaining news coverage produced by print media embedded in each of these systems, a relationship that many scholars have noted we know little about (e.g. Jones, 2007: 130). We derive hypotheses from the aforementioned models and relate them directly to measurable characteristics of news content. We then compare the results of a content analysis with the expectations derived from the theoretical models. We are thus in a position to examine whether the historical and structural differences behind the models are reflected in political news coverage and whether there is a blurring of reporting styles over time due to globalisation, commercialisation, diffusion, and European integration.

Theoretical dimensions and hypotheses

The first content-related indicator that can be expected to differentiate journalistic output across Western press systems is *opinion-orientation* in the news (Benson and Hallin, 2007; Strömbäck and Dimitrova, 2006; Wessler et al., 2010). Journalism in continental European systems has often been found to be more opinionated than in liberal media systems

(Hallin and Mancini, 2004: 61–3). Surveys have also repeatedly shown that journalists from continental European systems subscribe to more active reporting roles and are more comfortable with advocating a political position than their Anglo-American colleagues who see themselves as detached observers (Donsbach and Patterson, 2004; Hanitzsch, 2011). The proximity of the journalistic profession to the literary field and the later differentiation from the political sphere have contributed to a greater emphasis on commentary and advocacy in European journalism – particularly in the Mediterranean countries – than in the Anglo-American tradition. We thus expect elements of opinion-orientation to be highest in newspapers from polarised pluralist systems. The second-highest level of opinion-orientation may be expected in newspapers from the democratic corporatist model where, due to a residual element of historical political parallelism and systems characterised by external pluralism, opinionated news will be more widespread than in the Anglo-American system (Wessler et al., 2010: 237). Finally, in line with the standardisation hypothesis discussed above, we expect the level of opinion-orientation in the news to converge over time, reflecting a growing professional consensus about the norms of news reporting, in particular with regard to the inclusion of journalistic voice.

H 1.1:   The degree of opinion-orientation in the news is highest in polarised pluralist news systems and lowest in the US news system.

H 1.2:   Due to globalisation and the spread of critical professionalism, the level of opinion-orientation in the news has converged in Western media systems over time.

The second concept that is assumed to distinguish the reporting pattern in the three models is *objectivity*. Vos (2012: 436) argues that objective journalism refers to 'an emphasis on verifiable facts, a factual arrangement of the news, reporting that accurately reflects events, impartial and balanced reporting and writing, a detached and impersonal point of view, and the separation of news and editorial functions of the news organization'. Objectivity is strongly rooted in the US context and distinguishes American journalism from a more interpretive European tradition (Donsbach, 1995). According to the US objectivity principle, journalists should report the news without commenting on it and present each side of a debate (Schudson, 2001: 150). Mancini (2000: 273) argues that it is far easier for Anglo-American journalists to exercise objectivity and political neutrality because of the limitation of political choice arising from the two-party system. The prompt transmission of facts, expert sources, and eyewitness accounts became the cornerstone of the Anglo-American model (Williams, 2005: 63), and this new press used a straightforward language, separating newspapers from more elite political outlets (Mancini, 2005: 79). Journalists claim objectivity by citing procedures they follow which exemplify the formal attributes of a news story. Such strategies enhance the credibility of news stories and help journalists defend themselves against outside criticism. These formal attributes are presentation of conflicting possibilities; presentation of supporting facts that speak for themselves; use of quotation marks; story structure that follows an inverted pyramid; and the formal separation of facts and opinion (Tuchman, 1972: 665–70). We expect these professional routines to be used the least in newspapers from polarised pluralist systems because journalistic professionalism is weaker, training standards lower, and rational-legal authority less developed in these countries – all characteristics that should result in less respect for norms and standardised procedures of behaviours (Mancini, 2007b: 15). We expect political news coverage in democratic corporatist systems to be slightly less objective than in Anglo-American systems due to the historically strong political parallelism that has left some commentary-oriented journalism in Northern Europe. US newspapers will use these techniques most frequently because they fit the higher levels of market orientation and journalistic professionalisation. Second, we assume a rise in objective reporting from the 1960s to today because of the growing commercialised character of Western media systems, rising educational standards, and the diffusion of particular professional norms (Hallin and Mancini, 2004: 272–3; Mancini, 2000: 268).

H 2.1: The use of professional routines demonstrating adherence to the ideal of objectivity is highest in US news stories and lowest in polarised Mediterranean news stories. Britain and France are borderline cases of their respective models.

H 2.2: Due to rising commercialisation, journalistic professionalisation, and the expanding recognition of objectivity as a key attribute of independent news, the level of objectivity has generally risen throughout Western media systems over time.

The third theoretical criterion is *negativity*, meaning a preference for bad instead of good news. It often comes in the form of reports on problems, failings, confrontations, attacks, scandals, or political incompetence. Research has identified certain 'drivers' that help predict levels of negativity in the news. First, journalists may simply reflect a political culture in which political institutions enjoy low levels of public confidence, polarised conflicts over fundamental ideological questions are frequent, or politicians attack each other regularly and stage controversy publicly in anticipation of its inherent news value. Second, a widely shared role perception of journalists being watchdogs of those holding political or economic power leads to a press coverage that keeps record of complaints, unresolved problems, and misbehaviours. Third, because negative political news can be presented in dramatic, eye-catching, and easy-to-understand ways it has an inherent appeal that may be exploited in commercially oriented media environments. Fourth, over time journalism may have undergone a generational shift towards critical scrutiny of politicians' motivations, exposing their strategies and blunders, and confronting each statement with a counterstatement by a known opponent. The desire to deconstruct politics is likely to be further enhanced by the presence of spin doctors and news management. The first driver is strong in the polarised pluralist systems whereas the other drivers are often associated with liberal systems. We therefore expect newspapers from the liberal systems to show the highest levels of negativity in the news, and the steepest increase over time. The newspapers from the polarised pluralist systems are expected to take a middle position and those from the consensus democracies of the corporatist model to rank lowest.

H 3.1: The level of negativity in the news is lower in the consensus-oriented democratic corporatist systems than in the Anglo-American or the Southern European systems.

H 3.2: Due to the spread of commercial pressures and critical professionalism the level of negativity in the news has increased across Western systems, with liberal systems showing the largest increase.

The three journalistic models should also diverge in terms of the access they grant to different *sources* in public discourse. Ferree and colleagues (2002: 86) use the term 'standing' to denote the voice given to actors in

201

the news. Standing is not the same as just being mentioned; it refers to actors being quoted or paraphrased in a story. Citing sources from direct observers is considered as a way of verification of the news, and as a method of providing competing arguments (Dimitrova and Strömbäck, 2009). Drawing on Wessler (2008), we expect the following threefold pattern. First, due to greater state intervention and closer relationships between the media and the political field, we assume political elite actors from parties and the state to be more prominent in Southern European media systems than in the Anglo-American ones (Benson and Hallin, 2007: 30; Ferree et al., 2002: 89). Second, we assume that organised social groups of civil society (i.e. trade union representatives, social movements, interest groups, employers' associations, religious organisations) play the largest role in newspapers of democratic corporatist systems and the smallest in Anglo-American countries (Hallin and Mancini, 2004: 74; Wessler, 2008: 231). Third, individual sources like ordinary citizens or experts are expected to be most prominent in the US press because of a greater emphasis on individual freedoms and interests (Ferree et al., 2002: 98; Wessler, 2008: 231).

H 4.1: (a) The standing of 'political elite sources' in the news is highest in polarised Mediterranean news systems and lowest in the Anglo-American ones. (b) The standing of 'organised social group sources' is highest in the corporatist systems and lowest in the Anglo-American ones. (c) The standing of 'individual sources' is highest in Anglo-American ones.

H 4.2: (a) The standing of 'political elite sources' in the news has shrunk in all news systems (due to a differentiation from the political field and due to new technologies for gathering information that reduce the journalists' dependence on official sources). (b) The standing of 'individual sources' has increased (due to an emphasis on vivid storytelling in the use of citizen sources, and a growing 'scientification' of the discourse in the use of expert sources).

Method

To systematically examine developments in print media coverage of politics in different media systems, we conducted a quantitative content analysis of 18 news outlets over a time span of five decades. The relevant details can be seen in Table 10.1. The USA, Britain, Germany, Switzerland, France, and Italy are selected to ensure that two countries from each of the three media system models developed by Hallin and Mancini are covered. The study examines randomly chosen routine phases of political affairs coverage from the years 1960–1 and 2006–7 to allow for long-time comparison. The early 1960s are commonly defined as the golden period of political press coverage characterised by large audiences and growing budgets whereas the late 2000s are marked by increasing global, digital, and commercial competition (see Tunstall, 1996, 2008).

From each of the six countries, we considered news outlets from three different print media sectors: national newspapers, regional newspapers, and weeklies. In each country we aimed for a national quality newspaper that serves as agenda setter, a regional paper to account for the regional structure of the press market, and a widely read and influential weekly.

Table 10.1 Sample of news outlets for cross-country analysis (1960s/2000s)

Models	Countries	News outlets	No. of articles	
			1960s	2000s
Liberal Anglo-American	United States (USA)	New York Times	130	88
		St. Louis Post-Dispatch	101	86
		Time Magazine	50	41
	Great Britain (GBR)	The Times	124	65
		Birmingham Mail	79	44
		Observer	114	67
Corporatist Germanic	Germany (GER)	Frankfurter Allgemeine Zeitung	120	193
		Rheinische Post	142	147
		Spiegel	30	50
	Switzerland (SWI)	Neue Zürcher Zeitung	59	96
		Berner Zeitung	49	112
		Weltwoche	48	51
Polarised Mediterranean	France (FRA)	Le Monde	76	128
		Ouest France	89	74
		L'Express	31	87
	Italy (ITA)	Corriere della Sera	60	231
		Resto del Carlino	57	154
		Espresso	46	93

Sample N=3,212 articles.

The peculiar British press market does not fit these selection criteria well. We opted for a regional tabloid that was exceptionally strong in the first half of our study period but which has subsequently come under massive pressure (like the great majority of British regionals); and we opted for a Sunday paper because the unusually strong British Sunday market has prevented news magazines (in the tradition of *Time*, *Spiegel*, and *L'Express*) from gaining a foothold.

We analysed two 24-month periods (1960–1 and 2006–7). From every second month of these periods we selected a randomly chosen issue from each newspaper and analysed all articles that contained political actors and were either printed or mentioned on the front page – irrespective of whether they offered news, commentary, or interviews. The focus on the front page ensures that all the articles considered most important by editors and most likely to be noticed by readers are included in the analysis (Strömbäck and Dimitrova, 2006).[1] For weeklies printed in magazine format the sampling procedure was adjusted to include: (a) the cover story plus those articles linked to the cover story in the table of contents, (b) all other stories mentioned on the cover, and (c) all articles prominently highlighted in the table of contents. This procedure yielded a total of N=3,212 political articles. They constitute the universe of this study (see Table 10.1).

Our data analysis is guided by our hypotheses, and the relevant concepts were operationalised as follows.

Opinion-orientation

Drawing on Benson and Hallin's (2007) study we coded each article with respect to its main journalistic function and included the following revised categories: 'straight news' (descriptive, concise); 'long news with background' (providing context); 'interpretation and analysis' (explanation, speculation); 'opinionated stories' (formal commentaries or information pieces mixed with opinion); or 'interviews'. Here we are only interested in the category of 'opinionated stories' which includes editorials, personal columns, commentary, and other types of story that heavily mix information with subjective assessments and evaluations.

Objectivity

Drawing on Tuchman (1972) we measured objectivity as a professional strategy that guides reporters on how to write a story that will be recognised as objective. We adopted her criteria, revised them slightly, and coded them as dichotomous variables at the story level: the presentation of opposing 'pro and con' viewpoints; the use of 'expert sources'; the use of 'direct quotations and indirect speech'; and a 'hard-facts-first structure'. Based on how often these four indicators were coded in stories from the six countries, we created an aggregate objectivity index for each story that sums up the four dichotomous sub-variables and ranges (based on a standardised formula) from 0 to 1.[2] For simplicity we will only report the aggregate indices in our analysis.

Negativity

We operationalised negativity by four sub-variables. First, we coded 'negative tone' if the tonality in a news report is pessimistic (for instance by referring to threats, risks, undesirable trends, antagonism, gloom). Second, we coded whether a 'conflict frame' was imposed on a story (for instance by zooming in on disputes and disagreements between political actors). Third, we coded 'political incompetence' if a story centres on political weaknesses and failings or displays scepticism toward the capabilities of a political actor. Fourth, we coded 'political scandals' if a story reports intense public communication about a real or imagined defect or misbehaviour in politics that provokes widespread indignation or outrage. As before, we constructed a standardised aggregate index from these four indicators that ranges (based on the same mathematical formula) from 0 to 1.

Use of sources

Sources are actors in a news story who are quoted with direct or indirect speech. Our coding categories are based on a typology developed by Benson and Hallin (2007) to which we added some minor modifications. To rate the prominence of 'political elites' in the news we measured quotations and paraphrases of the executive, legislative, and judiciary. To determine the salience of 'organised social groups' from civil society we coded the presence of trade union representatives, social movements or interest groups, employers' associations, and religious organisations. Finally, we measured the use of 'individual sources' in the form of quotes or paraphrases from ordinary citizens or experts.[3]

Results

News organisations are embedded – or institutionalised – in national environments that shape the practices within those organisations. Institutionalisation occurs through processes that are influenced by the political economy of the national media markets, national policy styles and regulatory approaches, and national reception prisms that audiences use to process political news as relevant. These and other forces have a socialisation effect on journalists that leads them to report the news in ways that are at least partially country specific. This means that the nation is a still meaningful framework for comparative analysis (see Donsbach and Patterson, 2004; Hallin and Mancini, 2004; Hanitzsch, 2011; Weaver, 1998) and a nationally comparative approach is adopted here as well.

Opinion-orientation

Hypothesis 1.1 presumes the degree of opinion-orientation (either in the form of clearly labelled commentaries or stories mixing information and opinion) to be lowest in news outlets embedded in the US press system and highest in outlets from polarised Mediterranean systems. As can be seen from Figure 10.1, the news coverage of the 1960s clearly supports Hypothesis 1.1. However, by the late 2000s the distinctions between the journalistic styles have become blurred and the use of opinion-oriented story types in the different press systems has become more similar.[4] Still, and as expected by our discussion of the journalism models, the frequency of opinionated news remains lowest in the US press throughout the entire period under investigation. In the 1960s, French and Italian newspapers do share a great fondness for opinionated journalism which clearly seems to reflect the partisan tradition of polarised pluralist systems. It also supports the results of an earlier comparative content analysis by Benson and Hallin (2007: 37) which found a higher inclination for opinion in French than US papers. This can be explained by commentary being traditionally the most celebrated form of writing in French news journalism (Chalaby, 1996: 315).

Hypothesis 1.2 expects the degree of opinion-orientation to converge in Western press systems. This is also clearly supported by our results. The US and particularly the British press have significantly increased their use of opinion-oriented stories and become more European in this regard. The French press, on the other hand, has significantly scaled

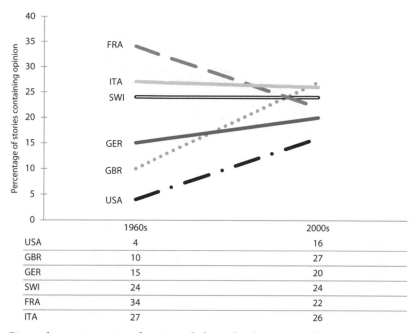

	1960s	2000s
USA	4	16
GBR	10	27
GER	15	20
SWI	24	24
FRA	34	22
ITA	27	26

Figure shows proportion of stories coded as either 'commentary' or 'stories mixing information with opinion'. Not depicted are the other story types: 'straight news', 'long background news', 'analysis and interpretation', and 'interview'. Based on N=3,212 stories.

Figure 10.1   Use of opinion in political coverage (1960s/2000s)

back its preference for opinion, presumably under the influence of global diffusion of professional values and transnational coorientation in the news media business. These findings also offer tentative support for our suspicion that Great Britain and France are borderline cases of their respective models.

Objectivity

Hypothesis 2.1 predicts that features associated with the strategic rituals of objectivity will be most visible in US news reports and least visible in Mediterranean stories, and it expects to find support for classifying Great Britain and France as mixed cases. These assumptions are supported by the results reported in Figure 10.2. Objectivity-related news practices are most

207

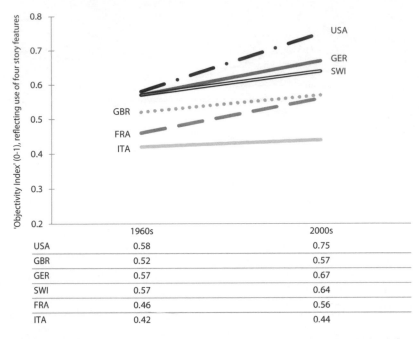

	1960s	2000s
USA	0.58	0.75
GBR	0.52	0.57
GER	0.57	0.67
SWI	0.57	0.64
FRA	0.46	0.56
ITA	0.42	0.44

Figure shows average frequency of four elements in political stories: inclusion of opposing 'pro and con' viewpoints, use of 'expert sources', use of 'direct quotations and indirect speech', a 'hard-facts-first structure' (aggregated to index; see method section). Based on N=3,009 stories.

Figure 10.2   Use of objectivity-related elements in political coverage (1960s/2000s)

prevalent in US papers and least so in French and Italian papers, although some interesting qualifications apply. First of all, British and French newspapers confirm their status as borderline cases that make them hard to classify. This is particularly true for the British press which has removed itself from the US understanding of objectivity considerably and makes the notion of an Anglo-American model of journalism (as championed by Chalaby, 1996) increasingly hard to sustain. The German papers show, on the other hand, that they have internalised the lessons provided by American instructors after World War II and diligently integrated them in their in-house training programmes. At least that is what the data suggest. The Swiss-German papers studied show great affinity with the press in neighbouring Germany.

Proceeding to Hypothesis 2.2 we find also clear support for our expectation that from the 1960s to the 2000s the ideal of objectivity has been increasingly disseminated and recognised in the Western press. The use of objectivity-related news practices has not declined in any of the six systems but it is remarkable that throughout the entire period the Italian press stays far behind in last place. The fact that objectivity-related reporting strategies have risen cross-nationally does not mean, however, that the press systems have become more similar in this respect. On the contrary: the gap between 'objective' and 'non-objective' news cultures has continued to grow.[5] In sum we can conclude that both our objectivity-related hypotheses have been confirmed.

Negativity

Our findings in Figure 10.3 illustrate that in the 1960s the levels of negativity in political news coverage varied significantly between the six press systems and that the levels of negativity have become even more dissimilar over time.[6] In the 1960s, the news stories in the consensus democracies of the democratic corporatist systems were the least negative, confirming our prediction in Hypothesis 3.1. However, counter to our expectations, we find that newspapers from the polarised pluralist systems report politics more negatively than newspapers from the liberal systems. We assumed the effects of commercialisation and critical professionalism in the Anglo-American systems would induce roughly similar levels of negativity to those produced by the effects of polarisation and inter-party contestation in the polarised systems. But it appears as if the effects of the political systems are stronger than those of the media system. We have no reason to believe that this somewhat surprising result is influenced by our methodology.[7] In fact, it is broadly in line with findings reported by Benson and Hallin (2007) and Benson (2010) who also describe French news reports as containing more critical coverage than US newspaper reports. This common finding seems to underscore that the high degree of ideological diversity in a multi-party system, the existence of anti-system political parties, and a tendency to question the legitimacy of political institutions foster high values of negativity in the polarised model.

Hypothesis 3.2 expects a growth in media negativity in all six press systems due to increased market-orientation, journalistic autonomy, and critical professionalism. However, this assumption is only partly supported. Negativity has risen significantly in the commercialised US

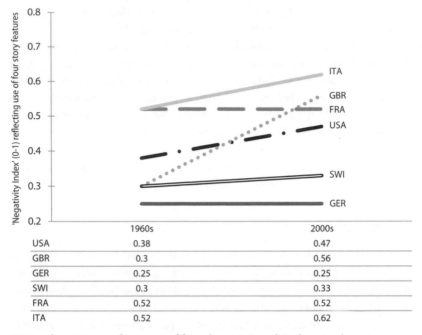

	1960s	2000s
USA	0.38	0.47
GBR	0.3	0.56
GER	0.25	0.25
SWI	0.3	0.33
FRA	0.52	0.52
ITA	0.52	0.62

Figure shows average frequency of four elements in political stories: 'negative story tenor', 'conflict-oriented frame', 'incompetence frame', and 'scandalisation frame' (aggregated to index; see method section). Stories clearly relating to other countries than their own were excluded from this analysis. Based on N=1,626 stories.

Figure 10.3   Use of negativity in political coverage (1960s/2000s)

and British press systems, particularly due to intensified coverage of 'political incompetence' and 'political scandals'. Despite a considerable boost in British and US papers, negativity is less intensive than in Italian newspapers which paint politics in fairly dark, pessimistic colours. This contrasts most conspicuously with the situation in Germany and Switzerland where the newspapers express a remarkably steady sobriety in their political coverage. In sum, the extremely diverse developments run contrary to the assumption of homogenising tendencies in terms of negativity.

News sources

US newspapers integrate a higher number of sources per article, measured as actors being either quoted or paraphrased in a news story, than newspapers of the other press systems (see Table 10.2). This result is consistent with Donsbach's (1995) finding that US journalists make much greater use of eyewitnesses, experts, spokespersons, and ordinary citizens as news sources than journalists in other Western systems.[8] The reliance on news sources increases strongly in most systems (with the exception of Italy) but so far the appreciation of source- and research-intensive reporting is still weaker at European than American papers.

Moving to a more in-depth analysis presented in Table 10.3 we observe a significant association between the six press systems and the variety of sources presented in the news.[9] Our prediction in Hypothesis 4.1(a) that 'political elite' sources are utilised more frequently in media systems shaped by greater state intervention and closer proximity of the political field is only weakly supported, because the French newspapers counter expectations by using them the least in the 2000s. In contrast, Italian newspapers show the highest preference for political elite sources, supporting our expectations.

Table 10.2 Frequency of news sources in political coverage (1960s/2000s)

		USA	GBR	GER	SWI	FRA	ITA
Average number of sources per article	1960s	4.0[a]	2.8[b]	2.4[b]	2.6[ab]	3.2[ab]	3.5[ab]
	2000s	7.0[a]	4.3[b]	4.0[bc]	3.4[c]	4.4[b]	3.4[c]
Change		+ 3.0***	+ 1.5***	+ 1.6***	+ 0.8	+ 1.2**	− 0.1
Total N=1907 articles	1960s	193	122	169	13	94	74
	2000s	149	131	270	150	195	347

Table shows average frequency of directly or indirectly quoted sources. Based on N=1,907 stories; stories clearly relating to other countries than their own were excluded from this analysis. Means with different superscript letters are significantly different; means with the same superscript are not statistically different (1960s: post-hoc Dunnett's T3 test; 2000s: post-hoc LSD test) at $p < .05$ level. Differences between the 1960s and 2000s: * $p < .05$; ** $p < .01$; *** $p < .001$.

211

Hypothesis 4.1(b) expects that 'organised social groups' from civil society play the biggest role in the corporatist systems and the smallest role in the liberal systems. However, the use of organised social group sources does not differ substantially across systems. The data provide only limited support for the corporatism hypothesis as Swiss newspapers show indeed the highest amount of 'organised social groups' during the 1960s, whereas the German press does not integrate many organised sources. Meanwhile, the organised sources have come to be most common in Italian political news reports, thus disconfirming Hypothesis 4.1(b). Another study by Wessler (2008) also failed to establish a greater standing of organised groups in democratic corporatist news systems. We conclude that their greater de facto significance in corporatist systems does not translate to greater media prominence – on the contrary, organised groups may prefer to conduct their lobby work outside the media spotlight.

In an effort to address Hypotheses 4.1(a) and 4.2(b) from another angle, we determined each story's topic profile under three basic categories: 'policy issues' (e.g. economy, security, education, social problems); 'political elites' (e.g. government, parties); and 'organised social groups' (e.g. trade unions, employers' associations, social movement groups, religious organisations). Space constraints prevent us from presenting detailed results, but the breakdown provides weak support for our hypothesis on political elite and no support for our hypothesis concerning attention to organised social groups in democratic corporatist systems. The relationship between these source groups and news coverage is obviously much less linear and direct than the theoretical model would lead us to believe.

Hypothesis 4.1(c) predicts that the standing of 'individuals' is greater in Anglo-American news outlets than in those from continental Europe. Again, the findings in Table 10.3 provide only limited support for this. Individual sources are represented prominently in the US, but relatively infrequently in the British press. Contrary to our expectations, the French papers focus quite intensively on individual sources and differ clearly from Italian news practices. Nonetheless, there is one common conclusion that can be drawn from the sourcing patterns in the Mediterranean systems: polarised, fragmented multi-party systems increase the likelihood of a broad range of voices entering the news arena. In times of controversy the French journalists may invite reactions from notables, public intellectuals, and spokespeople ('individuals'), while in Italy organised groups from outside the established party system seize every news opportunity (including unions, protest groups, and the Church).

Table 10.3   Types of sources in political coverage
(1960s/2000s)

(%)		USA	GBR	GER	SWI	FRA	ITA
Political elite[a]	1960s	62	57	59	61	58	74
	2000s	51	53	65	57	42	66
Individuals[b]	1960s	09	06	03	11	07	02
	2000s	18	09	11	13	22	04
Organised	1960s	07	11	07	14	07	07
social groups[c]	2000s	10	06	07	10	11	18
Media[d]	1960s	03	04	14	11	05	13
	2000s	03	02	03	05	04	04
Business	1960s	03	08	04	03	04	04
	2000s	04	04	06	05	09	04
Unnamed	1960s	05	10	05	00	11	02
sources[e]	2000s	02	19	03	03	05	02
Other	1960s	11	06	07	00	08	02
sources	2000s	12	08	05	08	07	03
Total %	1960s	100%	100%	100%	100%	100%	100%
	2000s	100%	100%	100%	100%	100%	100%
Total N=7,352	1960s	(781)	(339)	(409)	(36)	(298)	(257)
of sources	2000s	(1,044)	(565)	(1,080)	(512)	(864)	(1,167)

Based on N=1,907 stories; items clearly relating to other countries than their own were excluded from this analysis. Totals can be different from 100% due to rounding. Most stories were coded for multiple number of sources (e.g. if two trade unions were quoted both were counted as organised social groups). Percentages are based on all sources mentioned in one national system.
a. President and prime minister, cabinet members, other government officials, legislators, political party officials, judiciary.
b. Ordinary citizens, experts.
c. Trade unions, employers' associations, religious organisations, social movement groups.
d. Journalists and other media, news agencies.
e. Undisclosed and unidentifiable sources.

Hypothesis 4.2(a) is supported as the standing of political elite sources in the news has receded in all systems except Germany. Hypothesis 4.2(b) is also supported as the standing of individual sources in the news has increased in all systems. This can be attributed to a more popularised reporting style that values personal narratives, or to a growing scientification of the political discourse that integrates specialist knowledge from experts.

Conclusion

This study is informed by two theoretical perspectives on long-term development in political journalism: one focuses on those forces pushing for the convergence of systems and homogenisation of news practices and content; the other focuses on deep-seated differences in structures and cultures that serve as brakes on this path and ensure that original contours of models are preserved over time. Focusing on the situation in Western press systems, we started by outlining the three most elaborate models found in the comparative literature so far, namely those developed by Hallin and Mancini, and derived a set of hypotheses on how differences in press *systems* (and change over time) may play out in news *content*. Here our study makes a clear contribution to a better understanding of these models as the content-specific, discursive elements have so far received little attention in comparative media systems research. The theoretically grounded indicators used to examine system-related differences in reporting styles are opinion-orientation, objectivity, negativity, and sourcing patterns. To further examine whether we find more support for a convergence or maintenance of models we employed a longitudinal design comparing print outlets from six Western systems (USA, Great Britain, Germany, Switzerland, France, and Italy) in 1960–1 and 2006–7. While we find clear convergence in the preference for opinionated stories in covering politics, the use of objectivity-related and negativity-related reporting features continues to differentiate journalism models more or less according to our theoretical expectations.

With regard to opinion-orientation, the emerging shared tendency of Western newspapers to devote about one quarter of their top political stories to opinionated journalism may be explained by a gradual blending of European influences (with a high appreciation for commentary) and American influences (with a growing appreciation for interpretation). Objectivity is a reporting convention that originates in the US but is increasingly gaining traction in democratic corporatist systems. At the same time, it is gradually separating US and British newspaper journalism, making the myth of a coherent Anglo-American ideal less and less sustainable. In fact, British newspapers seem to be aligning more and more with French and Italian papers in their use of opinion, objectivity, and negativity. The US, on the other hand, stands out as a press system that values opinion the least and the use of sources and other objectivity-related story elements the most. For all Western systems it is noteworthy that the growing use of objectivity and opinion developed in parallel without mutually excluding each other. This points to a potentially more complex and hybrid style of political coverage, a style that is not necessarily detrimental to democracy.

Negativity is highest in those systems that are marked by high levels of political polarisation (Italy, France) and/or high levels of media commercialisation (USA, Great Britain). Further analyses will be needed to draw new groupings of press systems based on their reporting patterns. One area calling for further research is the use of sources, where the patterns found here are only partly reconcilable with our theoretical expectations. Contrary to what Hallin and Mancini's term 'corporatist media system' leads one to expect, our analysis provides no evidence that corporatist groups play significantly larger roles in German and Swiss public discourse than in other media systems. Also, the idea that presumably more individualistic 'liberal' systems grant more media attention to individuals turns out to be unfounded.

We conclude that political reporting practices cannot be integrated without contradiction into existing media system typologies. System differences do not map directly onto differences in how journalists cover politics. However, we are able to confirm several expectations derived from the work by Hallin and Mancini, including their suspicion that France and Great Britain are borderline cases. While both the liberal and the polarised pluralist systems lose internal consistency over time, our analysis reveals a remarkable similarity and stability of the reporting patterns at German and Swiss newspapers. We can also conclude that similar technological and economic changes around the world as well as growing transnational exchanges between the national models have not led to an across-the-board, wholesale homogenisation of news practices. This only further underlines the relevance of comparative research. The arguably most important implication our conclusions have for comparative research is that the institutional aspects of media systems should not be expected to be directly reflected in content. While systemic contexts influence news production, journalism remains an autonomous force that is as much shaped by internal values of the profession ('agency') as it is constrained by the outside environment ('structure').

Acknowledgement

This study was supported by the National Center of Competence in Research on 'Challenges to Democracy in the 21st Century' (NCCR Democracy), funded by the Swiss National Science Foundation.

Notes

1 A necessary adaptation concerned the front page of *The Times* which in 1960–1 was reserved for advertisements and obituaries; in those years we coded political articles from the inside pages (only those half a page or larger, or accompanied by a picture or a very bold headline; N=124).

2 To standardise the aggregate objectivity index, the following formula was applied: $(x_i - min_{[th]}) / (max_{[th]} - min_{[th]})$; x_i refers to the empirical value of the aggregate objectivity index x, $min_{[th]}$ to the minimal theoretical value of the aggregate index (here 0), and $max_{[th]}$ to the maximal theoretical value (here 4).

3 All news articles were analysed by international student coders who received extensive training prior to coding. Inter-coder reliability tests were calculated separately for all language groups. Average Cohen's *kappa* coefficients within each language group were 0.81–1.0 for all format-based variables and 0.61–0.80 for all content-based variables.

4 The visual message of Figure 10.1 is also statistically confirmed by univariate analyses of variance which found highly significant differences in country means for the 1960s ($F(5, 1399) = 21.94$, $p < .001$, R^2-*adj.* = .069) and much less robust – albeit still significant – differences for the 2000s ($F(5, 1801) = 2.53$, $p < .05$, R^2-*adj.* = .004). The decrease in cross-national variance is clearly expressed in the R^2 values.

5 This can be demonstrated statistically by way of another univariate analysis of variance. It finds much stronger differences across the six nations' objectivity indices in the 2000s ($F(5, 1686) = 63.88$, $p < .001$, R^2-*adj.* = .157) than in the 1960s ($F(5, 1311) = 14.32$, $p < .001$, R^2-*adj.* = .048) as expressed by the R^2 values.

6 The divergence of the 1960s ($F(5, 547) = 9.65$, $p < .001$, R^2-*adj.* = .073) was surpassed by the divergence of the 2000s ($F(5, 1067) = 37.37$, $p < .001$, R^2-*adj.* = .145) as expressed in the R^2 values of two analyses of variance.

7 To prevent historic events from distorting our data we worked with extended 24-month data-gathering periods in the 1960s and 2000s. While 'negative' events may have taken place on the days of our analysis, coders were instructed

to assess the *presentational style* of the stories and not the inherent quality of the underlying events.

8   The mean averages reported in Table 10.2 differ significantly between the six countries, both in the 1960s ($F(5, 659) = 5.46$, $p < .001$, R^2-*adj.* $= .033$) and in the 2000s ($F(5, 1236) = 21.26$, $p < .001$, R^2-*adj.* $= .075$).

9   This association for the 1960s is $\chi^2 = 98$, $df = 35$, $p < .001$; for the 2000s it is $\chi^2 = 345$, $df = 35$, $p < .001$.

11

International Journalism in Transition

Kevin Williams

Introduction

The structural changes that are taking place in political journalism are acutely experienced at the international level. News organisations are closing their overseas bureaus and making foreign correspondents redundant. The news hole for international news is 'shrinking' (Shaw, 2001). Studies from various parts of the world observe a decrease in the mass media's attention to international issues.[1] The decline in the amount of international news is accompanied by the perceived deterioration in the quality of what is reported. Stories of entertainment and human interest are replacing news of diplomacy and politics, and increased immediacy is detrimental to considered and thorough reporting. Many practitioners are asking whether there is a future for foreign news (Hargreaves, 2000). They believe the product is on the verge of 'extinction' (Kalb, 1990) and its primary gatherer, the foreign correspondent, is 'vanishing' (Hiatt, 2001). According to former BBC news executive Richard Sambrook (2011: 1): 'for more than a hundred years the principal means of learning about events has been through the reporting of journalists based abroad [...] and now we are entering a new era where they may no longer be central to how we learn about the world'.

This chapter examines the nature of the changes that are taking place in international journalism, and in particular the notion that decline best describes what is happening. Drawing on historical analysis it notes that 'putative lapses in foreign news coverage are, in fact, the norm' in the history of international journalism (Allen and Hamilton, 2010: 634). The demise of the foreign correspondent has to be placed in the context of the emergence of new types of international newsgatherers

(Hamilton and Jenner, 2004). Bloggers, citizen journalists, and non-government organisations are filling the void and compensating for the disappearance of on-the-spot expertise and knowledge. How far, however, is the proliferation of alternative newsgatherers transforming international journalism?

International newsgathering is a dynamic process which throughout its history has adjusted and adapted to developments such as technological innovation, new economic circumstances, and the changing nature of international relations. Technology emerges as a primary driver of change. The advent of the telegraph, the rise of radio broadcasting, and the arrival of the internet have modified the practices and performance of international newsgatherers. The present modifications are seen as unprecedented. Not only has the speed at which international news is gathered and disseminated been transformed, but the traditional paradigm of international journalism has broken down as digitally connected citizens can acquire and exchange news and information from and about everywhere in the world. Digital technology facilitates the emergence of new types of newsgatherers, provides the opportunity to produce and consume more international news, and encourages a greater diversity of voices unencumbered by the traditional conventions of international journalism. In particular, citizens in the global South are able to communicate unmediated by Western interests, thereby redressing the inequalities of the international information order. The way in which people learn about international affairs has been revolutionised.

The focus on the ever-growing possibilities of new technology and on the decline of traditional practices obscures the fact that international journalism today is an amalgamation of the 'old' and 'new' which is characterised as much by 'continuity' with the past as by change. The pattern of international news – where it is from and who and what it is about – has remained remarkably constant. Many of the basic principles that shape the selection, gathering, and dissemination of international news are shared by established correspondents and alternative newsgatherers. New actors and innovative practices sit alongside traditional themes and established values. The composition of international news, the basis for determining the newsworthiness of events, and the role of international agencies in the digital world would be remarkably familiar to the foreign correspondents of 150 years ago.

Continuity results from journalism's ideological entrenchment in an information order established in the middle of the nineteenth century.

The history of international reporting indicates that newsgathering has been conducted through a national prism while rooted in a global perspective (Rantanen, 2007). The growth of the present international information order was driven by the 'first engine of globalisation', the expansion of the European powers and in particular the British Empire (Kaul, 2011). Journalism was a vital component in the news and information networks which connected up the colonial village, conveying the values that acted as the community cement and providing the intelligence that informed the exercise of power. New technology may increase the speed of news, diversify the range of views that can be accessed, and enable people to communicate directly with each other, but how we perceive and understand each other and decide what is important is intimately tied up with the legacy of 'colonialism'. International journalism today could be described as entering a phase of digital colonialism.

Decline as the norm

Searching for a 'golden age' of well-resourced international newsgathering is unfulfilling (Allen and Hamilton, 2010). The most dramatic cuts in foreign news staff in the British press took place in the 1970s. The 1977 Royal Commission on the Press identified a 30 per cent decline in the number of British newspaper staff correspondents based overseas since 1945 (Boyd-Barrett et al., 1977: 16). Dorman (1986: 421) traces the demise of US foreign correspondents abroad from the end of World War II: 'between the end of World War II and the mid-1970s, the number of U.S. correspondents overseas dropped from about 2,500 to 430'. The 1930s are often considered the 'heyday' of the foreign correspondent, when legendary reporters such as Sefton Delmer of the *Daily Express* or Herbert Matthews of the *New York Times* roamed the world to warn of the dangers and threats arising from the international instability and political extremism of the era. Yet a study of American newspapers in 1927 found that international news took up a relatively small proportion of column inches; the average share of available news space devoted to foreign news in the 40 newspapers sampled was 4.7 per cent (cited in Allen and Hamilton, 2010: 635).

Renowned foreign correspondents of the 1930s referred to the difficulties of getting their copy into the newspaper. Vernon Bartlett (1937:

88) realised 'how very lucky any foreign correspondent was to have his message put in the paper and not on the spike'. Bartlett, who worked for the *News Chronicle*, *The Times*, and the BBC, sounded a familiar refrain when he complained that 'technical developments have robbed the newspaper man's job of its romance and dignity' (1937: 113). He worried about the pressure that 'compels' correspondents 'to rush off to places by air in order to telephone back messages which must be sufficiently highly coloured to justify the expense'. The rising costs of foreign news exercised the concerns of editors locked into the bitter newspaper circulation wars of the 1930s. The *New York Herald Tribune* fielded an outstanding corps of correspondents in the 1930s, which suffered 'a gradual decline' as a result of cost cutting that 'crimped the ability of correspondents to write at length' (Hamilton, 2009: 156). The situation of the international news agency Reuters also illustrates the uncertain nature of international newsgathering during the interwar years. The number of Reuters bureaus fell during these two decades: in 1920 there were 43 offices throughout the world, but by 1932 this had dropped to 27 (Read, 1992: 195). The agency 'could never afford to maintain as many news bureaux or to appoint as many full-time correspondents as it needed' (Read, 1992: 195). The lack of an adequate number of correspondents on the ground led to the charge that Reuters simply recycled propaganda from foreign agencies and governments 'disguised as pure news' (Read, 1992: 156).

Concern about international news in the interwar years was accentuated by the arrival of a new media technology: wireless broadcasting. In the early years of the medium, the press and news agencies were reluctant to allow broadcasters to report news. The immediacy of live news posed a threat to newspaper sales and the demand for news agency copy. A bitter conflict, for example, ensued in the United States and Canada with the Associated Press issuing a notice to its members in 1922 that its news bulletins were not to be used for the purposes of broadcasting (Storey, 1951: 180). Efforts by the BBC to extend its news service and deploy its own correspondents were resisted up until World War II. How to respond to the challenge of the new technology considerably exercised Reuters – and other agencies – in the 1930s. The almost instantaneous communication of news meant that by 1938 a study found that radio gave relatively more attention than newspapers to international news (Lazersfeld, 1940: 210). Developing transmission services and managing the costs incurred in deploying these services were at the forefront of the efforts of international journalism to come to terms with the limitlessness of the new medium in its ability to communicate directly with audiences all over the world.

Tracing the history of international journalism back to its origins in the mid-nineteenth century, we find most national newspapers in Europe struggling to gather news from overseas. Few newspapers in the 1850s and 1860s had their own international newsgathering operations. *The Times* of London and John Gordon Bennett's *New York Herald* were exceptions. Most newspapers had to lift stories from other competitors or rely on the word of mouth of itinerant voyageurs of one kind or another – diplomats, merchants, and tourists. The reliability of such sources was problematic, hence the effort of newspapers to have their own special correspondent on the spot (Hohenberg, 1995: 13). The rapid growth in newspaper titles throughout Europe in the second half of the nineteenth century generated more competition and more pages to fill. Newspapers came to rely on news agencies to provide domestic and international copy. By 1870, *The Times* found Reuters' foreign news service 'indispensable' (Palmer, 1978: 208) and newspapers across Europe reproduced Reuters' 'latest telegrams', thereby extending their news coverage at minimum cost (Read, 1992: 20). Primarily as a result of the international news agencies, by 1890 *The Times* had lost its pre-eminence as the supplier of foreign news (Palmer, 1978: 214). From its earliest days international journalism operated amidst concerns about the amount of international news and the high costs involved in gathering such news.

International news cycle

Regular expressions of concern about reductions in international news draw attention away from the increase over time in the amount of international news in most media systems. Longitudinal research indicates that 'foreign news coverage [...] grew considerably between the 17th and 20th centuries' in the European and North American press (Wilke, 1987: 154). This steady growth of international news has been punctuated by periodic cycles of decline. The scarcity of the product in the American press is the norm for peacetime (Hamilton, 2009: 128). Only at times of war, conflict, and crisis does international news feature more prominently. Large increases in the number of US correspondents based abroad have coincided with American military involvement overseas, most notably World War II and Vietnam. The contemporary decline in international

223

news and foreign correspondents has been interspersed with 'big stories' such as the overseas incursions in Iraq and Afghanistan.

Comparative research indicates the cyclical nature of international news; peaks and falls are manifested in different ways. The US media system is exceptional; there is less international news and it is 'quite different from anywhere else in the world' in its composition (Wilke et al., 2012: 317). Woodward (1930) found that American newspapers devoted much less space to international news in the interwar years than their European counterparts. At 8.95 per cent the *New York Times* had in Woodward's study the highest proportion of international news space of the US newspapers examined; this contrasted with the five British, French, and German newspapers studied which dedicated 23–25 per cent of their news space to foreign stories. Wilke's study (1987: 156) of three centuries of international news concludes that 'international news coverage in the American newspapers remained without exception negligible and in part was reduced over time'.

The amount of international news in European media systems has always been more substantial. A higher proportion of foreign news stories has consistently appeared in German and French newspapers over time compared to their Anglo-American counterparts (Wilke, 1987: 154). A study of Flemish newspapers between 1986 and 2006 found that despite a gradual decline in the 1990s overall foreign news remained 'fairly steady' notwithstanding exceptional news events (Joye, 2010). The 'drastic fall' in international news on US network television following the Cold War (Norris, 1995) was not mirrored on European screens. Kolmer and Semetko (2010) show how German television provides a relatively high level of foreign news. The share of foreign news fell, but was still higher than other comparable countries including the US (Kolmer and Semetko, 2010: 708–9). There has not been a general decline in foreign news coverage on the main German channels; even the commercial channels devote a relatively high share of their news output to foreign news. The Danish media system in the 1990s witnessed more coverage of foreign affairs, the hiring of more foreign correspondents and stringers, and the growth of the foreign desks (Holm, 2001). Only in the last decade has the number of correspondents started to fall (Rasmussen, 2012). The greater supply of international news on European TV screens appears to owe much to the public service nature of the continent's television systems.

Studies of media systems in non-Western countries tend to show a relatively high amount of international news. A 1983 study commissioned by UNESCO[2] indicates that there is in general more international news in media systems in Latin America, Asia, and Africa (Sreberny-Mohammadi, 1984). The higher proportion of international news stories in these systems reflects their well-documented 'dependency' on Western news sources, especially the international news agencies (INas). Many media systems in Africa use international news to fill their pages to avoid the political dangers of covering domestic news and to overcome the high economic cost of providing their own services. International news has become more prominent. In their study of foreign news in the *New York Times* over 22 years, Riffe and his colleagues (1994) found that the average length of international news stories had increased. Allen and Hamilton (2010) note that the decline in the number of foreign news articles in the US press is accompanied by a 'greater supply' of front-page stories. Kester (2007: 130) describes how a quality or up-market Dutch newspaper *NRC-Handelsblad* devoted more front-page attention to international news from the 1960s, contrasting with popular newspapers which increasingly pushed their international coverage back into the inside pages of the newspaper. Decline is more acute in the popular press and on commercial television stations, but there has been a qualitative shift from a hard to soft news focus in international coverage in most media systems (Aalberg et al., 2013).

Changing production process

The focus on decline masks shifts within the editorial process. The closure of news bureaus has resulted in a redrawing of the international newsgathering map. Some regions have seen an influx of correspondents and an increase in news coverage in recent years, reflecting a change in power and political influence, which is a significant determinant of newsworthiness. For example, Brussels has grown as a news beat, with the number of reporters covering the EU doubling between 1976 and 1987 (Raeymaeckers et al., 2007: 105). This was due to the increasing political importance of NATO and the European Union; the accession to the EU of every new member state has brought in more reporters. Since a high point in 2005, however, when the Brussels press corps numbered over 1,300 correspondents, there has been a clear decline: by 2010 the number had dropped to 800 (International Press Association, 2010).

Over the longer term there has been a concentration of newsgathering resources in Europe and North America. News organisations have retrenched their resources on major news centres such as New York, Washington, and London. Decline has been less severe in these centres, if it has taken place at all, than in most parts of Asia, Latin America, and Africa. Reaction to the shifting balance of economic and political power in the contemporary world has been uneven. There has been a growth of correspondents in Beijing, which has corresponded with the exodus of full-time correspondents and the closure of bureaus in Moscow following the end of the Cold War (Fleeson, 2003). However, the growing influence of China and India has not been fully embraced in news terms; national news organisations in some systems have been slow to increase their presence in Beijing, while others have withdrawn from India – for example, the Dutch quality newspaper *De Volkskrant* closed its operations there in 2004 (Tuinstra, 2004).

The decline in permanent correspondents has consequences for the structure of foreign news desks and the editorial process. Editors today rely less on permanent staff and more on freelancers, home-based reporters, ad hoc bureaus, and amateur information gatherers. Simon Rasmussen (2012) refers to a shift from a fixed to a flexible model of international newsgathering. Flexibility is evident in several ways: cooperation between news organisations to use or employ correspondents; setting up temporary bureaus to cover specific events; employing more freelance reporters; and relying more on travelling home-based reporters, often referred to as 'parachute' journalism. Cost-cutting has provided the context for this change. Ad hoc arrangements and parachute journalism are seen as a cheaper option than posting long-stay correspondents abroad. A parachute journalist drops into a country for a relatively short period of time, usually at a time of crisis, files a story or handful of dispatches, and then leaves (Martin, 2011). The term is often used pejoratively: journalists touch down in places they know nothing about; they have no understanding of the people, politics, language, and culture; and they have no time to cultivate local sources to make sense of the story. Breaking news may be covered well, but the evaluation of the causes and consequences suffers. Yet not everyone subscribes to this assessment. For instance, Erickson and Hamilton (2007: 141) refer to 'the broad, undifferentiated criticism' of parachute journalism which ignores the variety of different kinds of roving reporters; they highlight the ways in which parachute journalism can be 'additive', providing 'more not less expertise' and helping to connect with the audience.

The growth of freelance reporters is another response to a cost-cutting environment. The ability to pursue a part-time career as a foreign correspondent is facilitated by new technology. Armed with laptop, mobile phone, smaller cameras, and access to satellites, freelancers can report from the most distant places. Cheaper-to-employ, younger, and often less experienced freelance reporters have swelled the ranks of international journalism with what is again seen as a detrimental impact on the profession. Freelance reporting is defended on the grounds that it provides opportunities for a wider array of voices and that the freelance is less in the thrall of news desks, having more independence to follow the stories they want to cover. There is an increasing reliance on local fixers who, it is argued, add local voices and perspectives to a Western-dominated portrayal of the world (Murrell, 2010). They allow foreign correspondents to connect with local culture and be aware of the nuances of situations and circumstances on the ground. However, for correspondents it means information comes to them through a series of filters based on translation and leads to the production of secondhand accounts (Murrell, 2010: 134).

Whatever their merits as newsgatherers, home-based correspondents and freelance reporters do not represent a transformation in international journalism. Erickson and Hamilton (2007) describe how reporters travelled the world prior to the age of air travel, using a range of transportation from ships and trains to horse and cart. The speed of travel has changed, but the intent to travel has always been there. Travel has also been an essential component of the work of long-stay correspondents. Long-stay reporters in many parts of the world are peripatetic, responsible for large and often culturally diverse beats such as 'Africa' and the 'Middle East'. Foreign correspondents have always relied on local fixers and stringers to navigate their beats. The team nature of bureau journalism is often forgotten; fixers, freelancers, and translators have 'remained relatively unknown outside media circles' (Murrell, 2010: 127) and their contribution to the practice and performance of foreign correspondents has been neglected. Relying more on such actors has implications for the ability to develop specialist knowledge and could lead to the standardisation of what is reported. It does not represent a fundamental change in international journalism. Hamilton and Jenner (2004) argue that more attention should be paid to alternative news sources and assessing their ability and capacity to report international events and issues.

New international newsgatherers

It is the emergence of new types of newsgatherer that is seen as transforming international journalism. Many commentators have argued that the deficiencies of traditional media would be overcome with the advent of new media technologies. The exponential growth of the internet, the mobile phone, and social media provides a different form of connectivity. They are inherently participatory technologies, encouraging anyone connected to send messages and receive them. People everywhere are able to create their own content for public consumption, greatly increasing the number of people able to report on international events. Bloggers and citizen journalists can cover the world from their sitting rooms. Through the internet and social media they have access to information about what is happening in every corner of the world. This has enabled those caught up in breaking news stories to send back instant coverage. Many major news organisations have come to incorporate the reports of citizen journalists into their accounts of breaking news or local reaction to international events (Heinrich, 2008). Such developments have led to speculation about a new age of international journalism.

New media technology has spawned a huge number of new news outlets. From aggregators such as Google News to specialist international news sites such as GlobalPost to individual bloggers, sources of international news have blossomed. The expansion of the blogosphere and social media has been remarkable. As of July 2011, there were an estimated 164 million blogs (Treanor, 2011). At the end of 2012 it was estimated that nearly 1.9 billion people were using social networks (Griessner, 2012). Individuals can access sources previously unavailable to them. Those interested in Africa are now able to access the websites of local newspapers across the continent. AllAfrica.com, which aggregates and indexes content from over 130 African news organisations, is an example of how locally produced content is made globally available. Such activity is seen as not only generating more information, but changing the nature of international news and the structure of international newsgathering. More information is clearly available. Online websites of mainstream outlets carry more international stories from more places (Gasher and Gabriele, 2004). Bloggers are able to post information from locations around the world and citizens can access websites providing information on the most remote of places.

Yet to what extent is this contributing to a greater supply and diversity of international news? For many the answer is not much. International news in the new media is similar to that in the mainstream media and there are problems in accessing and understanding news on the web. The research conducted tends to point to international news remaining anchored in traditional news values, with the focus on certain parts of the world, negative stories, and limited representations of many parts of Africa, Asia, and Latin America. Chris Paterson's study (2007) of international news on the internet concludes that to a great extent online international news replicates the inequities and limitations of the traditional news media. A 2007 study of online versions of four mainstream media outlets found that in quantitative terms the imbalance between developed and developing countries was 'still evident' and news about 'elite nations' was 'dominant in the foreign news sections of the four online newspapers' (Chia, 2007). Examining the two most visited news websites in the US, Denis Wu (2007: 549) concludes that their international news output 'does not seem to deviate much from that of their traditional counterparts'. His findings show 'significant overlaps between most covered nations' and that 'Middle-Eastern countries, economic elites and military powers still dominate the news space on the web'. Bloggers do not significantly deviate from the established pattern of international news reporting. A study of Blogpulse found that the references to nations in blogposts strongly correlate with their appearance in mainstream news outlets (Zuckerman, 2004). The geography of online international news thus reflects the imbalances of the traditional mainstream media.

This is also apparent with the value-added components of new media technology. The hyperlink allows the user to access other documents and sites, thereby assisting the acquisition of more information and increasing the potential for greater understanding of issues in the news. Easy to establish and, as a result of more powerful search engines, easy to find, hyperlinks can be seen as essential to claims that the internet expands our knowledge and understanding of international relations. However, Tsan-Kuo Chang and his colleagues (2009: 149) found in their study of international news stories from 28 online news media in 15 countries that the use of hyperlinks to external websites in foreign news stories was 'infrequent'. This is supported by Paterson's research (2007: 57), which found that the sources of international news most consulted by online users are two international news agencies.

The main providers of international news on the web are the agencies. Ben Scott (2005: 95) notes how the INAs 'very quickly' became major players in the internet news market, 'supplying ideally suited digital content [...] to the portal aggregators, start-up news web sites and traditional news vendors looking to strengthen their online presence'. The net generates a small proportion of the original reporting which rests in the hands of a small number of organisations, primarily Associated Press, Agence France-Presse, and Reuters. Research has found that 43 per cent of what was published on the most popular websites run by major media organisations was drawn almost verbatim from the INAs, while for the major internet portals the figure rose to 85 per cent (Paterson, 2006, 2007). They are the main suppliers of international news for old *and* new media. The new media technologies 'have undergone 'a rapid incorporation into familiar structures of inequity and commercial exploitation' (Golding, 1998: 79).

There are limits to the capacity of citizens to access and use new technology. Nearly half of the world's bloggers are US-based; and almost one in three is European (Treanor, 2011). Internet usage is predominantly a feature of the world's wealthiest countries. Despite the increased presence of new technology in many parts of the global South – China, South Korea, and Brazil are amongst the top ten countries for internet use – there is still a 'digital divide', with many millions of people in Asia, Africa, and Latin America having no access to new media. In addition a 'participation gap' has been identified, with a relatively small group of highly skilled users who create and share content (Hargittai and Walejko, 2008). Zuckerman (2008a) argues that, even with access, much of what is available is not necessarily comprehensible. As the blogosphere has grown, he points out, it has morphed from a community in which everyone shares a similar set of suppositions and language into a number of separate spheres characterised by different languages and cultures. Every day more content is created in a variety of languages, erecting a growing number of linguistic barriers. Material can be translated, but there remains a problem of comprehending opinions and perspectives. There is a limited understanding of the context of locally produced content. Blogs, websites, and online newspapers (like most media products) are compiled and written with a specific audience in mind – not a global audience. They assume a degree of knowledge of actors, circumstances, and context without which stories are not immediately comprehensible. Finally, there is what Zuckerman refers to as the problem of authentication. Online content, blogs, Facebook, Twitter, and other social media are unfiltered; it is difficult to identify their political agenda or how they relate to their society. Casual users are not able to easily assess the extent to which the views they access online are representative or marginal.

Pattern of international news

The failure of a supply-side transformation means that the pattern of international news we have today has not changed significantly since the nineteenth century. Best summed up by the MacBride report (1980), some parts of the world and some people receive disproportionate coverage. The geography of international news is skewed to elite nations and elite people (Galtung and Ruge, 1965). Other parts of the world are notable for their absence. Africa – rich in people and resources, and making up a significant slice of the world's land mass – is under-represented in news terms. Moreover, when the continent is reported, it is often at times of crisis and in negative terms; even in African newspapers the reporting of the continent is skewed to negative stories (Obijiofor and Hanusch, 2003). New media technology has not significantly changed this pattern of reporting. According to Suzanne Franks (2010: 72) 'many parts of Africa are less understood and less well reported than they were several generations ago'. Familiar stereotypes and narrow geographical spread are found in the blogosphere and online, which according to critics is 'highly derivative' of mainstream media coverage (Zuckerman, 2008a).

This can be seen in the sources of information cited in international news. Much of the legwork to obtain information is not done by the newsgatherer but by his or her sources. Most journalism is not eyewitness but depends on the testimony of others. Tracking down personal contacts to provide such accounts is time-consuming and resource intensive. Foreign correspondents have found it more difficult to do this than other specialist reporters (Tunstall, 1971). As a result they have come to rely on the local press and media in the country or countries to which they are accredited *and* institutional or official sources of information (Boyd-Barrett, 1980; Morrison and Tumber, 1985). Advances in communication technology are supposed to have enhanced the ability to access a greater diversity of sources. However, accounts on the web and stories in the traditional media tend to focus on similar sources. Citizen journalists today, like correspondents throughout history, plough through the local press and media to identify stories – the only differences are the way in which it is done, where it is done from, and the speed at which it is done. The assessment that a foreign correspondent is only 'as good as the local media allow' (Morrison and Tumber, 1985: 466) equally applies to the citizen journalist.

Research into the changing sourcing of news over time is sparse, but what there is indicates that the reliance on official sources by US newspapers has increased over time, particularly since the 1950s (Barnhurst and Mutz, 1997: 34). There is in the US media a 'trend toward more and broader sourcing, with official sources continually serving as the bedrock and mainstay of reporting overseas' (Hamilton and Lawrence, 2010: 695). The dependency reflects the need to supply the voracious appetite of newsrooms, a pressure recognised by foreign ministries earlier than other parts of government. The diplomatic service pioneered the techniques of news management. An example of the early institutionalisation of such techniques in Britain was the establishment of the News Department at the Foreign Office in 1916 (Taylor, 1999). The arrival of the press attaché in 1927 cemented the relationship between local diplomatic missions and the foreign press corps (De Jong, 1977). The interaction between official sources and correspondents reflects not only practical considerations, but also the close ties that have traditionally existed between the foreign correspondent and the diplomatic service (Vaughan, 1999; Volz and Lee, 2011).

The exponential increase in the sources of information on the internet has not necessarily changed this situation (Archetti, 2012). Attention is drawn to the diminished capacity of governments and other international agencies to promote their view of events in a media landscape dominated by the internet and real-time television news (Gowing, 2009). Yet much of the international news on the net is uploaded in one form or another by governments and official organisations. The vast amount of information and the anonymity of much of what appears make it easier for official sources to plant the information they are seeking to promote. The working environment of the foreign correspondent and new newsgatherers compounds this. The obstacles that militate against efforts of correspondents to cultivate a broad range of sources have increased. Meeting multiple deadlines for a variety of news platforms reduces the time for correspondents to check sources, search out stories, and produce in-depth news. Foreign correspondents, like other specialist disseminators of information, are becoming 'purveyors' rather than 'gatherers' of news. The capacity to interrogate sources is diminished. The new media technology presents 'the dangerous illusion of multiple perspectives which actually emanate from very few sources' (Paterson, 2006).

Digital colonialism

The hierarchy of nations in international news, with the core countries of the international system receiving more coverage than smaller, less developed, and less powerful peripheral nations, is a legacy of colonialism (Chang, 1998). Perceptions of audiences in the West as well as their counterparts in the global South are constrained by the history of their interaction. In an increasingly commercial system that places emphasis on giving audiences what they want, there is a tendency to reproduce values, perceptions, and hierarchies steeped in the history of international relations – a history of colonial interaction. Faraway places do not routinely become newsworthy as a result of the events that take place there; they are a product of a particular way of seeing and understanding what is important and what is worth communicating. Proximity, a news value emphasised by Galtung and Ruge (1965) in their study of the selection of news, is culturally constructed and steeped in a colonial past. For many countries the ties fostered by colonialism ensure greater attention; for example, the disproportionate reporting of Indonesia in the Dutch media (d'Haenens and Verelst, 2002), or East Timor (Monteiro, 2002) in the Portuguese media, or India and parts of Africa on the BBC is the result of the historical legacy of colonialism. Technology may change, but the mindset that influences how technology is used and applied evolves more slowly. Newsgatherers of all types might resist colonial values, but the legacy shapes the structures and culture within which they have to work. To paraphrase an African commentator, the legacy of 300 years of colonialism runs deep in international society, and international journalism is not isolated from this legacy (Mandaza, 1986: 133).

Understanding colonialism and its implications for international news and information flows in the digital age is a broad and complex discussion. Colonialism takes many forms, varies from country to country, and its contemporary relevance must take into account new ways of seeing. It is recognised that colonialism has had an important role in shaping the structures and processes that underpin international newsgathering and dissemination. Less attention is paid to how colonialism has shaped national audience perceptions in the West and global South of events, peoples, and places outside their borders. From the earliest times international journalism has been 'global'. We tend to emphasise the national dimension to the production of international news. What is supposedly different today is the 'global' perspective that shapes international journalism. New technology makes 'global communication possible' and attracts global audiences for international events; with growing interconnectedness these developments demand or facilitate the emergence of a globalised journalism (Berglez, 2008). This ignores the global nature of journalism since the inception of the foreign correspondent in the middle of the nineteenth century. This was a product of colonialism.

Foreign correspondence has always been 'cosmopolitan'. Rantanen (2007: 843) argues that the national/international division prevents us from 'seeing how early news was a product of *cosmopolitan* cities rather than of nation states'. Employed by newspapers and news agencies, foreign correspondents in the latter part of the nineteenth century tended to be cosmopolitan in their background, experience, and outlook. Often they were not natives of the countries whose media outlets they were reporting for – for example, *The Times*'s celebrated Paris correspondent Henri de Blowitz was born in Bohemia, spent his working life in France, and became a naturalised French citizen. They usually reported for more than one newspaper, compiling reports for the press in several countries, and were employed for their local knowledge, linguistic skills, and political contacts (Brown, 1985). Based in capital cities or major city centres, their reporting was shaped by sources in the city in which they were resident (Brown, 1985: 215). The INAs developed a system of connectivity between Europe's major cities, and as the telegraph and cable were extended they were linked together in a network of global cities (Pike and Winseck, 2004; Winseck and Pike, 2007, 2009). The bulk of international news emanated from these cities and it was in these news centres that correspondents congregated.

The expansion of the network was facilitated by the rise of European empires which determined that cities such as Bombay, Shanghai, and Hong Kong should become connected. Correspondents and stringers for the metropolitan press and news agencies in these locations were often drawn from the ranks of the local press. *The Times* 'frequently' recruited 'correspondents from among conservative sections of the Anglo-India press establishment' (Kaul, 1997: 74). Many went on to serve in Fleet

Street, such as Geoffrey Dawson as editor of *The Times* and Sir Roderick Jones who headed up Reuters. They were 'journalists for Empire' (Startt, 1991). The telegraph and the news bound the British Empire together; the essential unity of corporate life in the Empire was achieved by the supply of news of common imperial interest (Harris, 1981: 13). Foreign correspondents were central to a system of newsgathering that provided indigenous elites and European settlers with news of what was happening in their spheres of influence. They connected the global and the local, and the news they provided about other parts of the world was shaped by colonial considerations and perceptions.

In the digital era international journalism remains steeped in a global perspective shaped by the legacy of colonialism. Mobile phones and the internet deliver a seemingly constant stream of information, culture, and language from a variety of sources beyond the physical and socio-political setting of the user. More people are involved in generating international news and information, and democratising the process of communication. Local voices, the voices of those subjugated by colonialism, are able to be heard more clearly. Yet the flow of information, culture, and language remains unbalanced; the traffic is still predominantly from North to South. The supply of international news and information online is dominated by a small number of original newsgatherers and a relatively small number of content producers, primarily located in North America and Western Europe. What is there is not generated for a global audience but for local consumption. Bridging the gap between cultures and languages is the objective of some bloggers (Zuckerman, 2008b), but most users, like viewers, listeners, and readers, are searching out the familiar. Aggregators reinforce this by encouraging users to personalise their content provision online. Familiar faces (established news organisations), familiar places (established centres of power), and familiar stereotypes and representations are all part of the legacy of colonialism.

Conclusion

International journalism is in transition in media systems in Europe and around the world. The focus on the decline of the foreign correspondent conceals the shifts that are taking place as a result of technological change that encourages new working methods, business models, and distribution systems. The development of new and alternative newsgatherers is generating more information about what is happening in the world, and citizens everywhere now have the opportunity to access this information for themselves. However, the nature of this information and the problems of accessing and comprehending it are perhaps not making us better informed. An increased flow of information does not necessarily provide more knowledge and greater critical awareness of international affairs. The new media share many of the deficiencies of the old media, notably a pattern of news coverage that is located in a particular way of seeing the world.

Notes

1   This is, for example, well documented in the UK. A survey conducted by the Media Standards Trust in the UK in 2009 found that international news coverage across four leading UK national newspapers had fallen by 40 per cent since 1979, with international news making up only 11 per cent of the output of the national newspapers studied compared to 20 per cent in 1979. This reinforces a trend detected by researchers into television coverage of international events. Following deregulation the amount of foreign coverage provided by ITV current affairs fell by nearly 50 per cent between 1988 and 1998. Channel 4's foreign coverage dropped by nearly a third in the first five years of the first decade of the twenty-first century. Similar findings are apparent in other Western media systems. For a discussion of the methodological problems confronting this kind of research, see Wouters (2009).

2   This was based on a snapshot of a day of foreign news in 29 national media systems.

Bibliography

Aalberg, T., Aelst, P. van, and Curran, J. (2010) 'Media systems and the political information environment: A cross-national comparison', *International Journal of Press/Politics* 15/3: 255–71.

Aalberg, T., Papathanassopoulos, S., Soroka, S., Curran, J., Hayashi, K., Iyengar, S., Jones, P. K., Mazzoleni, G., Rojas, H., Rowe, D., and Tiffen, R. (2013) 'International TV news, foreign affairs interest and public knowledge: A comparative study of foreign news coverage and public opinion in 11 countries', *Journalism Studies*, DOI:10.1080/1461670X.2013.765636.

Abramowitz, A. (2010) *The Disappearing Center* (New Haven, CT: Yale University Press).

AgCom (2011 and 2012), *Relazione Annuale sull'Attività Svolta e sui Programmi di Lavoro*, annual report available at www.agcom.it/Default.aspx?message= contenuto&DCId=5.

AIM Research Consortium (ed.) (2007a) *Understanding the Logic of EU Reporting from Brussels: Analysis of Interviews with EU Correspondents and Spokespersons* (Bochum, Fribourg/Brsg.: Adequate Information Management in Europe), Working Papers, vol. 3.

——— (ed.) (2007b): *Comparing the Logic of EU reporting in Mass Media across Europe* (Bochum, Fribourg/Brsg.: Adequate Information Management in Europe).

——— (ed.) (2007c) *Reporting and Managing European News: Final Report of the Project 'Adequate Information Management in Europe' 2004–2007* (Bochum, Fribourg/Brsg.: Adequate Information Management in Europe).

Albæk, E., Hopman, D. N., and de Vreese, C. H. (2010) *Kunsten at holde balancen* (Odense: Syddansk Universitetsforlag).

Alexander, H. E. (1996) 'Financing presidential election campaigns', *Issues of Democracy* 1/13, available at http://cfinst.org/pdf/HEA/137_financinpre selectusis.pdf (accessed 12 August 2013).

Allan, S. (2006) *Online News: Journalism and the Internet* (Maidenhead: Open University Press).

Allen, C. and Hamilton, J. M. (2010) 'Normalcy and foreign news', *Journalism Studies* 11/5: 634–49.

Allern, S. and Blach-Ørsten, M. (2011) 'The news media as a political institution: A Scandinavian perspective', *Journalism Studies* 12/1: 92–105.

Almond G. and Powell, B. (1966) *Comparative Politics: System, Process, and Policy* (Boston: Little, Brown & Company).

Amedeo, F. (2012) 'Le match des candidats sur Internet', 22 April, available at http://elections.lefigaro.fr/presidentielle-2012/2012/04/22/01039-20120422 ARTFIG00211-lematch-des-candidats-sur-internet.php (accessed 15 August 2012).

American Journalism Review (2009) 'AJR's 2009 count of Statehouse reporters', available at www.ajr.org/article.asp?id=4722 (accessed 12 August 2013).

Anderson, C. W. (2013) *Rebuilding the News* (Philadelphia, IL: Temple University Press).

Antheaume, A. (2010) 'The French press and its enduring institutional crisis', in D. A. L. Levy and R. K. Nielsen (eds), *The Changing Business of Journalism and Its Implications for Democracy* (Oxford: Reuters Institute for the Study of Journalism), pp. 69–80.

Archetti, C. (2012) 'Which future for foreign correspondence?', *Journalism Studies* 13/5–6: 847–56.

Auletta, K. (2010) 'Non-stop news', *New Yorker*, 25 January, available at www.newyorker.com/reporting/2010/01/25/100125fa_fact_auletta (accessed 13 August 2013).

Baisnée, O. (2002) 'Can political journalism exist at the EU level?', in R. Kuhn and E. Neveu (eds), *Political Journalism: New Challenges, New Practices* (London: Routledge), pp. 108–28.

——— (2003) *La production de l'actualité communautaire* (PhD thesis: Université de Rennes 1).

Barile, P. and Rao, G. (1992) 'Trends in the Italian mass media and media law', *European Journal of Communication* 7/2: 261–81.

Barnett, S. and Gaber, I. (2001) *Westminster Tales: The Twenty-first-century Crisis in Political Journalism* (London: Continuum).

Barnett, S., Ramsay, G. N., and Gaber, I. (2012) *From Callaghan to Credit Crunch: Changing Trends in British Television News 1975–2009* (London: University of Westminster).

Barnett, S., Seymour, E., and Gaber, I. (2000) *From Callaghan to Kosovo: Changing Trends in British Television News* (London: University of Westminster).

Barnhurst, K. and Mutz, C. (1997) 'American journalism and the decline of event-centred reporting', *Journal of Communication* 47/4: 27–53.

Bartlett, V. (1937) *This is My Life* (London: Chatto & Windus).

Baugut, P. and Grundler, M.-T. (2009) *Politische Nicht-Öffentlichkeit in der Mediendemokratie: Eine Analyse der Beziehungen zwischen Politikern und Journalisten in Berlin* (Baden-Baden: Nomos).

Baum, M. A. (2002) 'Sex, lies, and war: How soft news brings foreign policy to the inattentive public', *American Political Science Review* 96/1: 91–109.

Baum, M. A. and Groeling, T. (2008) 'New media and the polarization of American political discourse', *Political Communication* 25/4: 345–65.

Belardelli G. (2012) *The political cultures of contemporary Italy*. Paper presented at the workshop 'The Media, Democracy and Political Culture', Perugia, 9 March.

Bennett, W. L. (1990) 'Toward a theory of press–state relations in the United States', *Journal of Communication* 40/2: 103–27.

Bennett, W. L. and Entman, R. M. (eds) (2001) *Mediated Politics: Communication in the Future of Democracy* (New York: Cambridge University Press).

Bennett, W. L. and Iyengar, S. (2008) 'A new era of minimal effects? The changing foundations of political communication', *Journal of Communication* 58/4: 707–31.

Benson, R. (1999) 'Field theory in comparative context: A new paradigm for media studies', *Theory and Society* 28/3: 463–98.

―――― (2010) 'What makes for a critical press? A case study of French and U.S. immigration news coverage', *International Journal of Press/Politics* 15/1: 3–24.

Benson, R. and Hallin, D. C. (2007) 'How states, markets and globalization shape the news: The French and U.S. national press, 1965–1997', *European Journal of Communication* 22/1: 27–48.

Benson, R. and Neveu, E. (eds) (2005) *Bourdieu and the Journalistic Field* (Cambridge: Polity Press).

Benson, R. and Powers, M. (2010) *Public Media and Political Independence: Lessons for the Future of Journalism from Around the World* (New York: Free Press Publication).

Benyahia-Kouider, O. (2011) *Un si petit monde* (Paris: Fayard).

Berger, P. and Luckmann, T. (1989) *La construction sociale de la réalité* (Paris: Méridiens-Klincksiek).

Berglez, P. (2008) 'What is global journalism?', *Journalism Studies* 9/6: 845–58.

Bhatti, Y., Hansen, K. M., and Olsen, A. L. (2013) 'Political hypocrisy: The effect of political scandals on candidate evaluation', *Acta Politica*, 12 April, DOI:10.1057/ap.2013.6. 1-21.

Binderkrantz, A. S. and Green-Pedersen, C. (2009) 'Policy or processes in focus?', *International Journal of Press/Politics* 14/2: 166–85.

Blach-Ørsten, M. (2011) 'Politiske Skandaler i Danske Medier 1980-2010', *Tidsskriftet Politik* 14/3: 7-16.

—— (2012a) *Skandalemaskinen* (Østerbro: Columbus).

—— (2012b) 'Pressen og EU-formandskabet', *Økonomi & Politik* 85/3: 51-62.

Blach-Ørsten, M. and Bro, P. (2009) 'Inde på Christiansborg: Den synkroniserede journalistik', in A. B. Lund, I. Willig, and M. Blach-Ørsten (eds), *Hvor kommer nyhederne fra?* (Århus: AJOUR), pp. 9-28.

Blumler, J. (ed.) (1992) *Television and the Public Interest: Vulnerable Values in West European Broadcasting* (London: Sage).

Blumler, J. and Gurevitch, M. (1995) *The Crisis of Public Communication* (London: Routledge).

Blumler, J. and Gurevitch, M. (2001) 'Americanization reconsidered: U.K.-U.S. campaign communication comparison across time', in W. L. Bennett and R. M. Entman (eds), *Mediated Politics: Communication in the Future of Democracy* (New York: Cambridge University Press), pp. 380-406.

Bond, P. (2011) 'Mitt Romney claims he'll cut off funding for PBS, says he wants advertisements on "Sesame Street"', *Hollywood Reporter*, 28 December, available at www.hollywoodreporter.com/news/mitt-romney-pbs-big-bird-sesame-street-276555 (accessed 21 August 2012).

Boyd-Barrett, O. (1980) *The International News Agencies* (London: Constable).

Boyd-Barrett, O., Seymour-Ure, C., and Tunstall, J. (1977) *Studies on the Press* (London: HMSO).

Brants, K. and Voltmer, K. (eds) (2011) *Political Communication in Postmodern Democracy: Challenging the Primacy of Politics* (Basingstoke: Palgrave Macmillan).

Brevini, B. (2010) 'Towards PSB 2.0? Applying the PSB ethos to online media in Europe: A comparative study of PSBs' internet policies in Spain, Italy and Britain', *European Journal of Communication* 25/4: 348-65.

Brown, L. (1985) *Victorian News and Newspapers* (Oxford: Claredon Press).

Brown, R. (2011) 'Mediatization and news management in a comparative institutional perspective', in K. Brants and K. Voltmer (eds), *Political Communication in Postmodern Democracy* (Basingstoke: Palgrave Macmillan), pp. 59-74.

Brüggemann, M. and Kleinen-von Königslöw, K. (2009) '"Let's talk about Europe": Why Europeanization shows a different face in different newspapers', *European Journal of Communication* 24/1: 27-48.

Bruno, N. and Nielsen, R. K. (2012) *Survival is Success: Journalistic Online Start-ups in Western Europe* (Oxford: Reuters Institute for the Study of Journalism).

Bruns, T. (2007) *Republik der Wichtigtuer: Ein Bericht aus Berlin* (Freiburg: Herder).

Canel, M. J., Holtz-Bacha, C., and Mancini, P. (2007) *Conflict as a frame in television coverage of politics: A comparative study in Italy, Spain and Germany.* Paper presented at ICE Annual Meeting, San Francisco, 24 May.

Carlyle, T. (1841) *On Heroes, Hero Worship, and the Heroic in History* (London: James Fraser).

Carton, D. (2003) *'Bien entendu ... c'est off'* (Paris: Albin Michel).

Castle, S. (2010) 'As the E.U. does more, fewer tell about it', *New York Times*, 22 March, available at www.nytimes.com/2010/03/23/business/global/23press. html?pagewanted=all&_r=0 (accessed 12 August 2013).

Censis (2010) *Rapporto sulla situazione sociale del Paese* (Milano: Franco Angeli).

Center for Responsive Politics (2012) '2012 election spending will reach $6 billion, Center for Responsive Politics predicts', available at www.opensecrets.org/ news/2012/10/2012-election-spending-will-reach-6.html (accessed 12 August 2013).

Chadwick, A. (2011) 'The political information cycle in a hybrid news system: The British prime minister and the "Bullygate" affair', *International Journal of Press/Politics* 16/1: 3–29.

Chalaby, J. K. (1996) 'Journalism as an Anglo-American invention: A comparison of the development of French and Anglo-American journalism, 1830s–1920s', *European Journal of Communication* 11/3: 303–26.

Chang, T.-K. (1998) 'All countries are not created equal to be news: World system and international communication', *Communication Research* 25: 528–66.

Chang, T.-K., Himelboim, I., and Dong, D. (2009) 'Open global networks, closed international flows: World system and political economy of hyperlinks in cyberspace', *International Communication Gazette* 71/3: 137–59.

Charon, J.-M. (2009) 'Le journalisme d'investigation et la recherche d'une nouvelle légitimité', in A. Mercier (ed.), *Le Journalisme* (Paris: CNRS Éditions), pp. 113–28.

Chemin, A. and Catalano, G. (2005) *Une famille au secret* (Paris: Stock).

Chia, L. (2007) *Foreign news coverage in four online newspapers* (Unpublished BA honours thesis: School of Journalism and Communication, University of Queensland, Brisbane).

Chupin, I., Hubé, N., and Kaciaf, N. (2009) *Histoire politique et économique des médias en France* (Paris: La Découverte).

Cocconi, G. (2010) 'Il giornalismo politico e i suoi paradossi', *Problemi dell'Informazione* 35/1–2: 116–20.

Cohen, A. (2012) *De Vichy à la Communauté européenne* (Paris: Presses Universitaires de France).

Cohen, P. and Lévy, E. (2008) *Notre métier a mal tourné* (Paris: Mille et une nuits).

COI (1979–2012) *The IPO Directory: Information and Press Officers in Government Departments and Public Corporations* (London: Central Office of Information).

Cook, T. E. (1998) *Governing with the News: The News Media as a Political Institution* (Chicago, IL: University of Chicago Press).

Cornia, A. (2010) 'The Europeanization of Mediterranean journalism practices and the Italianization of Brussels: Dynamics of interaction between EU institutions and national journalism cultures', *European Journal of Communication* 25/4: 366–81.

Couldry, N., Livingstone, S. M., and Markham, T. (2010) *Media Consumption and Public Engagement: Beyond the Presumption of Attention* (Basingstoke: Palgrave Macmillan).

Currah, A. (2009) *What's Happening to Our News* (Oxford: Reuters Institute for the Study of Journalism).

Curran, J. (2011) *Media and Democracy* (London: Routledge).

Curran, J. and Park, M. (eds) (2000) *De-Westernizing Media Studies* (London: Routledge).

Curran, J. and Seaton, J. (2003, 6th edn) *Power Without Responsibility* (London: Routledge).

Curran, J., Iyengar, S., Lund, A. B., and Salovaara-Moring, I. (2009) 'Media reporting, public knowledge and democracy: A comparative study', *European Journal of Communication* 24/1: 5–26.

Cushion, S. (2012a) *The Democratic Value of News: Why Public Service Media Matter* (Basingstoke: Palgrave Macmillan).

——— (2012b) *Television Journalism* (London: Sage).

Cushion, S. and Lewis, J. (2009) 'Towards a "Foxification" of 24 hour news channels in Britain? An analysis of market driven and publicly funded news coverage', *Journalism: Theory, Practice and Criticism* 10/2: 131–53.

Dakhlia, J. (2008) *Politique people* (Paris: Bréal).

Dalen, A. van (2012) 'The people behind the political headlines: A comparison of political journalists in Denmark, Germany, the United Kingdom and Spain', *International Communication Gazette* 74/5: 464–83.

Dalen, A. van and Aelst, P. van (2012) 'Political journalists: Covering politics in the democratic-corporatist media system', in D. H. Weaver and L. C. Willnat (eds), *The Global Journalist in the 21st Century* (New York: Routledge), pp. 511–25.

Dalen, A. van, Albaek, E., and de Vreese, C. H. (2011) 'Suspicious minds: Explaining political cynicism among political journalists in Europe', *European Journal of Communication* 26/2: 147–62.

Dalton, R. J. (2007) *Democratic Challenges, Democratic Choices: The Erosion of Political Support in Advanced Industrial Democracies* (Oxford: Oxford University Press).

D'Arma, A. (2010) 'Italian television in the multichannel age: Change and continuity in industry structure, programming and consumption', *Convergence* 16/2: 201–15.

Davies, N. (2008) *Flat Earth News* (London: Chatto & Windus).

Davis, A. (2002) *Public Relations Democracy: Public Relations, Politics and the Mass Media in Britain* (Manchester: Manchester University Press).

―――― (2007) *The Mediation of Power: A Critical Introduction* (London: Routledge).

―――― (2009) 'Journalist–source relations, mediated reflexivity and the politics of politics', *Journalism Studies* 10/2: 204–19.

―――― (2010a) *Political Communication and Social Theory* (London: Routledge).

―――― (2010b) 'New media and fat democracy: The paradox of online participation', *New Media & Society* 11/8: 1–19.

Davis, M. S. (1971) 'That's interesting! Towards a phenomenology of sociology and a sociology of phenomenology', *Philosophy of the Social Sciences* 1: 309–44.

De Jong, J. (1977) 'The press attaché: Background, status, task', *International Communication Gazette* 55/2: 171–84.

Deuze, M. (2002) 'National news cultures: A comparison of Dutch, German, British, Australian and US journalists', *Journalism Quarterly* 79/1: 134–49.

Diamanti, I. (2011) 'L'Italia sfiducia i Tg Rai-set e cerca libertà su Internet', *La Repubblica*, 12 December.

Dimitrova, D. V. and Strömbäck, J. (2009) 'Look who's talking: Use of sources in newspaper coverage in Sweden and the United States', *Journalism Practice* 3/1: 75–91.

Dobek-Ostrowska, B., Głowacki, M., Jakubowicz, K., and Sükösd, M. (eds) (2010) *Comparative Media Systems: European and Global Perspectives* (Budapest: CEU and COST A30 publication).

Domenach, N. and Szafran, M. (2011) *OFF: Ce que Nicolas Sarkozy n'aurait jamais dû nous dire* (Paris: Fayard).

Donsbach, W. (1995) 'Lapdogs, watchdogs and junkyard dogs', *Media Studies Journal* 9: 17–30.

Donsbach, W. and Patterson, T. E. (2004) 'Political news journalists: Partisanship, professionalism, and political roles in five countries', in F. Esser and B. Pfetsch (eds), *Comparing Political Communication: Theories, Cases, and Challenges* (New York: Cambridge University Press), pp. 251–70.

Dorman, W. (1986) 'Peripheral vision: U.S. journalism and the third world', *World Policy* Summer: 419–45.

Duverger, M. (1974) *La monarchie républicaine – ou comment les démocraties se donnent des rois* (Paris: Robert Laffont).

EBU (2011) *PSB TV News: Trends and developments*. EBU Research in collaboration with the Eurovision News Exchange Secretariat upon commission from the EBU News Committee, available at www.ebu.ch/CMSimages/en/Executive_summery_SIS_TV_NEWS_2011_A4_tcm6-73002.pdf (accessed 19 August 2012).

——— (2012) 'EBU viewpoint on PSM funding', EBU internal document.

Ehrlich, M. (1995) 'The competitive ethos in television newswork', *Critical Studies in Mass Communication* 12: 196–212.

Elmelund-Præstekær, C., Hopmann, D. K., and Nørgaard, A. S. (2011) 'Does mediatization change MP–media interaction and MP attitudes toward the media? Evidence from a longitudinal study of Danish MPs', *International Journal of Press/Politics* 16/3: 382–403.

Entman, R. (2012) *Scandal and Silence* (Cambridge: Polity).

Erickson, E. and Hamilton, J. (2007) 'Happy landings: A defense of parachute journalism', in D. Perlmutter and J. Maxwell Hamilton (eds), *From Pigeons to News Portals: Foreign Reporting and the Challenge of New Technology* (Baton Rouge, LA: Louisiana State University Press), pp. 130–49.

Esmark, A. and Blach-Ørsten, M. (2011) 'Et komparativ blik på den politiske kommunikationskultur i Danmark', *Økonomi & Politik* 84/1: 3–18.

Esmark, A. and Mayerhöffer, E. (2012) 'The personalisation puzzle: Linking personalization of media coverage to institutional and cultural factors in six European parliamentary democracies.' Unpublished working paper.

Esmark, A. and Ørsten, M. (2008) 'Media and politics in Denmark', in J. Strömbäck, M. Ørsten, and T. Aalberg (eds), *Communicating Politics: Political Communication in the Nordic Countries*, (Gothenburg: Nordicom), pp. 25–44.

Esser, F. (2008) 'Dimensions of political news cultures: Sound bite and image bite news in France, Germany, Great Britain, and the United States', *International Journal of Press/Politics* 13/4: 401–28.

Esser, F. and Hemmer, H. (2008) 'Characteristics and dynamics of election news coverage in Germany', in J. Strömbäck and L. L. Kaid (eds), *The Handbook of Election News Coverage around the World* (New York and London: Routledge), pp. 289–307.

Esser, F. and Pfetsch, B. (eds) (2004) *Comparing Political Communication: Theories, Cases and Challenges* (Cambridge: Cambridge University Press).

Esser, F., Reinemann, C., and Fan, D. (2001) 'Spin doctors in the United States, Great Britain, and Germany', *Harvard International Journal of Press/Politics* 6/1: 16–45.

Esser, F., de Vreese, C. H., Strömbäck, J., Aelst, P. van, Aalberg, T., Stanyer, J., Lengauer, G., Berganza, R., Legnante, G., Papathanassopoulos, S., Salgado, S., Sheafer, T., and Reinemann, C. (2012) 'Political information opportunities in Europe: A longitudinal and comparative study of thirteen television systems', *International Journal of Press/Politics* 17/3: 247–74.

Fengler, S. and Russ-Mohl, S. (2008) 'Journalists and the information-attention markets: Towards an economic theory of journalism', *Journalism* 9/6: 667–90.

Fenton, N. (ed.) (2010) *New Media, Old News: Journalism and Democracy in a Digital Age* (London: Sage).

Ferenczi, T. (1993) *L'invention du journalisme en France* (Paris: Plon).

——— (2005) *Le Journalisme* (Paris: PUF).

Ferree, M. M., Gamson, W. A., Gerhards, J., and Rucht, D. (2002) *Shaping Abortion Discourse: Democracy and the Public Sphere in Germany and the United States* (New York: Cambridge University Press).

Fieg (2012) *La Stampa in Italia*. Annual report, available at www.fieg.it/salastampa_item.asp?sta_id=702 (accessed 13 August 2013).

Findahl, O. (1999) 'Public service broadcasting: A fragile, yet durable construction', *Nordicom Review* 20/1: 13–19.

Fishman, M. (1980) *Manufacturing News* (Austin, TX: University of Texas).

Fleeson, L. (2003) 'Bureau of missing bureaus', *American Journalism Review* 25/7: 7–10.

Forcella, E. (1959) 'Millecinquecento lettori', *Tempo Presente* 6.

Fottorino, E. (2012) *Mon tour du 'monde'* (Paris: Gallimard).

Franklin, B. (1997) *Newszak and News Media* (London: Arnold).

——— (2005) 'McJournalism: The local press and the McDonaldization thesis', in S. Allan (ed.), *Journalism: Critical Issues* (Maidenhead: Open University Press), pp. 137–50.

——— (2012) 'The future of journalism: Developments and debates', *Journalism Studies* 13/5–6: 663–81.

Franks, S. (2010) 'The neglect of Africa and the power of aid', *International Communication Gazette* 72/1: 71–84.

Freedman, D. (2010) 'The political economy of the "new" news environment', in N. Fenton (ed.), *New Media, Old News: Journalism and Democracy in a Digital Age* (London: Sage), pp. 35–50.

Galtung, J. and Ruge, M. (1965) 'The structure of foreign news: The presentation of the Congo, Cuba and Cyprus in four Norwegian newspapers', *Journal of International Peace Research* 1: 64–91.

Gambaro, M. (2010) 'La difficile partita dei quotidiani politici. E la droga dei contributi pubblici', *Problemi dell'Informazione* 35/1–2: 91–115.

Gandy, O. (1982) *Beyond Agenda Setting: Information Subsidies and Public Policy* (Norwood, NJ: Ablex Publishing Corporation).

Gans, H. J. (1979) *Deciding What's News: A Study of CBS Evening News, NBC Nightly News, Newsweek and Time* (New York: Pantheon).

Gasher, M. and Gabriele, S. (2004) 'Increasing circulation? A comparative news-flow study of the *Montreal Gazette*'s hard copy and on-line editions', *Journalism Studies* 5/3: 311–23.

Genestar, A. (2008) *Expulsion* (Paris: Bernard Grasset).

Gerstlé, J. (2008, 2nd edn) *La communication politique* (Paris: Armand Colin).

Gitlin, T. (1980) *The Whole World is Watching* (Berkeley, CA: University of California Press).

Golding, P. (1998) 'Global village or cultural pillage? The unequal inheritance of the communications revolution', in R. McChesney, E. Meiksins Wood, and J. Bellamy Foster (eds), *Capitalism and the Information Age: The Political Economy of the Global Communication Revolution* (New York: Monthly Review Press), pp. 69–85.

Gorius, A. and Moreau, M. (2011) *Les gourous de la com* (Paris: La Découverte).

Gowing, N. (2009) *'Skyful of Lies' and Black Swans: The New Tyranny of Shifting Information Power in Crises* (Oxford: Reuters Institute for the Study of Journalism).

Graves, L. (2007) 'The affordances of blogging', *Journal of Communication Inquiry* 31/4: 331–46.

Green-Pedersen, C. and Stubager, R. (2010) 'Medierne og den politiske dagsorden: En tango med fører?', *Politica* 42/3: 326–44.

Griessner, C. (2012) *News Agencies and Social Media: A Relationship with a Future?* (Oxford: Reuters Institute for the Study of Journalism), available at https://reutersinstitute.politics.ox.ac.uk/fileadmin/documents/Publications/fellows__papers/2012-2013/NEWS_AGENCIES_AND_SOCIAL_MEDIA.pdf (accessed 13 August 2013).

Hachmeister, L. (2007) *Nervöse Zone: Politik und Journalismus in der Berliner Republik* (München: DVA).

d'Haenens, L. and Verelst, C. (2002) 'Portrayal of Indonesia's reform in the Dutch print media', *Gazette: The International Journal for Communication Studies* 64/2: 183–97.

Halimi, S. (2005, 2nd edn) *Les nouveaux chiens de garde* (Paris: Raisons d'Agir).

Hallin, D. C. (1992) 'The passing of the "high modernism" of American journalism', *Journal of Communication* 42/3: 14–25.

Hallin, D. C. and Mancini, P. (2004) *Comparing Media Systems: Three Models of Media and Politics* (Cambridge: Cambridge University Press).

Hallin, D. and Papathanassopoulos, S. (2002) 'Political clientelism and the media: Southern Europe and Latin America in comparative perspective', *Media, Culture & Society* 24: 175–95.

Hamilton, J. (2009) *Journalism's Roving Eye: A History of American Foreign Correspondence* (Baton Rouge, LA: Louisiana State University Press).

Hamilton, J. M. and Jenner, E. (2004) 'Redefining foreign correspondence', *Journalism: Theory, Practice and Criticism* 5: 301–21.

Hamilton, J. M. and Lawrence, R. (2010) 'Bridging past and present: Using history and practice to inform social scientific study of foreign newsgathering', *Journalism Studies* 11/5: 683–99.

Hanitzsch, T. (2011) 'Populist disseminators, detached watchdogs, critical change agents and opportunist facilitators: Professional milieus, the journalistic field and autonomy in 18 countries', *International Communication Gazette* 73/6: 477–94.

Hanitzsch, T. and Mellado, C. (2011) 'What shapes the news around the world? How journalists in 18 countries perceive influences on their work', *International Journal of Press/Politics* 16/3: 404–26.

Hansard (2009) *Audit of Political Engagement 6: The 2009 Report* (London: Hansard Society).

Hardy, J. (2008) *Western Media Systems* (London: Routledge).

Hargittai, E. and Walejko, G. (2008) 'The participation divide: Content creation and sharing in the digital age', *Information, Communication and Society* 11/2: 239–56.

Hargreaves, I. (2000) 'Is there a future of foreign news?', *Historical Journal of Film, Radio and Television* 20/1: 55–61.

Hargreaves, I. and Thomas, J. (2002) *New News, Old News* (London: ITC).

Harris, P. (1981) *Reporting Southern Africa: Western News Agencies Reporting from Southern Africa* (Paris: UNESCO).

Harrits, G. S. (2006) '"Men Jeg Vil Godt Bare Have Det Serveret Lidt Nemt": Om Praktiske Forskelle i Politisk Kommunikation', *Politica* 38/2: 173–86.

Hartley, J. M. (2013) 'The online journalist between ideals and audience', *Journalism Practice*, DOI:10.1080/17512786.2012.755386.

Hayward, J. and Wright, V. (2002) *Governing from the Centre* (Oxford: Oxford University Press).

Heffernan, R. (2003) 'Political parties and the party system', in P. Dunleavy, A. Gamble, R. Heffernan, and G. Peele (eds), *Developments in British Politics 7* (Basingstoke: Palgrave Macmillan), pp. 119–39.

Heinrich, A. (2008) *Network journalism: Moving towards a global journalism culture*. Paper presented to RIPE conference, Mainz, 9–11 October.

Hendricks, M. (2012) 'Newspaper websites see increases in unique and average daily visitors in first quarter', *Newspaper Association of America*, available at www.naa.org/News-and-Media/Press-Center/Archives/2012/Newspaper-Websites-See-Increases-In-Unique-And-Average-Daily-Visitors-In-First-Quarter.aspx (accessed 12 August 2013).

Henning, D. (2011) 'Netherlands budget cuts hit social services', *World Socialist*, 12 July, available at www.wsws.org/articles/2011/jul2011/neth-j12.shtml (accessed 20 August 2012).

Herrnson, P. S. (2004, 4th edn) *Congressional Elections* (Washington, DC: CQ Press).

Hiatt, F. (2001) 'The vanishing foreign correspondent', *Washington Post*, 29 January.

Hibberd, M. (2001) 'The reform of public service broadcasting in Italy', *Media, Culture & Society* 23: 233–52.

Hjarvard, S. (2007) 'Den politiske presse: En analyse af danske avisers politiske orientering', *Journalistica* 5: 27–53.

Hobsbawm, J. and Lloyd, J. (2008) *The Power of the Commentariat* (London: Editorial Intelligence).

Hofmann, G. (2007) *Die Verschwörung der Journaille zu Berlin* (Bonn: Bouvier Verlag).

Hohenberg, J. (1995) *Foreign Correspondence: The Great Reporters and Their Times* (Syracuse, NY: Syracuse University Press).

Holm, H.-H. (2001) 'The effect of globalization on media structures and norms: Globalization and the choice of foreign news', in S. Hjarvard (ed.), *News in a Globalized Society* (Göteborg: Nordicom), pp. 113–28.

Humphreys, P. (1996) *Mass Media and Media Policy in Western Europe* (Manchester: Manchester University Press).

International Press Association (2010) 'Brussels press corps "shrinking", journalists say', 22 March.

Iosifidis, P. (ed.) (2010) *Reinventing Public Service Communication: European Broadcasters and Beyond* (Basingstoke: Palgrave Macmillan).

Ipsos-MORI (2009) *Trust in People* (London: Ipsos-MORI), September.

Isimm Ricerche (2009) *2008: Un Anno di informazione televisiva* (Perugia: Morlacchi Editore).

Isimm Ricerche (2010) *2009: Un Anno di informazione televisiva* (Perugia: Morlacchi Editore).

Itanes (ed.) (2006) *Dov'è la vittoria? Il voto del 2006 raccontato dagli italiani* (Bologna: Il Mulino).

Iyengar, S., Hahn, K. S., Bonfadelli, H., and Marr, M. (2009) '"Dark areas of ignorance" revisited: Comparing international affairs knowledge in Switzerland and the United States', *Communication Research* 36/3: 241–58.

Jakubowicz, K. (2010) 'PSB 3.0: Reinventing European PSB', in P. Iosifidis (ed.), *Reinventing Public Service Communication: European Broadcasters and Beyond* (Basingstoke: Palgrave Macmillan), pp. 9–22.

Jamieson, K. H. and Cappella, J. N. (2008) *Echo Chamber* (Oxford; New York: Oxford University Press).

Jansen, C. and Maier, J. (2012) 'Die Causa zu Guttenberg im Spiegel der Printmedien: Ergebnisse einer Inhaltsanalyse zur Berichterstattung führender deutscher Tageszeitungen über den Plagiatsskandal', *Zeitschrift für Politikberatung* 5: 3–12.

Jensen, J. (2006) 'The Minnesota e-democracy project: Mobilising the mobilised?', in S. Oates, D. Owen, and R. Gibson (eds), *The Internet and Politics: Citizens, Voters and Activists* (London: Routledge), pp. 34–51.

Jones, T. M. (2007) 'Book review: Hallin, D. C. and Mancini, P. (2004). *Comparing Media Systems: Three Models of Media and Politics*. New York: Cambridge University Press', *Comparative Political Studies* 2008/41: 128–31.

Joye, S. (2010) *Around the world in 8 pages? A longitudinal analysis of international news coverage in Flemish newspapers (1986–2006)*. Working papers Film & TV Studies, available at https://biblio.ugent.be/input/download?func=downlo adFile&recordOId=940464&fileOId=940470 (accessed 15 January 2013).

Kaciaf, N. (2013) *Les Pages 'Politique'* (Rennes: Presses Universitaires de Rennes).

Kalb, M. (1990) 'Foreword', in S. Serfaty (ed.), *The Media and Foreign Policy* (New York: St Martin's Press), pp. i–iii.

Katz, E. (1996) 'And deliver us from segmentation', *Annals of the American Academy of Political and Social Science* 546: 22–33.

Kaul, C. (1997) 'Imperial communications, Fleet Street and the Indian empire c1850s–1920s', in M. Bromley and T. O'Malley (eds), *Journalism: A Reader* (London: Routledge), pp. 58–86.

——— (2011) '"An imperial village": Communications, media and globalization in India', in P. Putnis, C. Kaul, and J. Wilke (eds), *International Communication and Global News Networks: Historical Perspectives* (New Jersey: Hampton Press), pp. 83–98.

Kepplinger, H. M. (2009) 'Rivalen um Macht und Moral: Bundestagsabgeordnete und Hauptstadtjournalisten', in H. Kaspar, H. Schoen, S. Schumann, and J. R. Winkler (eds), *Politik – Wissenschaft – Medien: Festschrift für Jürgen W.*

Falter zum 65. Geburtstag (Wiesbaden: VS Verlag für Sozialwissenschaften), pp. 307–21.

Kepplinger, H. M. and Maurer, M. (2008) 'Das fragmentierte Selbst: Rollenkonflikte im Journalismus – das Beispiel der Berliner Korrespondenten', in B. Pörsken, W. Loosen, and A. Scholl (eds), *Paradoxien des Journalismus: Festschrift für Siegfried Weischenberg* (Wiesbaden: VS Verlag für Sozialwissenschaften), pp. 165–82.

Kester, B. (2007) 'Windows on the world: The presentation of international news, 1880–1980', in M. Broersma (ed.), *Form and Style in Journalism: European Newspapers and the Presentation of News, 1880–2005* (Groningen: Peeters), pp. 115–32.

Kirchner, L. (2012) 'Scandinavian public media fight for their right to grow', *Columbia Journalism Review*, 31 May.

Köcher, R. (2011) 'Das Auseinanderdriften der sozialen Schichten als Herausforderung für Information und Kommunikation', available at www. ifd-allensbach.de/fileadmin/AWA/AWA_Praesentationen/2011/AWA2011_ Koecher.pdf (accessed 20 November 2012).

Kolmer, C. and Semetko, H. (2010) 'International television news: Germany compared', *Journalism Studies* 11/5: 700–17.

Kuhn, R. (2004) '"Vive la différence"? The mediation of politicians' public images and private lives in France', *Parliamentary Affairs* 57/1: 24–40.

—— (2010) '"Les médias, c'est moi": President Sarkozy and news media management', *French Politics* 8/4: 355–76.

—— (2011) *The Media in Contemporary France* (Maidenhead: Open University Press).

Kuhn, R. and Neveu, E. (eds) (2002) *Political Journalism: New Challenges, New Practices* (London: Routledge).

Kumar, M. J. (2007) *Managing the President's Message* (Baltimore, MD: Johns Hopkins University Press).

La Croix (2012) TNS Sofres, *Baromètre de confiance dans les media*, 2012 (Paris).

—— (2013) TNS Sofres, *Baromètre de confiance dans les media*, 2013 (Paris).

Ladd, J. M. (2012) *Why Americans Hate the Media and How It Matters* (Princeton, NJ: Princeton University Press).

Lafon, B. (2012) *Histoire de la télévision régionale* (Paris: INA Éditions).

Lagroye, J. (1997) 'On ne subit pas son rôle', interview with B. Gaïti and F. Sawicki, *Politix* 38: 7–17.

Lazersfeld, P. (1940) *Radio and the Printed Page* (New York: Duell, Sloan & Pearce).

Lee-Wright, P., Philips, A., and Witschge, T. (2012) *Changing Journalism* (London: Routledge).

Leibovich, M. (2010) 'Politico's Mike Allen, the man the White House wakes up to', *New York Times*, 21 April, magazine, available at www.nytimes. com/2010/04/25/magazine/25allen-t.html (accessed 13 August 2013).

Lengauer, G., Esser, F., and Berlganza, R. (2011) 'Negativity in political news: A review of concepts, operationalizations and key findings', *Journalism* 13/2: 179–202.

Lesmeister, C. (2008) *Informelle politische Kommunikationskultur: Hinter den Kulissen politisch-medialer Kommunikation* (Wiesbaden: VS Verlag für Sozialwissenschaften).

Leveson, B. (2012) *The Leveson Inquiry: An Inquiry into the Culture, Production and Ethics of the Press. Executive Summary* (London: HMSO).

Levy, D. A. L. and Nielsen, R. K. (eds) (2010) *The Changing Business of Journalism and Its Implications for Democracy* (Oxford: Reuters Institute for the Study of Journalism).

Lewis, C., Butts, B., and Musselwhite, K. (2012) 'A second look: The new Journalism Ecosystem', available at http://investigativereportingworkshop.org/ilab/story/ second-look (accessed 12 August 2013).

Lewis, J., Williams, A., and Franklin, B. (2008) 'A compromised fourth estate? UK news journalism, public relations and news sources', *Journalism Studies* 9/1: 1–20.

Lijphart, A. (1999) *Patterns of Democracy: Government Forms and Performances in Thirty Six Countries* (New Haven, CT: Yale University Press).

Löffelholz, M. and Weaver, D. (eds) (2008) *Global Journalism Research* (New York and London: Blackwell Press).

Lund, A. B. (2002) *Den redigerende magt* (Århus: Aarhus Universitetsforlag).

Lund, A. B. and Lindskow, K. (2011) 'Offentlig mediestøtte fra postprivilegier til licensforlig', *Økonomi & Politik* 48/1: 46–60.

Lund, A. B., Willig, I., and Blach-Ørsten, M. (2009) *Hvor kommer nyhederne fra?* (Århus: Forlaget Ajour).

Lünenborg, M. and Berghofer, S. (2010) 'Politikjournalistinnen und -journalisten', available at www.dfjv.de/fileadmin/user_upload/pdf/Politikjournalistinnen_ und_Journalisten.pdf (accessed 20 November 2012).

Macaulay, T. (1828) 'Hallam's constitutional history', *Edinburgh Review*.

MacBride, S. (1980) *Many Voices, One World: Communication and Society. Today and Tomorrow* (Paris: UNESCO).

Magnette, P. (2000) *L'Europe, l'Etat et la démocratie* (Paris: Editions Complexe).

Mancini, P. (1994) *Sussurri e Grida dalle Camere* (Milano: Franco Angeli).

—— (2000) 'Political complexity and alternative models of journalism: The Italian case', in J. Curran and M. J. Park (eds), *De-westernizing Media Studies* (London: Routledge), pp. 265–78.

—— (2002) *Il Sistema Fragile* (Roma: Carocci).

———— (2005) 'Is there a European model of journalism?', in H. de Burgh (ed.), *Making Journalists: Diverse Models, Global Issues* (London: Routledge), pp. 77–93.

———— (2007a) 'La Lottizzazione of Italian RAI: Between pluralism, consociational democracy and clientilism', in H. Bohrmann, E. Klaus, and M. Machill (eds), *Media Industry, Journalism Culture and Communication Policies in Europe* (Cologne: Herbert von Halem Verlag), pp. 107–24.

———— (2007b) *Journalism culture: A two-level proposal.* Paper presented at the ICA Annual Conference 2007 (24–28 May), San Francisco.

———— (2011) *Between Commodification and Lifestyle Politics: Does Silvio Berlusconi Provide a New Model of Politics for the Twenty-first Century?* (Oxford: Reuters Institute for the Study of Journalism).

Mandaza, I. (1986) 'News from the third world: Crossing the barrier', in P. Desbarats and J. Southerst (eds), *Information/Crisis/Development: News from the Third World* (Ontario: University of Western Ontario), pp. 132–41.

Marchetti, D. (2005) 'La fin d'un Monde? Les transformations du traitement de la "politique étrangère" dans les chaînes de télévision françaises grand public', in L. Arnaud et C. Guionnet (eds), *Les frontières du politique: Enquêtes sur les processus de politisation et de dépolitisation* (Rennes: Presses Universitaires de Rennes), pp. 49–77.

Martin, J. (2011) 'What's so wrong with "parachute journalism"?', *Columbia Journalism Review*, 26 May.

Masure, B. (2009) *Journalistes à la niche?* (Paris: Hugo & Co.).

Mazzoleni, G, Vigevani, G., and Splendore, S. (2011) *Mapping Digital Media: Italy.* Open Society Foundations Country Report, available at www.soros.org/reports/mapping-digital-media-italy.

McCarty, N. M., Poole, K. T., and Rosenthal, H. (2006) *Polarized America* (Cambridge, MA: MIT Press).

McChesney, R. (2000) *Rich Media, Poor Democracy: Communication Politics in Dubious Times* (New York: New Press).

McClellan, S. (2008) *What Happened* (New York: Public Affairs).

McLachlin, S. and Golding, P. (2000) 'Tabloidization in the British Press: A Quantitative Investigation into Changes in British Newspapers 1952–1997', in C. Sparks and J. Tulloch (eds), *Tabloid Tales: Global Debates over Media Standards* (Oxford: Rowman & Littlefield), pp. 75–90.

McQuail, D. (1987, 2nd edn) *Mass Communication Theory* (London: Sage).

Meier, W. A. (2011) 'From media regulation to democratic media governance', in J. Trappel, W. A. Meir, L. d'Haenens, J. Steemers, and B. Thomass (eds), *Media in Europe Today* (Bristol: Intellect), pp. 153–66.

Mele, M. (2011) 'Santoro torna e fa il pieno di telespettatori: share al 12%', *Il Sole 24 Ore*, 5 November.

Mentana, E. (2009) *Passionaccia* (Milano: Rizzoli).

Meyen, M. and Riesmeyer, C. (2009) *Diktatur des Publikums: Journalisten in Deutschland* (Konstanz: UVK).

Moe, H. and Syvertsen, T. (2009) 'Researching public service broadcasting', in K. Wahl-Jorgensen and T. Hanitzsch (eds), *Handbook of Journalism Studies* (New York and London: Routledge).

Monteiro, C. (2002) 'Covering the lost empire: The Portuguese media and East Timor', *Journalism Studies* 3/2: 277–87.

Morrison, D. and Tumber, H. (1985) 'Foreign correspondent: Dateline London', *Media, Culture & Society* 7/4: 445–70.

Mosca L. and Vaccari, C. (2011) *Nuovi Media, Nuova Politica? Partecipazione e Mobilitazione Online, da MoveOn al Movimento 5 Stelle* (Milano: Franco Angeli).

Murrell, C. (2010) 'Baghdad bureaux: An exploration of the interconnected world of fixers and correspondents at the BBC and CNN', *Media, War & Conflict* 3/2: 125–37.

Neuberger, C., vom Hofe, H. J., and Nuernbergk, C. (2011) *Twitter und Journalismus: Der Einfluss des 'Social Web' auf die Nachrichten* (Düsseldorf: Landesanstalt für Medien Nordrhein-Westfalen).

Neuman, W. R. (1991) *The Future of the Mass Audience* (Cambridge: Cambridge University Press).

Neuman, W. R., Crigler, A. N., and Just, M. R. (1992) *Common Knowledge* (Chicago, IL: University of Chicago Press).

Neveu, E. (2002) 'Quatre configurations du journalisme politique', in R. Rieffel and T. Watine (eds), *Les Mutations du journalisme en France et au Québec* (Paris: Editions Panthéon Assas), pp. 251–76.

—— (2009, 3rd edn) *Sociologie du journalisme* (Paris: La Découverte).

Newman, N. (ed.) (2012) *The Reuters Institute Digital News Report 2012* (Oxford: Reuters Institute for the Study of Journalism).

Newspaper Association of America (2013) 'Newspaper readership & audience by age and gender', available at www.naa.org/Trends-and-Numbers/Readership/Age-and-Gender.aspx (accessed 12 August 2013).

Nielsen, R. K. (2012a) *Ten Years that Shook the Media World* (Oxford: Reuters Institute for the Study of Journalism).

—— (2012b) *Ground Wars: Personalized Communication in Political Campaigns* (Princeton, NJ: Princeton University Press).

Nielsen, R. K. and Levy, D. A. L. (2010) 'The changing business of journalism and its implications for democracy', in D. Levy and R. K. Nielsen (eds), *The*

Changing Business of Journalism and Its Implications for Democracy (Oxford: Reuters Institute for the Study of Journalism), pp. 3–15.

Nikoltchev, S. and Blázquez, F. J. C. (2011) 'Funding', in O. Steenfadt (ed.), *Future or Funeral? A Guide to Public Service Media Regulation in Europe* (Open University Foundations), pp. 77–108.

Norris, P. (1995) 'The restless searchlight: Network news framing of the post-Cold War world', *Political Communication* 12/4: 357–70.

—— (2000) *A Virtuous Circle: Political Communications in Postindustrial Societies* (Cambridge: Cambridge University Press).

—— (2011) *Democratic Deficit: Critical Citizens Revisited* (Cambridge: Cambridge University Press).

NUJ (2006) *National Union of Journalists Survey of Members* (London: National Union of Journalists).

Obijiofor, L. and Hanusch, F. (2003) 'Foreign news coverage in five African newspapers', *Australian Journalism Review* 23/1: 145–64.

Ørsten, M. (2004) *Transnational politisk journalistik* (Roskilde: Skriftserie fra Journalistik på RUC), nr. 1.

Ortoleva, P. (1997) 'Il Capitalismo Italiano e i Mezzi di Comunicazione di Massa', in F. Barca (ed.), *Storia del Capitalismo Italiano* (Roma: Donzelli), pp. 237–65.

Osservatorio di Pavia (2008) *Politica e Giornalismo nei Telegiornali Rai.* Paper available at http://osservatorio.it/download/RicercaTg.pdf (accessed 13 August 2013).

Padovani, C. (2009) 'Pluralism of information in the television sector in Italy: History and contemporary conditions', in A. Czepek, M. Hellwig, and E. Nowak (eds), *Press Freedom and Pluralism in Europe: Concepts and Conditions* (Bristol/Chicago: Intellect Books), pp. 289–304.

Palestini, L. (2011) 'Exploit La7: Volano gli ascolti del "terzo polo" della TV', *La Repubblica*, 2 February.

Palmer, M. (1978) 'The British press and international news 1851–1899', in J. Curran, G. Boyce, and P. Wingate (eds), *Newspaper History: From the 17th Century to the Present Day* (London: Constable), pp. 205–19.

Pape, T. von and Quandt, T. (2010) 'Wen erreicht der Wahlkampf 2.0? Eine Repräsentativstudie zum Informationsverhalten im Bundestagswahlkampf 2009', *Media Perspektiven* 9: 390–98.

Paterson, C. (2006) 'News agency dominance in international news on the internet', *Papers in International and Global Communication* (Leicester: Centre for International Communication Research).

—— (2007) 'International news on the internet: Why more is less', *Ethical Space: The International Journal of Communication Ethics* 4/2: 57–65.

Patterson, T. E. (1993) *Out of Order* (New York: A. Knopf).

———— (2000) *Doing Well and Doing Good: How Soft News and Critical Journalism are Shrinking the News Audience and Weakening Democracy – And What News Outlets Can Do about It* (Harvard University, CT: John F. Kennedy School of Government).

Péan, P. and Nick, C. (1997) *TF1 un pouvoir* (Paris: Fayard).

Pedersen, O. K., Kjær, P., Esmark, A., and Carlsen, E. M. (2000) *Politisk journalistik* (Århus, AJOUR).

Penty, C. (2011) 'Spain raises taxes, cuts spending to trim deficit: Highlights', *Bloomberg News*, available at Bloomberg.com/news/2011-12-30/spain-raises-taxes-cuts-spending-to-trim-deficit-highlights?category= (accessed 19 August 2012).

Pew Research Center (2011) 'Press widely criticized, but trusted more than other information sources', available at www.people-press.org/2011/09/22/press-widely-criticized-but-trusted-more-than-other-institutions (accessed 12 August 2013).

Pew Research Center's Project for Excellence in Journalism (1998) *Changing definitions of news*, Pew Project for Excellence report, available at www.journalism.org/node/1090 (accessed 19 August 2011).

Pew Research Center's Project for Excellence in Journalism (2012) *The state of the news media: An annual report on American journalism*, available at http://stateofthemedia.org/files/2012/08/2012_sotm_annual_report.pdf (accessed 19 August 2012).

Pfetsch, B. (2001) 'Political communication culture in the United States and Germany', *International Journal of Press/Politics* 6/1: 46–67.

———— (2004) 'From political culture to political communication culture', in F. Esser and B. Pfetsch (eds), *Comparing Political Communication* (Cambridge: Cambridge University Press), pp. 344–66.

———— (2008, 2nd edn) 'Government news management: Institutional approaches and strategies in three western democracies reconsidered', in D. A. Graber, D. McQuail, and P. Norris (eds), *The Politics of News, The News of Politics* (Washington, DC: CQ Press), pp. 71–97.

———— (ed.) (2013) *Political Communication Cultures in Western Europe*, (Houndmills: Palgrave Macmillan).

Pfetsch, B. and Esser, F. (2013) 'Political communication in comparative perspective: Key concepts and new insights', in C. Reinemann (ed.), *Political Communication. Volume 17 of the Handbook of Communication Sciences* (Berlin: deGruyterMouton).

Pfetsch, B. and Mayerhöffer, E. (2011) 'Vordergründige Nähe: Zur Kommunikationskultur von Politik- und Medieneliten', *Medien und Kommunikationswissenschaft* 59/1: 40–9.

Philips, A. (2010) 'Old sources, new bottles', in N. Fenton (ed.), *New Media, Old News: Journalism and Democracy in a Digital Age* (London: Sage), pp. 87–101.

Pike, R. and Winseck, D. (2004) 'The politics of global media reform, 1907–23', *Media, Culture & Society* 26/5: 643–75.

Pilichowski, H. (2012) *Sarkozy et la presse* (Paris: JC Lattès).

Plasser, F. and Lengauer, G. (2008) 'Television campaigning worldwide', in D. W. Johnson (ed.), *Routledge Handbook of Political Management* (New York: Routledge), pp. 253–71.

Plasser, F. and Plasser, G. (2002) *Global Political Campaigning* (Westport, CT: Praeger).

Plunkett, J. (2012) 'Newsnight: How years of cuts have hit the programme', *Guardian*, 12 November.

Pontzen, D. (2006) *Nur Bild, BamS und Glotze? Medialisierung der Politik aus Sicht der Akteure?* (Münster: Lit).

Prior, M. (2003) 'Any good news in soft news? The impact of soft news preference on political knowledge', *Political Communication* 20/2: 149–71.

——— (2007) *Post-broadcast Democracy: How Media Choice Increases Inequality in Political Involvement and Polarizes Elections* (New York: Cambridge University Press).

Quatremer, J. (2012) *Sexe, mensonges et médias* (Paris: Plon).

Raeymaeckers, K., Cosjin, L., and Deprez, A. (2007) 'Reporting the European Union: An analysis of the Brussels press corps and the mechanisms influencing the news flow', *Journalism Practice* 1/1: 102–19.

Raeymaeckers, K. and Golding, P. (2007) 'News agenda of EU-related news: A comparative research programme for ten European countries (7–28 March 2005)', in AIM Research Consortium (ed.), *Comparing the Logic of EU Reporting in Mass Media across Europe* (Bochum, Fribourg/Brsg.: Adequate Information Management in Europe), pp. 9–22.

Rantanen, T. (2007) 'The cosmopolitanization of news', *Journalism Studies* 8/6: 843–61.

Rasmussen, S. (2012) *Is There Anybody Out There? Crisis and Collaboration in Foreign Reporting* (Oxford: Reuters Institute for the Study of Journalism), available at https://reutersinstitute.politics.ox.ac.uk/fileadmin/documents/Publications/fellows__papers/2011-2012/Is_there_anybody_out_there_.pdf (accessed 13 August 2013).

Read, D. (1992) *The Power of News: The History of Reuters* (Oxford: Oxford University Press).

Reese, S., Rutigliano, L., Hyun, K., and Jeong, J. (2007) 'Mapping the blogosphere: Professional and citizen-based media in the global news arena', *Journalism: Theory, Criticism and Practice* 8/3: 235-61.

Regards sur l'actualité (2009) *La presse après les États généraux* (Paris: La documentation française), 350: 1-78.

Reinemann, C. (2003) *Medienmacher als Mediennutzer: Kommunikations- und Einflussstrukturen im politischen Journalismus der Gegenwart* (Köln: Böhlau).

———— (2004) 'Routine reliance revisited: Exploring media importance for German political journalists', *Journalism and Mass Communication Quarterly* 81/4: 857-76.

———— (2011) *Ökonomisierung = Entpolitisierung? Die Politik- und Wirtschafts berichterstattung der Bild-Zeitung 1984-2006.* Paper presented at the 3rd Joint Congress of the German, Swiss, and Austrian Sociological Societies, Innsbruck, Austria, 9 September-1 October.

Reinemann, C. and Fawzi, N. (2010) 'The shrinking news agenda: How market forces have shaped 24-hour television news channels in Germany', in S. Cushion and J. Lewis (eds), *The Rise of 24-Hour News Television* (New York: Peter Lang), pp. 299-318.

Reinemann, C. and Wilke, J. (2007) '"It's the debates, Stupid!" How the introduction of televised debates changes the portrayal of German chancellor candidates in the German press 1949-2005', *International Journal of Press/Politics* 12/4: 92-111.

Reinemann, C., Stanyer, J., Scherr, S. and Legnante, G. (2011) 'Hard and soft news: A review of concepts, operationalizations and key findings', *Journalism* 13/2: 221-39.

Richardson, K., Parry, K., and Corner, J. (2013) *Political Culture and Media Genre: Beyond the News* (Basingstoke: Palgrave Macmillan).

Ridet, P. (2008) *Le président et moi* (Paris: Albin Michel).

Rieffel, R. (1984) *L'élite des journalistes: les hérauts de l'information* (Paris: Presses Universitaires de France).

———— (2010) *Mythologie de la presse gratuite* (Paris: Le Cavalier Bleu).

———— (2012) 'L'évolution des pratiques journalistiques', in R. Le Champion (ed.), *journalisme 2.0* (Paris: La Documentation française), pp. 31-8.

Riffe, D., Aust, C. F., Jones, T. C., Shoemaker, B., and Sundar, S. (1994) 'The shrinking foreign newshole of *The New York Times*', *Newspaper Research Journal* 15: 74-88.

Rosen, J. (2006) 'The people formerly known as the audience', *PressThink*, 27 June, available at http://archive.pressthink.org/2006/06/27/ppl_frmr.html (accessed 13 August 2013).

Ryfe, D. (2006) 'Introduction: New institutionalism and the news', *Political Communication* 23/2: 135–44.

―――― (2012) *Can Journalism Survive?* (Cambridge: Polity).

Sambrook, R. (2011) *Are Foreign Correspondents Redundant?* (Oxford: Reuters Institute for the Study of Journalism).

Sani, G. (1980) 'The political culture of Italy: Continuity and change', in G. Almond and S. Verba (eds), *The Civic Culture Revisited* (Boston, MA: Little, Brown & Company), pp. 273–324.

Sartori, G. (1976) *Parties and Party Systems: A Framework for Analysis* (Cambridge: Cambridge University Press).

Schmidt, H. (2011) 'Journalismus 2.0 – Informationsströme durch das Social Web', available at http://de.slideshare.net/HolgerSchmidt/journalismus-20-informationsstrme-durch-das-social-web (accessed 15 November 2012).

Schneidermann, D. (2010) *Crise au Sarkozistan* (Paris: arretsurimages.net).

Schneller, J. (2012) 'Totgesagte leben länger', available at www.ifd-allensbach.de/awa/ergebnisse/2012.html (accessed 20 November 2012).

Schrøder, K. and Kobbernagel, C. (2012) *Danskernes brug af nyhedsmedier 2011* (Roskilde: Centre for Nyhedsforskning).

Schudson, M. (2001) 'The objectivity norm in American journalism', *Journalism* 2/2: 149–70.

―――― (2003) *Sociology of News* (New York: W.W. Norton & Co.).

Scott, B. (2005) 'A contemporary history of digital journalism', *Television & New Media* 6/1: 89–126.

Scott, D. K. and Gobetz, R. H. (1992) 'Hard news/soft news content of the national broadcast networks, 1972–1987', *Journalism Quarterly* 69/2: 406–12.

Seghetti, R. (2010) 'Comunicazione e informazione in Italia: Gli assetti proprietari ed economici', *Problemi dell'Informazione* 35/1–2: 29–62.

Semetko, H. A., Blumler, J. G., Gurevitch, M., Weaver, D. H., Barkin, S., and Wilhoit, G. C. (1991) *The Formation of Campaign Agendas: A Comparative Analysis of Party and Media Roles in Recent American and British Elections* (Hillsdale, NJ: Lawrence Erlbaum).

Servergnini, B. (2010) 'L'ossessione del nemico: La ricerca continua della rissa', *Il Corriere della Sera*, 15 October.

Shaw, D. (2001) 'Foreign news shrinks in era of globalization', *Los Angeles Times*, 20 September.

Shehata, A. and Strömbäck, J. (2011) 'A matter of context: A comparative study of media environments and news consumption gaps in Europe', *Political Communication* 28/1: 110, DOI:10.1080/10584609.2010.543006.

Siebert, F. S., Peterson, T., and Schramm, W. (1956) *Four Theories of the Press: The Authoritarian, Libertarian, Social Responsibility, and Soviet Communist Concepts of What the Press Should Be and Do* (Urbana and Chicago, IL: University of Illinois Press).

Sigal, L. V. (1973) *Reporters and Officials: The Organisation and Politics of Newsmaking* (Lexington, MA: Lexington Books).

Sjøvaag, H. (2012) 'Regulating commercial public service broadcasting: A case study of the marketization of Norwegian media policy', *International Journal of Cultural Policy* 18/2: 223–37.

Smith, A. (1997) 'Des élites sans territoires: les commissaires européens', *Pôle sud* 7: 48–56.

—— (2004) *Le gouvernement de l'Union européenne: Une sociologie politique* (Paris: LGDJ).

Sobieraj, S. (2010) 'Reporting conventions: Journalists, activists and the thorny struggle for political visibility', *Social Problems* 57/4: 505–28.

Sondage Ipsos Public Affairs (2013) 'France 2013: les nouvelles fractures', *Le Monde*, 25 January.

Soroka, S., Blake, A., Aalberg, T., Iyengar, S., Curran, J., Coen, S., Hayashi, K., Jones, P., Mazzoleni, G., Rhee, J. W., Rowe, D., and Tiffen, R. (2012) 'Auntie knows best? Public broadcasters and current affairs knowledge', *British Journal of Political Science*, published on Ifirst, 1–21, 6 December 2012.

Spanier, G. (2010) 'What will the BBC cut in its budget cull?', *Evening Standard*, 20 October, available at www.thisislondon.co.uk/markets/article/23889636-what-will-the-bbc-cut-in-its-budget-cull.do (accessed 20 August 2012).

Sparrow, B. H. (1999) *Uncertain Guardians: The News Media as an Institution* (Baltimore, MD: Johns Hopkins University Press).

Sreberny-Mohammadi, A. (1984) 'The "world of news"', *Journal of Communication* 34: 121–34.

Stanyer, J. (2013) *Intimate Politics* (Cambridge: Polity Press).

Starkman, D. (2010) 'The hamster wheel', *Columbia Journalism Review*, available at www.cjr.org/cover_story/the_hamster_wheel.php (accessed 13 August 2013).

Startt, J. (1991) *Journalists for Empire* (Westport, CT: Greenwood Press).

Statham, P. (1996) 'Television news and the public sphere in Italy: Conflicts at the media/politics interface', *European Journal of Communication* 11/4: 511–56.

Stella, G. A. (2009) 'Mentana: così dissi addio a Mediaset', *Il Corriere della Sera*, 13 May.

Storey, G. (1951) *Reuters Century 1851–1951* (London: Max Parish).

Strömbäck, J. and Dimitrova, D. V. (2006) 'Political and media systems matter: A comparison of election news coverage in Sweden and the U.S', *Harvard International Journal of Press/Politics* 11/4: 131–47.

Stroud, N. J. (2011) *Niche News: The Politics of News Choice* (New York: Oxford University Press).

Taylor, P. (1999) *British Propaganda in the Twentieth Century* (Edinburgh: Edinburgh University Press).

Tewksbury, D. and Rittenberg, J. (2012) *News on the Internet* (New York: Oxford University Press).

Thompson, J. B. (2000) *Political Scandal: Power and Visibility in the Media Age* (Cambridge: Polity Press).

Tiffen, R. (1989) *News and Power: The Role of the Media in Australian Politics* (Sydney: Allen & Unwin).

Total Press Search (1997) *European Voice subscriber study*.

Tracey, M. (1998) *Decline and Fall of Public Service Broadcasting* (Oxford: Oxford University Press).

Treanor, T. (2011) *2011 Blogging Statistics*, available at www.rightmixmarketing. com/right-mix-blog/blogging-statistics (accessed 13 August 2013).

Tuchman, G. (1972) 'Objectivity as strategic ritual: An examination of newsmen's notions of objectivity', *American Journal of Sociology* 77/January: 660–70.

—— (1978) *Making News* (New York: Free Press).

Tuggle, C. A., Casella, P., and Huffmann, S. (2010) 'Live, late-breaking and broken', in S. Cushion and J. Lewis (eds), *The Rise of 24-Hour News Television* (New York: Peter Lang), pp. 133–150.

Tuinstra, F. (2004) 'Caught between the Cold War and internet', *Nieman Reports*, available at http://nieman.harvard.edu/reportsitem.aspx?id=101905 (accessed 29 January 2009).

Tunstall, J. (1971) *Journalists at Work: Specialist Correspondents, Their News Organisations, News Sources and Competitor-Colleagues* (London: Constable).

—— (1996) *Newspaper Power: The National Press in Britain* (Oxford: Oxford University Press).

—— (2008) *The Media were American* (New York: Oxford University Press).

Vaccari, C. (2011) 'The news media as networked political actors: How Italian media are reclaiming political ground by harnessing online participation', *Information, Communication & Society* 14/7: 981–97.

Vaughan, C. (1999) 'Reporting from imperial frontiers: The making of foreign correspondents a century apart', *Asia Pacific Media Educator* 7/3: 37–52.

Vedel, T. (2013) 'Processus d'information des électeurs et suivi de campagne: le paradoxe des campagnes électorales', in P. Perrineau (ed.), *La décision électorale en 2012* (Paris: Armand Colin), pp. 59–68.

Viansson-Ponté, P. (1976) *Lettre ouverte aux hommes politiques* (Paris: Albin Michel).

Volz, Y. and Lee, C. C. (2011) 'Semi-colonialism and journalistic spheres of influences: British–American press competition in early twentieth-century China', *Journalism Studies* 12/5: 559–74.

Vos, T. P. (2012). '"Homo journalisticus": Journalism education's role in articulating the objectivity norm', *Journalism* 13/4: 435–49.

Watt, H., Marsden, S., Ross, T., and Swinford, S. (2012) 'Leveson Report: the verdict on individual newspapers', *Daily Telegraph*, 29 November, available at www. telegraph.co.uk/news/uknews/leveson-inquiry/9713061/Leveson-Report-the-verdict-on-individual-newspapers.html (accessed 4 September 2012).

Weaver, D. (1998) 'Journalists around the world: Commonalities and differences', in D. Weaver (ed.), *The Global Journalist: News People around the World* (Cresskill, NJ: Hampton Press), pp. 455–80.

Webster, J. G. (2008) 'Structuring a marketplace of attention', in J. Turow and L. Tsui (eds), *The Hyperlinked Society* (Ann Arbor, MI: University of Michigan Press), pp. 23–38.

Weischenberg, S., Maja, M., and Armin, S. (2006) *Die Souffleure der Mediengesellschaft: Report über die Journalisten in Deutschland* (Konstanz: UVK).

Wessler, H. (2008), 'Mediale Diskursöffentlichkeit im internationalen Vergleich – ein Forschungsprogramm', in G. Melischek, J. Seethaler, and J. Wilke (eds), *Medien und Kommunikationsforschung im Vergleich* (Wiesbaden: VS Verlag), pp. 219–36.

Wessler, H., Skorek, M., Kleinen-von Königslöw, K., Held, M., Dobreva, M., and Adolphsen, M. (2010) 'Comparing media systems and media content: Online newspapers in ten Eastern and Western European countries', in B. Dobek-Ostrowska, M. Glowacki, K. Jakubowicz, and M. Sükösd (eds), *Comparative Media Systems: European and Global Perspectives* (Budapest: Central European University Press), pp. 233–60.

Wheeler, M. (2004) 'Supranational regulation: Television and the European Union', *European Journal of Communication* 19/3: 349–69.

Who Makes the News? (2010), report from WACC, available at http://whomakesthenews.org/who-is-wacc.html.

Wilke, J. (1987) 'Foreign news coverage and international news flow over three centuries', *Gazette* 39: 147–80.

261

Wilke, J., Heimprecht, C., and Cohen, A. (2012) 'The geography of foreign news on television: A comparative study of 17 countries', *International Communication Gazette* 74/4: 301–22.

Williams, B. A. and Delli Carpini, M. X. (2011) *After Broadcast News: Media Regimes, Democracy, and the New Information Environment* (New York: Cambridge University Press).

Williams, K. (2005) *European Media Studies* (London: Hodder Arnold).

—— (2006) 'Competing models of journalism? Anglo-American and European reporting in the information age', *Journalistica* 2: 43–65.

Willig, I. (2011, 2nd edn) *Bag Nyhederne* (Frederiksberg: Samfundslitteratur).

Winseck, D. and Pike, R. (2007) *Communication and Empire: Media, Markets and Globalisation* (Durham, NC: Duke University Press).

Winseck, D. and Pike, R. (2009) 'The global media and the empire of liberal internationalism, circa 1910–30', *Media History* 15/1: 31–54.

Wojcieszak, M. E. and Mutz, D. C. (2009) 'Online groups and political discourse: Do online discussion spaces facilitate exposure to political disagreement?', *Journal of Communication* 59/1: 40–56.

Woodward, J. (1930) *Foreign News in American Morning Newspapers: A Study in Public Opinion* (New York: Columbia University Press).

World Bank Group (2009), report available at www.worldbank.org (accessed 18 January 2010).

World Values Survey (2005–8) World Values Survey 5th Wave, available at www. worldvaluessurvey.org (accessed 18 January 2010).

Wouters, R. (2009) 'The nature of foreign news: Conceptual consideration about analysing foreign news over time', available at www.m2p.be/ publications/1314357859.pdf (accessed 13 August 2013).

Wu, H. D. (2007) 'A brave new world for international news? Exploring the determinants of the coverage of foreign news on US websites', *International Communication Gazette* 69/6: 539–51.

Zuckerman, E. (2004) 'Using the internet to examine patterns of foreign coverage', *Nieman Reports* Fall: 51–2, available at www.nieman.harvard.edu/reportsitem. aspx?id=100530 (accessed 2 February 2010).

—— (2008a) *International news: Bringing about the golden age.* Paper of the Berkman Center for Internet and Society at Harvard University, available at http://cyber.law.harvard.edu/sites/cyber.law.harvard.edu/files/ International%20News_MR.pdf (accessed 2 February 2010).

—— (2008b) 'Meet the bridgebloggers', *Public Choice* 134/1–2: 47–65.

Index

RISJ/I.B.TAURIS PUBLICATIONS

CHALLENGES

Transformations in Egyptian Journalism
Naomi Sakr
ISBN: 978 1 78076 589 1

Climate Change in the Media: Reporting Risk and Uncertainty
James Painter
ISBN: 978 1 78076 588 4

Women and Journalism
Suzanne Franks
ISBN: 978 1 78076 585 3

EDITED VOLUMES

Media and Public Shaming: The Boundaries of Disclosure
Julian Petley (ed.)
ISBN: 978 1 78076 586 0 (HB); 978 1 78076 587 7 (PB)

Political Journalism in Transition: Western Europe in a Comparative Perspective
Raymond Kuhn and Rasmus Kleis Nielsen (eds)
ISBN: 978 1 78076 677 5 (HB); 978 1 78076 678 2 (PB)

Transparency in Politics and the Media: Accountability and Open Government
Nigel Bowles, James T. Hamilton and David A. L. Levy (eds)
ISBN: 978 1 78076 675 1 (HB); 978 1 78076 676 8 (PB)

The Ethics of Journalism: Individual, Institutional and Cultural Influences
Wendy N. Wyatt (ed.)
ISBN: 978 1 78076 673 7 (HB); 978 1 78076 674 4 (PB)